A GIFT FOR

_____

FROM

_____

DATE

_____

BILLY GRAHAM

TRUTH
for Each Day

THOMAS NELSON
Since 1798

Truth for Each Day

© 2023 Billy Graham Literary Trust

Portions of this book were excerpted from the Billy Graham "My Answer" column, found at https://billygraham.org/answers/.

Published in Nashville, Tennessee, by Thomas Nelson. Thomas Nelson is a registered trademark of HarperCollins Christian Publishing, Inc.

Thomas Nelson titles may be purchased in bulk for educational, business, fund-raising, or sales promotional use. For information, please email SpecialMarkets@ThomasNelson.com.

Unless otherwise noted, Scripture quotations are from the New King James Version®. Copyright © 1982 by Thomas Nelson. Used by permission. All rights reserved.

Scripture quotations marked ESV are from the ESV® Bible (The Holy Bible, English Standard Version®). Copyright © 2001 by Crossway, a publishing ministry of Good News Publishers. Used by permission. All rights reserved.

Scripture quotations marked KJV are from the King James Version. Public domain.

Scripture quotations marked NASB are from the New American Standard Bible® (NASB). Copyright © 1960, 1962, 1963, 1968, 1971, 1972, 1973, 1975, 1977, 1995, 2020 by The Lockman Foundation. Used by permission. www.Lockman.org

Scripture quotations marked NIV are from the Holy Bible, New International Version®, NIV®. Copyright © 1973, 1978, 1984, 2011 by Biblica, Inc.® Used by permission of Zondervan. All rights reserved worldwide. www.zondervan.com. The "NIV" and "New International Version" are trademarks registered in the United States Patent and Trademark Office by Biblica, Inc.®

Scripture quotations marked NLT are from the Holy Bible, New Living Translation. Copyright © 1996, 2004, 2015 by Tyndale House Foundation. Used by permission of Tyndale House Ministries, Carol Stream, Illinois 60188. All rights reserved.

Any internet addresses, phone numbers, or company or product information printed in this book are offered as a resource and are not intended in any way to be or to imply an endorsement by Thomas Nelson, nor does Thomas Nelson vouch for the existence, content, or services of these sites, phone numbers, companies, or products beyond the life of this book.

ISBN 978-1-4002-4438-6 (audiobook)
ISBN 978-1-4002-4437-9 (eBook)
ISBN 978-1-4002-4436-2 (HC)

Printed in India

23 24 25 26 27 REP 10 9 8 7 6 5 4 3 2

January

Bright Hope

"I know the plans I have for you," declares the Lord, "plans to prosper you and not to harm you, plans to give you hope and a future."
JEREMIAH 29:11 NIV

"Out with the old, in with the new" is often the slogan of a new year, followed by many resolutions made by people determined to "turn a new page" and do better than the year before. Sadly, most New Year's resolutions die before the end of January.

Jesus Christ had memorable slogans that have endured through the ages, and we would all do well to pay attention to them and adhere to them. Jesus announced His great society, "His kingdom," which was the promise of Heaven and eternal life with Him—forever. It will endure because the kingdom of God is not built on a false promise—but the Word of the Lord. Conversion is a requirement of citizenship in this wonderful place. Many people say that it doesn't matter what's believed [to get to Heaven]. But Jesus Christ said, "Unless you are converted . . . you will by no means enter the kingdom of heaven" (Matthew 18:3).

Are you holding on to the solid Rock, Jesus the Savior? Do not delay. Start the new year off with a sure thing: God's promise to give you a hope and a future.

How God Speaks to Us

I will bless the LORD who has given me counsel.

PSALM 16:7

God speaks to those who belong to Him through His Holy Word—He is the Word! The authors of Scripture made it clear that God was speaking to them and through them. More than three thousand times they said, "Thus saith the Lord" or its equivalent. And because "all Scripture is given by inspiration of God" (2 Timothy 3:16), we are taught what is right and wrong. God's purpose is to train us in His righteousness. We must not let anything or anyone take the place of the Bible to guide our lives.

God also speaks to us in nature. When He created the heavens and the Earth, He gave us an incredible, complex, beautiful, orderly universe. "Since the creation of the world His invisible attributes are clearly seen, being understood by the things that are made" (Romans 1:20).

God speaks through Jesus Christ, who is revealed for us in the pages of the Bible. He is the Word of God incarnate, and He speaks to us by the Holy Spirit. This may be the "still small voice" of the conscience that will not let us go until we do what is right—or it may be a loud, clear conviction of what God wants us to do. We must never silence that inner voice. We must check what we believe it is saying against the Scriptures to be sure it is true to God's Word.

SALVATION FOR ALL

There is no distinction between Jew and Greek, for the same
Lord over all is rich to all who call upon Him.
ROMANS 10:12

God's message of salvation is for all people. He died for the sins of the whole world. "Whoever calls on the name of the LORD shall be saved" (Romans 10:13). God our Savior "desires all men to be saved and to come to the knowledge of the truth" (1 Timothy 2:4).

This word *whoever* is a wonderfully big word; it speaks of the grace of God and His invitation that extends to all people.

Christianity is centered on the gospel that brings comfort and the assurance that God will forgive sin. Now this doesn't mean that all people will indeed call upon the name of the Lord for salvation. The majority of people resist Him, block His voice out, and ultimately reject Him.

The Bible teaches that life is only a vapor that appears for a moment and then vanishes (James 4:14). This is why God calls out to the nations of the world to get right with Him. History will someday come to an end, rendering the world's system dominated by evil a total failure. Wickedness in every form will cease: hatred, greed, jealousy, war, and death. This "day of the Lord" will be glorious, when He comes to bring peace to the "whosoevers." Be part of this wonderful host of people who love Him.

KNOWING THE TRUTH

Study to shew thyself approved unto God, a workman that needeth
not to be ashamed, rightly dividing the word of truth.
2 TIMOTHY 2:15 KJV

People have all kinds of ideas about truth. Some think that there is no absolute truth. Whatever the view, wisely study and believe what Jesus taught about truth. He taught not only that there is truth, but that He is the Truth. Through prayer ask Him to give you the faith to believe and put into practice His absolute truth, and pray the same for others.

Scripture tells us to study to show that we are approved to God—that our beliefs line up with His. We are to know God's Word, believe it, obey it, and live by it. Great blessing and comfort come in the midst of a conflicted world embroiled in turmoil.

There are those who are offended by absolute truth, but it doesn't change with the blowing of the wind. "The Spirit of truth . . . will guide you into all truth" (John 16:13). Jesus made the bold claim, "I am the way, the truth, and the life. No one comes to the Father except through Me" (John 14:6).

People question whether the Bible is really the Word of God. But the truth is clear: from beginning to end the Bible is God's Word, inspired by the Holy Spirit who will teach us, and we can know the truth, and the truth will set us free (John 8:32).

REFERENCE POINT

We . . . rejoice in God through our Lord Jesus Christ, through whom we have now received the reconciliation.

ROMANS 5:11

As sin has progressed and gained momentum, we seem to have lost our ability to be shocked. Behavior that was once considered abominable is now acceptable.

One thing is certain, however. There are many new sinners today, but there aren't any new sins. The Old Testament speaks of a time when "everyone did what was right in his own eyes" (Judges 17:6).

It doesn't have to be this way. Where we start determines where we end. Each new year brings hope and a new opportunity for change. We can reset our starting line. Take the compass, for instance. If the compass is not accurate, the traveler will lose his way. If the sun and the stars were not ordered in their stations, no mariner could depend on them to find his way through the oceans of the world. If there are no absolutes, no fixed reference points, there can be no certainty.

This is why God's Word is good news, because the absolute truth is that Jesus came and died on the cross and rose from the dead, to save us from sin. We can be reconciled to God and put back in a right relationship with Him by accepting His provision for sin, His Son, Christ the Lord. There is hope, there is certainty, and there is a reference point, and it all begins with God.

WISDOM AND KNOWLEDGE

Does not wisdom cry out, and understanding lift up her voice?
PROVERBS 8:1

The eighth chapter of Proverbs is deep and wide because it is the voice of wisdom speaking to our hearts. It is the Lord Jesus Himself gathering up His eternal attributes that call out to us with His understanding, truth, righteousness, knowledge and instruction, prudence and discretion, reverence, counsel, strength, love, riches and honor, justice, rejoicing, blessing, wisdom, and eternal life.

Knowledge is fact-gathering; wisdom is applying knowledge with discernment and good judgment. The Bible says, "The LORD gives wisdom; from His mouth come knowledge and understanding" (Proverbs 2:6).

But the blessing of knowledge becomes a curse when we pervert it. If ever a generation was bequeathed the knowledge of God, it has been the generations of today. Yet we are throwing away the glorious heritage on self-pleasure and satisfying immediate gratification. Our worldly wisdom has made us calloused and hard. Our natural wisdom comes not from God but is earthly, sensual, and devilish. In spite of the knowledge young people have accumulated, they are more confused, bewildered, frustrated, and without moral moorings. Today, society is turning its face against God, ignoring Him as the Source of all knowledge and wisdom.

The only right place to turn is God's Word to learn about knowledge and wisdom and how to apply them to life. "According to your word [O LORD,] teach me knowledge and good judgment" (Psalm 119:65–66 NIV).

THE SOURCE OF PEACE

"These things I have spoken to you, that in Me you may have peace."
JOHN 16:33

The human race continues its futile search for peace in all the wrong places. Today there is little personal, domestic, social, economic, or political peace anywhere. Why? Mankind has within it the seeds of suspicion, violence, hatred, and destruction.

Peace will not come to the world until Christ returns. "Do you suppose that I came to give peace on earth? I tell you, not at all, but rather division" (Luke 12:51). Jesus was not saying that He prevented peace; He was giving fair warning that His message would divide people. After all, who likes to be told they are sinners who must repent? When Christ began His earthly ministry, He showed love, gave comfort, and brought healing. The people's response was to oppose Him, reject Him, arrest Him, and kill Him.

Satan does everything in his power to steer peace seekers away from the Peacemaker, Jesus Christ. The same people who talk of peace, lobby for it, and convene peace conferences are often the same people who are blinded by Satan, who does not want the world to recognize the Source of peace.

But personal peace can be realized in the here and now. The future does not hinge on the world situation, however grim it might become. It depends on what each person does about Jesus Christ.

Overcoming Anger

Be angry, and do not sin.
EPHESIANS 4:26

It takes a great deal to stir God's anger, but when it happens, it is holy anger because God is pure and righteous. When the Bible tells us that God "is slow to anger" (Nahum 1:3), it simply means that He is patient beyond man's capability. The prophet Nahum preached that God "will not at all acquit the wicked" (v. 3). Who are the wicked? Those who break the law of God, and we have all broken God's law.

We must not think that we get away with anything. Sin will bring us to repentance or retribution. When His anger is stirred, He often uses the power of nature to demonstrate His pending doom. "The LORD has His way in the whirlwind and in the storm, and the clouds are the dust of His feet. . . . The earth heaves at His presence" (Nahum 1:3, 5).

So the storm clouds are swift, as holy feet stir up the dust of anger against man's sin and disobedience, because God's plan is to have fellowship with the human race, not conflict.

Man's anger, however, is sinful. It leads us into bitterness and hurts everyone. Can we overcome our anger, instead of constantly being overcome by it? Yes! With God's help.

Anger makes us lash out at others, destroying relationships. The history of the human race is largely the history of its anger. Anger flees when the Spirit of God fills our hearts.

WALKING WITH GOD

Nebuchadnezzar spoke, saying, "Blessed be the God of Shadrach, Meshach, and Abed-Nego, who sent His Angel and delivered His servants who trusted in Him."
DANIEL 3:28

God has not only promised to be with us in the good times; He has promised to be with us through difficult times. It doesn't mean that we will always be delivered from troubles, but He has promised to go with us through the trouble: "Yea, though I walk through the valley of the shadow of death, I will fear no evil; for You are with me" (Psalm 23:4).

Walk with God as Noah did, when the flood came. Noah was saved amidst the scorn and rejection of his neighbors. Walk with God as Moses did in the solitude of the desert. When the hour of judgment fell upon Egypt, Moses was prepared to lead his people to victory.

Walk with God as David did as a shepherd boy. When he was called to rule his people, he was prepared for the task of kingship. Walk with God as Daniel and his three young friends did to the palace of Babylon's king. When the fiery furnace and the lion's den came, God was beside them and delivered them.

As these faithful men of God walked, Christ wants to give us hope for the future. He wants us to know what it means to walk with Him every day. This is not possible unless we first come to Christ and receive His salvation. Walking with Him is the very fountainhead of joy.

THE GIFT OF THE GOSPEL

The gospel . . . is not according to man. . . . It came through the revelation of Jesus Christ.

GALATIANS 1:11–12

Before God could use Jonah, Jonah first had to humble himself and repent. Only then would God use him to preach the gospel to a pagan culture. Jonah was one who thought he could escape from the Lord. He found out differently. He was called to preach to rebellious Nineveh (the area today that is known as Mosul, in modern-day Iraq), but instead he rebelled against God's call.

Jonah was called to preach God's Word, but in a very different way from other prophets who preached to Israel. Jonah resented the fact that God was sending him to the "great city" (Jonah 1:2), the capital of Israel's pagan neighbor, Assyria. He didn't believe the people of Nineveh deserved God's salvation. So he did the very thing he was called to preach against: he disobeyed God and did what was in his heart.

God reprimanded Jonah and, in graciousness, expressed His compassion and love for those drowning in sin. This is a demonstration of the long arm of God's salvation extended to those who turn from rebellion and receive the Lord's mighty message of forgiveness.

The gospel is not just for those who receive it but to bring the whole world to salvation. The gospel shows us our sins and points us to the Savior.

BY FAITH ALONE

If we say that we have fellowship with Him, and walk in
darkness, we . . . do not practice the truth.
1 JOHN 1:6

There are many among us today who acknowledge Jesus as a historical figure. Many even claim to follow Him, but their lives are not transformed. Possessing salvation in Christ by faith alone is what proves that He is the Redeemer of souls.

Someone wrote that Buddha never claimed to be God. Moses never claimed to be Jehovah. Mohammed never claimed to be Allah. Yet Jesus claimed to be the living God. Buddha said, "I am a teacher in search of the truth." Jesus said, "I am the Truth." Confucius said, "I never claimed to be holy." Jesus said, "Who convicts me of sin?" Mohammed said, "Unless God throws his cloak over me, I have no hope." Jesus said, "Unless you believe in me, you will die in your sins." While it is captivating to read what others say about Jesus, faith is still the key to believing in Christ.

Years ago in a monastery in India, old relics that had been dug up were worshiped by Buddhists in the area. Muslims point with pride to Mecca, where the body of their prophet, Mohammed, is buried. Followers of Confucius revere the remains of their master, buried in an imposing tomb in China. We don't need a religion that worships the dead; we need the living Savior. Christianity is the faith of the empty tomb.

GOD'S TENDER COMFORT

Blessed be the God . . . of all comfort, who comforts us in all our tribulation,
that we may be able to comfort those who are in any trouble.

2 CORINTHIANS 1:3–4

It pleases God when He sees us reach out to others in need. He intends for people to have fellowship, to challenge and help one another. He gave us relationships to bring us joy.

We are created to need others in our lives. There was a popular song years ago: "People who need people." But more than that, we need Jesus Christ in our lives.

When we are comforted and encouraged by the Lord, He expects us to do the same for those who cross our paths. Humanity cries out for comfort in its sorrow, light in its darkness, peace in its turmoil, rest in its weariness, and healing in its sickness and diseases.

Ask God for help in communicating His comfort to those who need support. Point them to the God of all comfort through His Word. We are told that He is a refuge for the oppressed (Psalm 9:9), an ever-present help in trouble (Psalm 46:1), and His promises give life (Psalm 119:50).

Ask the Lord to make you a blessing to others. Many times this is most evident when we share our own struggles and testify to how God helps us. Our own witness of Christ meeting our needs speaks to those who need a tender touch from the Savior.

OUR HEAVENLY HOME

"In My Father's house are many mansions."
JOHN 14:2

Heaven is beyond the reach of our satellites and telescopes, but that doesn't mean it is beyond the reach of our hearts. The key to finding Heaven is finding Christ. Today's technology is performing things past generations would have never thought possible. GPS alone has changed how people travel.

But there is something far greater that has been available to man since the beginning of time: a heavenly GPS that will bring you safely to your eternal destination. It is called the gospel plan of salvation. It only has one direction—up—and the Navigator, the Lord Jesus Christ, is "the way" (John 14:6). He appoints the time of arrival and has prepared all that is necessary to welcome us.

By nature, people are bent toward home. When we finish our day and evening activities, we generally head for our homes. Far better than any dream you can imagine is the supernatural transformation that will take place for all God's people when He transports us to His heavenly home. We are assured that in Heaven we will be living in God's dwelling place forever, and it will be glorious beyond description. It will be greater than any earthly palace or mansion. Technology will never surpass the glories of this place that Jesus is preparing for His people.

TRUTHFUL OPTIMISM

If we say that we have no sin, we deceive ourselves, and the truth is not in us.

1 JOHN 1:8

Admiral Jim Stockdale served in Vietnam and spent time as a prisoner of war in the infamous "Hanoi Hilton." He once was asked which men didn't make it out of the prison. His answer was surprising: "The optimists." He went on to explain. "You must never confuse faith that you will prevail in the end."

While optimism can strengthen our resolve to persevere, it can also mislead us when we deny facts. A CNN documentary reported that optimism can take on the tone of arrogance. For instance, when bad weather approaches and the warning goes out to evacuate an area, the optimist might "opt" to stay put instead of getting out of harm's way. It might work for them, even many times, but then one fateful day the storm hits hard and they suffer greatly.

This happens with those who put God out of their thinking. They are optimistic that since they lead a good life, they will cross the finish line into Heaven. Their optimism leads them astray. They are not willing to acknowledge before God they are sinners and need salvation.

Truth is not always pleasant, but it is always right. Truth is absolute. The Bible tells us to be on the alert and not be arrogant. The true optimist will heed warnings and be wisely led by the Word of God.

THE PRIVILEGE OF PRAYER

And the LORD *said to him: "I have heard your prayer and*
your supplication that you have made before Me."
1 KINGS 9:3

Praying in Jesus' wonderful name reminds us—and those listening—that Jesus has opened the door to Heaven for us. We can approach Him, and speak directly to Him, only because of what He has done for us. The phrase "in Jesus' name" is not a magic formula we add in order to make God answer our prayers. God answers our prayers solely because of His Son Jesus Christ.

God knows what is best for us. When we pray, therefore, we seek God's will in our prayers. This pleases Him because He wants to show us the way to life, the way to peace—the way to Him. We gain access to the Lord by faith in Him, and He brings us into His wonderful grace (Romans 5:1–2).

Thank God for the wonderful privilege of prayer. It should be an integral part of our lives at all times. "We will give ourselves continually to prayer" (Acts 6:4).

In the morning, prayer is the key that opens to us the treasures of God's mercies and blessings; in the evening, it is the key that envelops us under His protection and safeguard.

Throughout Scripture we see Jesus demonstrating the power of prayer as He prayed to His Father in Heaven. How much more should we go to Him in prayer? Nothing can replace a daily time spent alone with God in prayer.

Re-Creation

If anyone is in Christ, he is a new creation; old things have passed away; behold, all things have become new.

2 CORINTHIANS 5:17

We live in a revolutionary, changing world. Man's moral capacities lag far behind his technological skills and discoveries. The greatest need in the world is to bring about the transformation of human nature, something man cannot do.

Many of our technologists are saying there is a great need for a new breed of man. Even the political radicals and the humanists talk about the "new man." From this it is clear that they acknowledge that man, as he is, is not good enough. So they look for the arrival of the new man who, they say, will come into being when society has been changed so that a new environment can produce him. There are also the technocrats who believe that technology is now advancing so rapidly that mankind will be able to create an entirely new human race. Some genetic engineers believe that they will be able to create any type of person they want.

But there is only one ultimate answer. Science and technology cannot change man's basic nature. Economic restructuring cannot change man's basic nature. No amount of self-improvement or wishful thinking can change man's basic nature. Only God the Creator can re-create us. And that is precisely what He does when we humble ourselves and submit to Jesus Christ.

PUT ON THE NEW LIFE

Put off . . . the old man which grows corrupt according to the deceitful lusts, and be renewed in the spirit of your mind, and . . . put on the new man which was created according to God.
EPHESIANS 4:22-24

There is a mindset today that if people believe in God and do good works, they are going to Heaven. But this leaves many questions that must be answered. It should not be surprising if people believe easily in a God who makes no demands, but this is not the God of the Bible. Satan has cleverly misled people by whispering that they can be saved without being changed, but this is the devil's lie.

There are many religions in the world and there is enormous confusion about where to find truth. Many preach that God is love, not a God of wrath. People proclaim that Heaven is real but Hell is only a figment of imagination.

God created Heaven for those who humble themselves before God, and Hell is created for Satan and those who serve him. A loving warning comes from Heaven: "Prepare to meet your God" (Amos 4:12). How is this done?

The Bible tells us that when we submit our lives to Christ, He gives us the ability to take off our former life and put on the new life He gives.

We must admit our sin and turn from it through faith in Jesus Christ and obey Him. The greatest joy and peace come to those who take this important step.

WHERE CONTENTMENT LIES

In lowliness of mind let each esteem others better than himself.
PHILIPPIANS 2:3

Envy, jealousy, and covetousness are interrelated. Discontent with our position and possessions often indicates a self-centered attitude, which leads to intolerant, resentful, and even malicious feelings toward a real or imagined rival. We may covet the success, personality, material possessions, good looks, or position of another. Then, in order to compensate for a frustrated ego, we make unkind and destructive remarks and submerge ourselves in self-pity, anger, bitterness, and depression.

Recognizing it and admitting it takes courage and truth. Being convicted is the first step toward the Savior. It pleases Jesus when we acknowledge our sin. There is nothing more healing than to take our minds off ourselves and put them on others.

Some people may appear to "have it all," but everyone suffers to some extent in their lives. There are many things that can hide behind a beautiful face, a sweet spirit, and talent. We think that they are always accepted and treated special, but often such people harbor pain of some kind. How wonderful when we can show love. For those who are truly happy, they will bring joy to others. A beautiful spirit is apparent when we submit ourselves completely to God, who is "able to make all grace abound toward you, that you, always having all sufficiency in all things, may have an abundance for every good work" (2 Corinthians 9:8).

HOPE OF HEAVEN

Hope does not disappoint, because the love of God has been
poured out in our hearts by the Holy Spirit.
ROMANS 5:5

Heaven will be a place in which its inhabitants will be freed from the fears, insecurities, and disappointments that plague us in the present life. We will be free from financial pressures that burden us down here, free from the fear of personal harm. There will be no fear of personal failure. Our relationship with God will be intimate and direct.

It pleases God that His children would long for His heavenly home that He is preparing for us; not as a place of escape but as a place where we will enjoy His presence forever.

But we mustn't shirk our responsibilities in this life. God intends for us to live full lives and to be engaged with others. We do not have to look far to find those who are more disappointed than we are or perhaps in worse health. Life is not about us; it is about learning to get along with our fellow man, and most of all, life is about what we decide concerning the Lord Jesus Christ. A true Christian spirit desires to spend eternity with God in Heaven and wants to tell as many people about this great hope so others can also enjoy the rewards of Heaven and the glory of God Himself. Until then, be faithful to proclaim this great message.

Healing Words

Speak evil of no one, [be] peaceable, gentle, showing all humility to all.

TITUS 3:2

M any people are quick with the deadly thrust but slow with the ointment of healing. The harsh criticism of others and unfair appraisals of those about us sting with pain. The unjust condemnation of others has a boomerang effect. When we hurl vindictive indictments with the hope of crippling others, we discover that we hurt ourselves more.

Many people are conflicted today because they are driven away by their own bitterness and harsh words from those who may also need a kind word. Many people go through their entire lives with a chip on their shoulder, carrying hurts and resentments over things that were said or done decades ago. Like a poison, their bitterness has made not only their own lives miserable but the lives of those around them. They have never learned the secret of forgiveness and forbearance.

The Bible warns us to be on guard "lest any root of bitterness springing up cause trouble" (Hebrews 12:15). Meekness and forbearance are "musts" if we are to live harmoniously in society and develop healthy homes, families, and friendships. While Christians must always speak the truth, we must do it in love.

God wants to help us overcome the bitterness that we feel. "Everyone must be quick to hear, slow to speak, and slow to anger" (James 1:19 NASB).

Big Needs, Big God

*"I will dwell in them and walk among them. I will be
their God, and they shall be My people."*
2 CORINTHIANS 6:16

God created animals first, and then God said, "Let Us make man in Our image,
according to Our likeness" (Genesis 1:26). He gave man dominion over every
living thing on Earth.

Man has three attributes that animals do not have: reason, conscience, and
will. Animals are motivated by instinct. Their behavior patterns are instinctive, not
intelligent.

The first man, Adam, used all three of these attributes. First, he reasoned that
his own judgment was as good as God's, and he ate the forbidden fruit. In that act,
the will of man came into play, for he could have decided either way. Then, after
he broke God's command—not to eat of the fruit—he felt conscience-stricken and
ran away to hide. Man has been following the same pattern through the centuries—
willfully disobeying God and running away.

Within these God-given attributes are life or death, happiness or sorrow, and
peace or conflict. If he dissipates the powers that God has given him, he is of all
creatures most miserable. People are little creatures with big capacities, finite beings
with infinite desires, deserving nothing but demanding all. God made people with
this huge capacity and desire in order that He might come in and completely satisfy
that desire. God wants to commune with mankind.

Hope in the Midst of Trouble

*"In the world you will have tribulation; but be of
good cheer, I have overcome the world."*

JOHN 16:33

Only in fairy tales do people live charmed lives. We may think that some people have it all, but if we turn the pages of their lives, we may see a very different picture.

Life touches some people with bouquets and others with thorn bushes. But the first may find a wasp in the flowers, and the second may discover roses among the thorns.

The Bible never promised that life would be fair. As we pray, we can give thanks when storms finally subside, or when the pain of ill health lets up, but the reality is that new troubles will come. While we should not anticipate trouble at every turn, some people spend so much time worrying about what might happen that they never enjoy what is happening; they never see what lies beyond trouble—perhaps the opportunity to comfort someone or to help someone. We can water the seed of hope in those around us and pray that the Lord will help prepare us for new challenges ahead.

Trouble is different for all of us. For Christians, we are blessed to have the promise that Jesus will be with us in the midst of our problems. He gives us the power to overcome whatever circumstances come our way.

WELL ARMED

"When a strong man, fully armed, guards his own palace, his goods are in peace."
LUKE 11:21

It is impossible to believe anything into existence. Try it. Who can simply "believe" that they can inherit a million dollars and it happens? Who can say that they can believe a child into existence?

People who make such claims are deceivers. Their motive is to draw others into believing lies. This is just what Satan did in the Garden of Eden, and Adam and Eve fell prey.

There are many authors, talk show hosts, and newscasters who become wealthy or famous by using high-sounding words that seem like the epitome of scholarship and culture. They are intellectually clever and crafty, adept at beguiling thoughtless men and women. The Bible tells us to be on the alert, "because your adversary the devil walks about like a roaring lion, seeking whom he may devour" (1 Peter 5:8).

Be on your guard. Arm yourself with the Word of God. It will guide and protect you. Believers are to test the various aspects and doctrines that abound, including the theories of others. Most of all, we are to test them against the standard of the Word of God.

Put your belief in the one true God. Have faith in Him. He is the One who spoke into existence the sun, moon, and stars—and yes, your very life. Reject the pride of man and embrace the man Jesus Christ.

KEEPING WORK IN ITS PLACE

Whatever you do, do all to the glory of God.
1 CORINTHIANS 10:31

The story is told about R. G. LeTourneau, an industrialist who received an order from the government for a very complicated machine to be used in lifting airplanes. No machine of this type had ever been designed. LeTourneau and his engineers could not come up with a plan. After some time, everyone was becoming tense and nervous. Finally, on a Wednesday night, LeTourneau told his staff that he was not going to work, that he was going to a prayer meeting. The engineers were upset, because they had a deadline and the boss was deserting them.

"But," he said, "I've got a deadline with God." He went to the prayer meeting, sang the hymns, and prayed. Afterward, as he was walking home, the design of the machine in complete detail came into his mind. He needed time with God and creative silence to bring it to the surface.

Sometimes we try so hard to solve our problems without taking them to God, and we become agitated or depressed. It pleases God when we express to Him our thanks and gratitude for His guidance and direction. But one caution: our work was never meant to become the center of our lives. That place belongs only to God, but He did give man work to do. There is dignity in work.

HERE FOR A PURPOSE

"By this My Father is glorified, that you bear much fruit; so you will be My disciples."
JOHN 15:8

For those who follow Jesus Christ, our ultimate destination is where Jesus is—Heaven. But He has chosen in His sovereignty that we remain on Earth for a time to be His light in a dark world. Just as the light of His gospel has driven truth into the hearts of believers, so He intends to use us to shine His light to others who have not yet found Him as Lord and Savior.

If God took us immediately into eternity to spare us all the problems and heartaches of this life, we'd never again have to experience worry or sorrow or suffering, and all the burdens and temptations that trouble us now would vanish. So why are we left here for a time? The reason is simple: God still has work for us to do right here. Heaven is our goal, but until that final moment when He takes us home to Himself, God has a purpose in keeping us here.

Earth isn't just Heaven's waiting room, where we sit around doing nothing; Earth is the stage on which the drama of the ages is being played out. It is the demonstration of Christ's victory over sin and death and Hell and Satan. And no matter who we are, we have a God-given role to play in that divine drama.

THE FEAR OF GOD

As high as the heavens are above the earth, so great is his love for those who fear him.

PSALM 103:11 NIV

Fear and anxiety have become the hallmarks of our age. They are like baby tigers; the more we feed them, the stronger they grow. Fear can banish faith, but faith can banish fear. We must ask ourselves where our faith rests—in ourselves and circumstances or in almighty God.

Seasons change. The calendar changes every month. Circumstances change. But God's Word never changes; God changes not. What a wonderful thought.

"Heaven and earth will pass away, but My words will by no means pass away" (Matthew 24:35).

God knows what is best for us, and He knows the fears that often overtake us. Only God's Word shows us who He is and gives us a settled hope for the future. His message—the Bible—is able to calm our spirits. The power—and truth—of His Word will lead people to discover their need for God and the need of His salvation.

There is a good and healthy fear: the fear of the Lord. Some may say that it is a terrible thing to fear the Lord, but the Bible says that God's love is great toward those who fear Him (Psalm 103:8, 11). This type of fear is a reverent respect and awe of His power in the world and in our lives. This is a wonderful promise.

OUR DIVINE RIGHT

As many as received Him, to them He gave the right to become children of God.
JOHN 1:12

Atheists say they do not believe in God at all, while an agnostic is not sure whether or not God exists. Skeptics attack the Bible and retreat in confusion; agnostics scoff at its teaching but are unable to produce an intellectually honest refutation. Atheists have denied its validity but must surrender to its historical accuracy and archaeological verification.

A distinguished anthropologist was once asked if he had ever found a tribe or group of people anywhere in the world that did not believe in God or in some type of higher power. He admitted he had not. Though he claimed to be an atheist, he reluctantly said that belief in a divine power was universal.

Not only can we know that God exists, but everyone can have a personal relationship with Him. God has shown Himself to us through His Son, Jesus Christ. He came to us in human flesh. He is the image of the invisible God (Colossians 1:15, 19). This was confirmed when Jesus Christ was raised from the dead by His Father in Heaven.

The privilege is ours to know Him as our Savior. Don't miss the love of God by rejecting the sacrifice His Son made for us on the cross of Calvary. He has done everything necessary to remove the barriers between God and humanity.

THE HUMAN HEART

"I, the LORD, search the heart, I test the mind."

JEREMIAH 17:10

The Bible speaks very specifically about the human heart. It devises wicked imaginations (Proverbs 6:18), is deceitful above all things (Jeremiah 17:9), is far from God (Matthew 15:8), and is foolish and darkened (Romans 1:21). This is a sad state, for the heart is the seat of emotion and the seat of belief. It symbolizes the center of life.

But God has not left the human heart in this state. He devised a way to make Himself known. He came to get at the very heart of man's disease—*sin*. This was the sole purpose in Jesus coming to Earth, to save us from the sin that can destroy us.

When we seek the Lord and turn from sin, He comes into every facet of life and transforms our thinking, our speaking, our deeds, our relationships, our desires, and He replaces our fears with trust. He changes our hate into love. He makes our hearts new.

It is God who evaluates the state of our hearts. He is the One who ponders our hearts (Proverbs 21:2 KJV) and searches our hearts. He also weighs our hearts, and we come up short (Romans 3:23).

But the heart of Christ, full of compassion and love, bled on the cross for our sinful hearts. His pure, perfect, and tender heart made a way for us to have clean hearts before Him.

RELATIONSHIP VERSUS RELIGION

"I am the LORD, and there is no other; there is no God besides Me."
ISAIAH 45:5

When Socrates was about to die, one of his disciples mourned that he was leaving his followers orphans. The leaders of the world's religions were unable to promise that they would never leave their followers. Jesus said, "I will not leave you orphans; I will come to you" (John 14:18). When it comes to promises, it's interesting to contrast God's words with religious and philosophical leaders' words.

The Bible is the gospel of the Lord Jesus Christ, and believing His truth and following Him leads us into a personal relationship with the one and only true God. "He who believes in Me, believes . . . in Him who sent Me. . . . I have not spoken on My own authority; but the Father who sent Me" (John 12:44, 49).

Christianity is not a religion but a relationship. It is not a Western religion, nor is it a message of one culture or political system; it is a message of life and hope for all the world! It carries the truth of redemption by the death of our Savior for our sins on the cross. It carries the fact that Christ rose again. Religion can be anything. But true Christianity is God coming to mankind in a personal relationship, and this is where His promise is certain: "I will never leave you nor forsake you" (Hebrews 13:5). Trust in Him today.

THE SOURCE OF HAPPINESS

I have learned in whatever state I am, to be content.

PHILIPPIANS 4:11

The Bible says, "He who heeds the word [God's Word] wisely will find good . . . happy is he" (Proverbs 16:20). The person who has learned the secret of being content with whatever life brings him is a happy person, though he may be faced with sorrow and disappointment. Contented people rejoice in the simple and beautiful things.

A seventy-five-year-old man, one of the wealthiest in the world, once said, "I am the most miserable man in the world. I have everything anyone could ever want. I can go anywhere. I have my own yacht and private plane, but deep down inside I'm miserable and empty." Another elderly man who didn't have a penny to his name said, "I may not have much in this life, but I'm the happiest man in the world!"

What makes the difference? The message of Christ proclaims that there is happiness when a person realizes his spiritual poverty because in this acknowledgment, the heart is open to God's truth and makes Jesus the center of life. God knows the heart of mankind. He knows that an uncontrolled life is an unhappy life. The psalmist wrote, "Those who seek the LORD shall not lack any good thing" (Psalm 34:10).

We need hearts filled with love and peace and joy, and that is why Jesus came into the world.

OUR THOUGHT LIFE

Do not be conformed to this world, but be transformed by the renewing of your mind.
ROMANS 12:2

God knows our thoughts better than we know them. Many people struggle with negative thoughts or impure thoughts but never think to take them to the Lord in prayer, and many people never think to open up God's Word to read what He has to say to us about our minds.

The answer is that God wants us to fill our minds with the things of Him, with thoughts and emotions that are good and pure, that reflect Him instead of the evils of this world.

But first, we must confess our sinful thoughts and desires and ask the Lord to forgive us of our sin. We must believe Jesus is who He says He is—the Son of God—who died for our sins to bring us to salvation and eternal life. When this happens, God sends the Holy Spirit into our lives to help us walk with Him in obedience. He has given us His Word to lead and guide us. He has opened the way for us to humble ourselves before Him in prayer and receive His strength and power to live a holy life. It is God's desire that we be conformed to the image of His Son and have pure minds and Christlike hearts.

When God empowers us, we refuse to let sin have its way in us.

FEBRUARY

IN THE WORLD BUT NOT OF IT

Do not love the world or the things in the world. If anyone
loves the world, the love of the Father is not in him.
1 JOHN 2:15

If you add food coloring to water and then put the stems of white flowers in the water for about eight hours in the daytime, they will turn the color of the water! As the water in the flowers evaporates, the stems "drink up" the colored water, and the flowers change color.

This little science experiment is a good example of why Christians should be careful about how we live among people who do not know the Lord—yet.

Nearly everyone Jesus spent time with was an outcast—someone most people treated in an unfriendly way. But His relationship with them was not just about friendship. He wanted to bring them to God.

Like Jesus, we are to be in the world, but not of the world. When we reach out to others in the name of the Lord—giving them the truth—we are participating in the world, showing that we care. But if we start acting like the world, participating in their questionable behavior, bad language, or exposing our minds to destructive entertainment, then we are worldly. Our purpose in being in the world is to be God's light—to let others see Jesus in us. We must ask if we are loving people in the world without being changed by them.

WHERE YOUR TREASURE IS

The love of money is a root of all kinds of evil.
1 TIMOTHY 6:10

The Bible does not condemn wealth, but Jesus did speak of the deceitfulness of riches. Those who have great wealth may tend to feel independent. It can be the stumbling block in surrendering their lives to Christ.

Riches can take our minds off the things of God, and God Himself. How we think about money generally speaks of how we think about God. The Bible warns that money cannot buy happiness, true pleasure, peace of mind; it certainly cannot buy our way into the kingdom of God.

Today we are putting our hopes in materialism, in technological progress, and in freedom from moral absolutes. They have all failed because they've been powerless to change the human heart. Many people teach that prosperity and a high standard of living are the highest goals attainable. The Bible, however, teaches that materialism apart from God will destroy a nation as well as an individual.

There is nothing wrong with people possessing riches. The wrong comes when riches possess people. God desires that we store up riches in Heaven, storing up what counts most for eternity. It is God who owns everything, and we are but stewards of His property during the brief time we have on Earth. For those who experience wealth in this life, may they use it to honor and glorify God.

THE VALUE OF PATIENCE

Let patience have its perfect work, that you may be
perfect and complete, lacking nothing.
JAMES 1:4

There was a young Christian woman who, though good in many respects, was very impatient. Her pastor one day spoke to her husband about his soul, and the man replied, "My wife is a good woman, but if religion would make me as impatient as she is, I want no part of it." The minister had a frank talk with the woman, and in tears and humility she confessed that her sin was the sin of impatience. She began to pray that the Lord would help her. She took to heart that exhibiting patience with her husband, and before her husband, would be a way to testify that God is in the business of transforming people.

Thomas à Kempis said, "All men commend patience, although few be willing to practice it." John F. Newton wrote, "Be patient enough to live one day at a time as Jesus taught us, letting yesterday go, and leaving tomorrow till it arrives."

We live in a high-strung, neurotic, impatient age. This fast-paced age energizes hyper personalities and creates jangled nerves that affect relationships.

Impatience has produced a new crop of broken homes and a million or more new ulcers and set the stage for culture wars. In no area of our lives has it been more damaging than on the domestic scene.

We must practice patience with everyone, especially our families.

POINT OF ENTRY

"I stand at the door and knock. If anyone hears My voice
and opens the door, I will come in to him."

REVELATION 3:20

Jesus opened Heaven's door for us by His death on the cross. He is the entry place for mankind to receive His forgiveness and to enjoy His love.

Every house and building has at least one entrance. Every nation has points of entry. The kingdom of God also has an entrance—only one—and it is Jesus Christ. He proclaims, "I am the door. If anyone enters by Me, he will be saved" (John 10:9).

The human heart has an entrance as well, but many have it bolted, defiantly refusing to let Christ come in.

God formed our hearts and wants to dwell there, but many have locked theirs up, ignoring the Savior who says, "I am the way, the truth, and the life. No one comes to the Father except through Me" (John 14:6).

When the crew of Apollo 15 returned to Earth's atmosphere in 1971 after a journey of nearly three hundred hours and almost half a million miles, they had to reenter the atmosphere through a corridor less than forty miles wide. This illustrates what Jesus said: "Enter by the narrow gate; for wide is the gate and broad is the way that leads to destruction" (Matthew 7:13).

Jesus Christ opened Heaven's door for us. When He knocks on your door, do not turn Him away.

CLEAN HEARTS

Let us draw near [to God] with a true heart in full assurance of
faith, having our hearts sprinkled from an evil conscience.
HEBREWS 10:22

Our thoughts are the most reliable indication of what we are really like. And when we face our thoughts and our motives honestly, we have to admit we are not as good as we would like other people to believe.

One of the great truths in the Bible is that God wants to change us—not only our outward actions but our innermost thoughts, because He knows that when we do wrong it is because we have first allowed evil thoughts to control us. Jesus said that out of the overflow of the heart the mouth speaks, and the evil man brings evil things out of evil stored up inside of him (Matthew 12:34–35). If we will ask the Lord to wash us clean of our sins, He will change us.

Imagine a bucket of stagnant water. The only solution is to empty it and clean it—and then fill it with fresh water. That is what Christ will do if we commit our lives to Him and let His Word, the Bible, fill our hearts with His truth.

Two conflicting forces cannot exist in one human heart. When doubt reigns, faith cannot abide. Where hatred rules, love is crowded out. Our hearts are big enough for Christ to live in, if we will only make room for Him.

GOD WORKS ALL THINGS FOR OUR GOOD

You meant evil against me; but God meant it for good.
GENESIS 50:20

Situations often come into our lives that seem unfair. As believers it is important to first ask where we might have gone wrong. This is difficult but it pleases God because the Bible says that every man seems right in his own eyes but the Lord weighs the heart (Proverbs 21:2). If we are willing to do this, we will gain wisdom and make better choices in the future.

Then there are times when we are indeed treated unfairly in the workplace. Remember, for those who love God and are called according to His purpose, He causes all things to work for good (Romans 8:28). By keeping this truth in focus, it will guard us against bitterness and anger. The Bible tells us that we must not allow bitter roots to sprout up in our lives because it causes us trouble (Hebrews 12:15). We must not give the devil a foothold in our lives. When we let circumstances cause us to react in an ungodly way, we are contributing to his success—no Christian wants that.

Often our self-esteem is tied to our work. In our culture, men and women often define themselves by their jobs. A job tells you nothing about a person's character or value. Be an overcomer and realize that God may be using what seems detrimental as a stepping stone to something better.

COMFORT IN PAIN

May the God of all grace . . . after you have suffered a while,
perfect, establish, strengthen, and settle you.
1 PETER 5:10

No one is exempt from the touch of tragedy. Crossing all racial, social, political, and economic barriers, suffering reaches out to unite mankind. Suffering in life can uncover untold depths of character and unknown strength for service to others. People who go through life unscathed by sorrow and untouched by pain tend to be shallow. Suffering, on the other hand, tends to plow up the surface of our lives to uncover the depths that provide greater strength of purpose.

The Bible does not promise that we will escape life's problems, but it does assure those who belong to Him that He will be with us in the midst, guiding and comforting. Some of the happiest Christians are those who have been lifelong sufferers. They have every reason to sigh and complain, yet they have found greater cause for gratitude and joy than many who experience fewer problems.

For those who do not know Jesus Christ as a personal Savior, turn to Him and walk with Him through life; not to escape all the problems of this life but to live life to the fullest. We all face difficulties in life, but for Christians our hope is found in the One who is with us no matter what comes. This is a great comfort to those who watch our lives.

THE POWER OF ENCOURAGEMENT

My soul melts from heaviness; strengthen me according to Your word.

PSALM 119:28

All around us are people whose lives are filled with trouble and sorrow. They need our compassion and our encouragement. It pleases the Lord when people want to lift others up. The psalmist wrote about finding encouragement through God's Word (Psalm 119:28). We can read books about compassion. We can listen to speeches about being encouragers. But nowhere will we find greater instruction than from the Bible. God is the One who teaches us to be more concerned about the needs and feelings of others than our own. We are to encourage our loved ones, friends, and associates, and God will help us do this. "'Not by might nor by power, but by My Spirit,' says the LORD" (Zechariah 4:6).

One of the attributes of the Holy Spirit is to encourage our hearts so that we can be a blessing to others. Those who follow Christ will learn what it means to minister to others, and this selfless act will show that you belong to Christ and are empowered by Him. Sometimes we encourage others without even being aware of it. No longer will our lives seem ordinary and indistinguishable from the rest of the world. You can be a real strength to others who need a word of encouragement. Look to Christ and you will find that in doing so you are pointing others to Him as well.

OUR EMOTIONS

Then God said, "Let Us make man in Our image."
GENESIS 1:26

Emotions in themselves are not wrong or sinful. God wove various personality traits into His created beings, and often the differences complement one another.

We shouldn't despise or deny these differences. If we didn't experience emotions, we couldn't know God's peace and joy. When Jesus was asked what the greatest commandment was, He replied that we should love the Lord our God with all our heart, soul, and mind (Matthew 22:37). These three traits make up the personality, and no people are exactly alike. Our Creator is unique, and everything He does is also unique.

It may be surprising to realize that God experiences emotion, but remember that we are all created in His image. This is a staggering thought but true. How empty life would be without emotions!

The psalmist declared, "I will praise You, for I am fearfully and wonderfully made" (Psalm 139:14). This does not refer only to the human body but everything about us—our minds and emotions. Each person is complex, and while we may have challenges in understanding one another, God perfectly understands everything about us.

We must admit, though, that our emotions can become twisted and even destructive, leading us to do or say things that are harmful to ourselves and others. We must rely on Christ to fill our minds with the things that please Him and bring glory to Him.

HEALTHY FEAR

"Peace I leave with you. . . . Let not your heart be troubled, neither let it be afraid."
JOHN 14:27

The Bible does not contradict itself. There can be many different meanings to one word. In the case of the word *fear* it can mean "to be afraid, have a feeling of terror," etc. But there is also a wonderful definition to this word and that is "to have reverence or respect" for something or someone. There are, of course, different kinds of fear. Not all fear is wrong.

The Bible indeed does tell us to fear God. That doesn't mean that we're to be in terror of Him—although we should fear His judgment—but it does mean we are to have reverence and respect for Him.

This can be a wonderful word study using Scripture. When we hear preachers or others talk about things of God, it pleases the Lord when it drives us to His Word. He Himself will teach us the truth about all things.

Think of the fears that so easily grip us, even keep us enslaved. There is the fear of problems we face and what might happen to us. Jesus declared, "These things I have spoken to you, that in Me you may have peace. In the world you will have tribulation; but be of good cheer, I have overcome the world" (John 16:33). Christ has come to take away the source of our fears.

TICKET TO HEAVEN

"Let him who thirsts come. Whoever desires, let him take the water of life freely."
REVELATION 22:17

Preparing for Heaven is much like going on a journey. First, we must decide we want to go there. Next, we must prepare for the trip by making things ready, even purchasing a ticket. We may say, "How is it possible to purchase a ticket to Heaven?" Others may ask, "How can we be good enough to be accepted into Heaven?" Still some may rely on the fact that they do volunteer work and give to the needy in hopes that good works will assure them of a place in Heaven.

The Bible says none of these will suffice because the ticket to Heaven is expensive—far too expensive for any human being to afford.

Does that mean we can never go there? No—and the reason is because Someone else has already purchased the ticket for us. That Person is Jesus Christ, and the price He paid was His own blood, shed on the cross for us.

Now He offers us the ticket to Heaven free and fully paid! Why refuse it? Why try some other way?

There is a transaction that takes place because this free gift is offered to those who are willing to repent of sin and turn to Christ. We turn from something to Someone and exchange sin for salvation. God's Holy Spirit makes this possible. Receive Him today.

CHEERFUL GENEROSITY

All things come from You, and of Your own we have given You.
1 CHRONICLES 29:14

God does not "need" our money to get His work done. He is sovereign and could do it without our help. Yet He has arranged it so that His work often is done through the generosity of His own people as a means to glorify Him in all that we do. He entrusts His people to be responsible and generous because it blesses Him and others.

At least two things happen when we give. First, when we give with the right attitude, God reminds us that what we have isn't really ours. He gives us everything we have; it actually belongs to Him.

Second, when we give, we help meet the needs of others whom God also loves. By giving to others we testify to God's love for them, and we point them to the greatest gift of all—God's gift of His Son for our salvation.

Someone has said that our lives should resemble channels, not reservoirs. A reservoir stores water; a channel distributes it. God wants us to be channels of blessing to others. We are only stewards of the world's resources. They are not ours; they are God's. When we find our security in Him, we can then give generously from what He has entrusted to us. This is our Christian duty, and the true believer gives with a cheerful heart (2 Corinthians 9:7).

CARING FOR THE SICK

"By this all will know that you are My disciples, if you have love for one another."
JOHN 13:35

A sick person has God-given worth. God is concerned about the way we treat people who may not have much to offer us. A person of influence may not have trouble getting loving treatment. But when Jesus was teaching His disciples that in doing for others they were doing deeds as unto the Lord Himself (Matthew 25:35–40), He did not show favoritism.

We can, and should, contribute to the God-given worth of a human life, keeping in mind how we would hope to be treated (Luke 6:31). Reaching out to someone in need is never wrong, but it is wise to ask God for His guidance and direction in how to go about it.

When someone is dying there is seldom opposition to words of comfort from a friendly voice. There are countless ways to comfort others, and God blesses those who have responsive compassion.

"Christians Who Care" should be the slogan and the banner for the body of believers. When others see the compassion we express for the suffering and bereaved, they will truly believe our faith means something. The Bible has much to say about comforting the sick. "[The] God of all comfort, who comforts us in all our tribulation, that we may be able to comfort those who are in any trouble" (2 Corinthians 1:3–4).

GOD SO LOVED THE WORLD

In this is love, not that we loved God, but that He loved us.
1 JOHN 4:10

Christ died for one reason: because of God's hatred of sin and His deep love for us, that He would make a way for the human race to be delivered from His judgment and to know His everlasting forgiveness. This is the amazing grace of God.

Few ever ask why the world hates Christ, and it's hard to understand when Jesus proclaimed: "For God so loved the world" (John 3:16). He indeed loves the world, yet the world hates God. Many people reject the God who created them and gave them life. They do not want to even think about Him, and so God gives them up to their own futile thoughts (Romans 1:21).

The gospel of John records these staggering words from Jesus: "[The world] hated Me" (John 15:18). There can be no question that the Scriptures teach that the devil is the "god of this age" (2 Corinthians 4:4), the present evil world system, and that the carnal mind is against God. Those who feed the flesh cannot please God. This is why God in Christ was despised and rejected by the world.

This hatred of mankind toward God and God's love toward the human race are fully displayed at the cross of Calvary, the glorious place where God reconciled the world to Himself and where Christ the Redeemer died that mankind might live.

VICTORY IN JESUS

Thanks be to God, who gives us the victory through our Lord Jesus Christ.
1 CORINTHIANS 15:57

Winning is something everyone wants to experience. The late Paul "Bear" Bryant, award-winning coach at the University of Alabama, said, "The price of victory is high, but so are the rewards." Another Paul, the apostle, said, "I press toward the goal for the prize of the upward call of God in Christ Jesus" (Philippians 3:14).

What is the greatest and most costly battle to ever take place? Who was the victor and what was the reward? The greatest battle ever fought was between good and evil. It took place at Golgotha—a rugged hillside outside of Jerusalem. But the day that Jesus Christ was nailed to the cross, even His closest friends thought the battle for good was lost. Jesus died and was buried in a tomb, sealed by a massive stone. Those who had followed Him walked away in total defeat.

But Jesus did not remain in that cold, dark tomb. He rose again and defeated death. He told His disciples that eternal life could only be found in the cross. He triumphed over death and taught His followers that their faith would be strengthened in weakness.

The most important prize ever to be won in this life is salvation that Christ offers to all, for then you will know victory that lasts.

WALKING WITH GOD

As you therefore have received Christ Jesus the Lord, so walk in Him.
COLOSSIANS 2:6

Parents who take their child for a walk generally want the child to stay close so that he or she does not stumble over rocks, slip into mud holes, or get hit by a car. Parents should guide the child and teach him or her how to anticipate problems ahead. This is what God wants us to do—stay close to Him. This is done by reading and knowing His Word and through prayer in the name of Jesus.

To *walk* means to place one foot in front of the other and to go forward one step at a time. If you stop doing this, you are no longer walking. You are standing still—or worse, going backward. Walking always implies movement, progress, and direction.

No wonder God commanded that we walk with Him. Doing so means we are moving forward in step with Him, confident that the way He is leading is best. Now, many people ask God to walk with them as they sprint through life, never consulting Him in prayer or by reading the Bible—God's road map to life.

We often do this because we are weak. We forget to look to our Guide. We stumble or get diverted, or get weary and stop moving forward. But the Spirit of God has been given to those who trust in Him to help us walk with Him.

The Incomprehensibility of God

Oh, the depth of the riches both of the wisdom and knowledge of God!
How unsearchable are His judgments and His ways past finding out!
ROMANS 11:33

Faith in God the Creator is far more important than having faith in education or experience. The Bible begins with the simple words: "In the beginning God . . ." (Genesis 1:1). These four words are the cornerstone of all existence and of all human history. Without God there could have been no beginning and no continuing. God was the creating power. By divine fiat He brought form out of shapelessness, order out of disorder, and light out of darkness.

We cannot rationalize God. There are mysteries about God that we will never understand in this life. We should not think it strange that it is impossible to comprehend God intellectually, when it is equally impossible to explain many mysteries in the realm of matter. Who can fathom the law of gravity? Newton discovered it, but he could not explain it.

There are many arguments we could marshal to give evidence of the existence of God. We see objects that have no intellect, such as stars and planets, moving in a consistent pattern, cooperating with one another. Hence it is evident that they achieve their movements not by accident but by design. If God can be fully proved by the human mind, then He is no greater than the mind that proves Him. Cry out to God, "Lord . . . help my unbelief!" (Mark 9:24).

THE BATTLE AGAINST EVIL

*Woe to those who call evil good, and good evil; who put
darkness for light, and light for darkness.*

ISAIAH 5:20

Christians understand that the world is embroiled in the great battle between right and wrong, just as the Bible says.

Christian responsibility is to speak truth in the midst of an unbelieving world. When God's people speak the truth from Scripture, it does offend. Some Christians may do this in the wrong spirit, but God's truth remains and God Himself will fight our battles. But this does not mean that Christians are to be silent when society assaults the Word of God. We must take a stand in light of truth—God's truth.

Mankind has a fighting spirit. There are many words that express this, and it is important to understand their meanings. From the beginning man has fought against God and His Word. There is an expression that says, "Don't fight it—it's bigger than both of us." But fighting sin is not wrong.

It is important to understand that "we do not wrestle against flesh and blood, but against principalities, against powers, against the rulers of the darkness of this age, against spiritual hosts of wickedness in the heavenly places" (Ephesians 6:12). The battles on Earth are far less than what is taking place in the heavenly realm known to God. But on Earth He empowers His people to be strong and to put on the armor of God.

IN OUR STEAD

Blessed is he whose transgression is forgiven.
PSALM 32:1

Imagine you committed a crime, were arrested, and were sent to jail. The day has come for you to appear in court. As you stand before the judge, there is absolutely no doubt: you are guilty of the charges against you. According to the law, you must pay for this crime, and in this case the penalty is a year in jail. The judge issues his verdict and pronounces your sentence. At once the bailiff comes over to lead you away to prison.

But then something almost beyond belief happens. The judge steps down from the bench, stops the bailiff, and takes your place. He is innocent—but he goes to prison and pays the penalty for the crime you committed. You, on the other hand, are free!

This is a picture of what Jesus Christ did for us. We are guilty before God and deserve nothing less than death. But the Judge—Jesus Christ—took our place. By His death on the cross, He took the penalty we deserve. Sin's penalty has been fully paid. But you must accept it! Believe it! Act on it!

When we are not willing to repent of sin against Him and humble ourselves, we are really rebelling against God and rejecting all that He has done for us. Not only will Christ forgive us, He also promises the hope of Heaven to all who receive Him.

GOD SEARCHES THE HEART

Every way of a man is right in his own eyes: but the LORD pondereth the hearts.

PROVERBS 21:2 KJV

There are many people who spend their lives doing good deeds. This, in fact, was the story of a young man in Scripture often referred to as the Rich Young Ruler. He wanted to have assurance that he would go to Heaven someday and have eternal life, so he worked very hard to meet a spiritual criterion as he believed it. Many people today work hard to satisfy this self-inflicted expectation while forgetting the reason behind "doing good."

Many believe they serve God, but they actually have little time for Him. They spend far more time watching television than reading the Bible. They spend far more time on social media than seeking wisdom from the Lord through prayer. There is no time for God, and their hearts are a long way from Him.

The Bible says that the Lord searches the heart. "I, the LORD, search the heart" (Jeremiah 17:10). He is in there probing. Scriptures tell us that God ponders the heart of every person.

We can rationalize the way we're living. But the Bible says God does not accept our evaluation and our judgment. He weighs our spiritual lives and accepts our repentance. Then He does a wonderful thing: He promises to give us a new heart if we will submit to Him and receive His salvation.

A WAY OF ESCAPE

Set your heart and your soul to seek the LORD your God.
1 CHRONICLES 22:19

Temptation is exactly the same for us as it was for Adam and Eve in the Garden of Eden. And Satan also tempts us in the same way that he tempted Jesus—through "the lust of the flesh, the lust of the eyes, and the pride of life" (1 John 2:16). Satan's attempt failed.

It is not a sin to be tempted, for everyone is tempted. The devil tempts, but he can tempt you only so far as God permits—and God always provides a way to escape (1 Corinthians 10:13). The sin is in yielding to temptation instead of seeking God's power to escape.

When you face temptation, follow Jesus' example. Jesus didn't argue with Satan; Jesus didn't debate with him; Jesus didn't rationalize. Instead, He replied, "It is written . . ." (Matthew 4:1–4). Jesus responded to the enemy's temptation with the simple but strong truth of God's Word.

The Bible tells us to be on the alert, for Satan is always looking for a way to trap us. "Sin lies at the door. And its desire is for you, but you should rule over it" (Genesis 4:7). How do we rule over it? By keeping our eyes on the Lord Jesus Christ. By keeping our hearts free from the things that can lead to temptation. Don't be trapped, but tap into the power that God grants to those whose hearts are bent toward Him.

CHILDREN OF LIGHT

The kingdom of God is not eating and drinking, but
righteousness and peace and joy in the Holy Spirit.
ROMANS 14:17

We should be a "glimmer" for someone who may be discouraged. While our tendency is to live in the past and sometimes dread the future, it is important to remember that the devil wants us to live discouraged lives. If we focus on what is bad, we pull the shade on future's light. We must put our eyes on others, and most important is to keep our eyes on Jesus.

Desire to live an outgoing, outflowing life in the context of eternity. When Jesus left this Earth after His resurrection, He said, "It is to your advantage that I go away; for if I do not go away, the Helper will not come to you; but if I depart, I will send Him to you" (John 16:7). That Helper is the Holy Spirit of the living God.

Do not be trapped by the world's darkness. If we belong to Jesus Christ, we are children of light. We must remember when we're discouraged how much more discouraged others are. Make a point to be pleasant and smile. People from every race and culture respond to a smile. Try it and you will see.

We will never be free from discouragement and despondency until we know and walk with the very fountainhead of joy, the Lord Jesus Christ as Savior and Lord.

Every Step Ordained

In their hearts humans plan their course, but the Lord establishes their steps.
PROVERBS 16:9 NIV

Some see their own life's journey as a series of unrelated events—some good, some bad. Others feel trapped like a leaf in a rushing stream, tossed about by circumstances beyond control. Many people may never have stopped to think about the road they are traveling.

Life is a journey—although sometimes we forget it. Life becomes so hectic, and we become so preoccupied with our immediate concerns, that we don't step back and see the whole picture. For many people life is a constant struggle just to survive. Others have everything they could ever want yet remain unsatisfied and unfulfilled.

But God didn't intend for our journey through life to be this way. Instead, He meant for it to be filled with joy and purpose, with even the most ordinary events being part of His plan. He also wants to guide us as we make decisions and give us hope for the future. Most of all, He wants to make this journey with us.

When we believe in the Lord Jesus and follow Him, we learn that He goes before us every step of the way.

THE GREATEST ANSWER

He who does not love does not know God, for God is love.
1 JOHN 4:8

Hatred abounds all over the world and often stems from jealousy. Satan's hatred of God was due to jealousy. He wanted to be exalted instead of exalting the God of the ages.

At no time in history was hatred on display more than during the time of Jesus on Earth. Herod hated Him because of fear that the baby Jesus would someday become King. Herod caused the slaughter of infant children in and around the village of Bethlehem so that the prophecy would not come to pass.

Hate knows no bounds. It is in motion at every level. Hatred is a social cancer that gnaws at the vitals of our people. It is rampant—a sign of the depravity of the human race. The Bible teaches hatred is sin.

The Bible also teaches that God is a God of love (1 John 4:8). Love is a basic part of God's nature. He loves us and He is waiting for each person to come to Him in repentance of sin. Rejection of Christ is hatred of Him. The greatest answer for life is to say an eternal "yes" to Christ and His offer of eternal life.

A Strong Foundation

Now is the day of salvation.
2 CORINTHIANS 6:2

As human beings we should all be wise in planning for life, whether that is getting a good education, preparing for marriage and a family, or something else. In fact, Jesus commended the wise man who built his house upon the rock instead of the sand (Matthew 7:24–26). He also asked the question, "For which of you, intending to build a tower [building], does not sit down first and count the cost, whether he has enough to finish it?" (Luke 14:28).

Planning and worrying are two different things. When we worry, we are not trusting God for our futures, but the Bible does teach the importance of preparation.

The most important preparation we can do in this life is to prepare for the next life—eternity. Where will we spend it? There are only two choices—Heaven or Hell. There is nothing in between. Do not wait until death approaches because no one knows what a day may bring. Today is the time to prepare for the future life. What a magnificent thought, and Jesus Christ has paid the cost. Do not delay.

Make it a goal to build strong foundations for life—foundations constructed from prayer and the truths of God's Word.

CHERISHING OUR RELATIONSHIPS

Be patient, bearing with one another in love.
EPHESIANS 4:2 NIV

A woman once wrote a letter describing how fortunate she was to have a kind, considerate husband. She then wrote four pages listing all his faults! How many marriages and other relationships grow cold and eventually are shattered because of fault finding?

We should thank God for the people in our lives. It is so easy to take other people for granted or to complain and become angry because they do not meet our every expectation. But we need to give thanks for those around us. We must also grasp that we do things that irritate others in our circle of friends and family.

How do we respond to this challenge? Do we go out of our way to let others know we appreciate them and are thankful for them? We should be diligent to thank God for others who touch our lives.

The Bible is the Book of books, and its pages are filled with examples of why and how relationships turn bad. It also tells us how to nurture friendship and overlook faults. God's Word instructs us to pray for discernment and wisdom, and to respond to others with understanding and mercy. Patience graciously, compassionately, and with understanding judges the faults of others without unjust criticism but in love. After all, this is what Christ has done for us, and we are told to "follow His steps" (1 Peter 2:21).

TRUE FAITH

"God is Spirit, and those who worship Him must worship in spirit and truth."
JOHN 4:24

In the era of social media, people are free in sharing their innermost thoughts. A young lady posted in a blog that as she searched for truth, she realized that the only life she belonged to was her own, saying, "I set about creating [a life] for myself . . . custom-built for me. And I fit perfectly in it." Another woman wrote that she believed in people, no matter their religion, who do good wherever they are.

If they are honest, they will one day post what King Solomon wrote: "I denied myself nothing my eyes desired; I refused my heart no pleasure. . . . Yet when I surveyed all that my hands had done . . . everything was meaningless, a chasing after the wind" (Ecclesiastes 2:10–11 NIV).

A religion designed to reflect one's personal desire is contrary to having a personal relationship with God, who puts within His true follower His desires. Professing faith in Christ is clearly not the same as possessing Christ, who is the Source of faith. Faith in the one true God will manifest itself in three ways: doctrine (what we believe), worship (our communion with God), and morality (how we live and behave).

Believe in Jesus Christ and obey His Word. This is living out true faith.

WHAT WILL WE CHOOSE?

See, I have set before you today life and good, death and evil.
DEUTERONOMY 30:15

Freedom of choice is debated a great deal and takes on various meanings. The very word *choice* presupposes at least two alternatives. We all face choices throughout life, and this is certainly a theme throughout the Bible.

God commands us to make choices, but only after providing us with sufficient information so that choices will be informed ones. Take, for instance, lending and labeling laws; one cannot apply for a loan or buy a product without being furnished certain information so that they are not deceived. This information is necessary in making intelligent choices.

God's given us information about Himself, including His holiness, man's sinfulness, and His provision for sin—redemption in Jesus Christ. Scores of promises to man about what will happen if he accepts God's promises and what will happen if he refuses God's promises are recorded in Scripture (see Galatians 6).

The great Old Testament leader Joshua, who led the Israelites, challenged them, saying, "Choose for yourselves this day whom you will serve" (Joshua 24:15). The choice was between the false god Baal or the one true God. Before the people answered Joshua he boldly declared, "As for me and my house, we will serve the LORD."

Making the right choice will affect our lives for the better.

REPENTANCE

*Repent . . . and turn to God, so that your sins may be wiped
out, that times of refreshing may come from the Lord.*
ACTS 3:19 NIV

There's a tendency for people to focus only on the love of God to the exclusion
of the other side of God's nature. God does love, but He also hates. One of the
definitions of *hate* is "to despise" something. And God despises sin in every form.

The Bible records that God hates pride, murder, the plans of the wicked, liars,
etc. (Proverbs 6), and God promises to judge sin with the fierceness of His wrath.
Why? Because He so loves the world that He desires for us to live in obedience. His
Word is truth and will provide for us His best.

God doesn't take sin lightly. We live in an age when sin is winked at; where
God is indulgent, softhearted, and tolerant of those who break His commandments.
People find it difficult to believe that God hates anything, much less sin.

Some people may be pretending that sin doesn't exist, but sin is present all
around us. When left unforgiven, sin sends men and women out into a timeless
eternity in Hell; but God is not willing that any should perish, but that all might
come to salvation in Him.

When we gladly receive God's forgiveness, He restores our souls and brings
peace and joy into our lives.

MARCH

THE LIGHT OF THE WORLD

With You is the fountain of life; in Your light we see light.
PSALM 36:9

The more knowledge we acquire, the less wisdom we seem to have. The more economic security we gain, the more boredom we generate. The more worldly pleasure we enjoy, the less satisfied and contented we are with life. We are like a restless sea, finding a little peace here and a little pleasure there, but nothing permanent and satisfying. So the search continues! Men will kill, lie, cheat, and steal to satisfy their quest for power, pleasure, and wealth in hopes of gaining peace, security, and happiness.

Yet inside us a little voice keeps saying, "We were not meant to be this way—we were meant for better things." We have a mysterious feeling that there is a fountain somewhere that contains the happiness that makes life worthwhile. We keep saying to ourselves that somewhere, sometime we will stumble onto the secret. Sometimes we feel that we have obtained it, only to find it elusive.

The happiness that brings enduring worth to life is not the superficial happiness that is dependent on circumstances. It's contentment that fills the soul even in the midst of the most distressing circumstances and the most adverse environments. The only Source of peace and contentment is in the Lord Jesus.

Jesus provides the only ray of hope that shines as an ever-brightening beam in a darkened world.

BEYOND THE CLOUDS

The LORD my God will enlighten my darkness.
PSALM 18:28

One of the great therapies to overcoming disappointments is to be thankful that we are spared results of bad decisions. Stories of dashed hopes and dreams have often been used to redirect our lives. Multitudes have survived what seemed to be hopeless.

It's not always easy to trace God's designs in our ill-planned dreams. But for those who love God, all things do work together for good. Who are we to dictate which way the winds will blow, or how God will maneuver our ship through life's storms? The psalmist wrote that God guides by His skillful hand (Psalm 78:72).

Clouds will come. They are part of life. But by God's grace, we need not be depressed by their presence. Just as clouds can protect us from the brightness of the sun, life's clouds can reveal the glory of God, and from their lofty height God speaks to us.

When our lives seem to crumble and life is dismal and gloomy, we must look up, beyond the clouds, and know that Christ can turn those dark clouds inside out. Many may be discouraged because of things they can't overcome. Sin also can hang over us like a cloud, causing turmoil and despair. When faced with the clouds of defeat, we need to open our hearts and let Christ take the clouds away and restore our hope in Him.

A Pure Heart

"Blessed are the pure in heart, for they shall see God."
MATTHEW 5:8

Matthew 5:8 is a wonderful passage from Jesus' Sermon on the Mount, and it tells us how to live for Him in this world. More important than doing what we want is to do what God wants, and He wants us to live life with pure hearts. He will strengthen us to obey Him. This is what it means to be conformed to the image of His Son. If Christ lives within us, we experience true success and contentment. Many times, He will give us the desires of our heart, but the important thing is that our desires become His because He will bless the desires that bring glory to Him.

What does this mean? Jesus had a humble heart. If He abides in us, pride will never dominate our lives. Jesus had a loving heart. If He dwells within us, we will learn to follow Him obediently. But even more, Jesus' one desire was to do His Father's will.

We may say, "That's a big order!" Yes, and it would be impossible if we had to measure up to His desires by our own strength. Paul recognized that he could never do the right things by his own strength and wrote, "I can do all things through Christ who strengthens me" (Philippians 4:13). May we always strive to live according to the Lord's desire for us.

The Most Important Relationship

Therefore submit to God.
JAMES 4:7

What is troubling people today? Heavy burdens because of some problem that threatens to overcome? Anxiety and worry about something? As children of God, we can turn these over to Christ, knowing that He loves us and He is able to help.

Many people never learn the secret of taking every care to God daily in prayer. Even a short time alone with God every morning can change our outlooks and recharge our batteries. But these unlimited benefits that flow from the storehouse of Heaven are contingent upon our relationship to God—the most important relationship one can ever have. We also live lives that are more contented when we turn thoughts from ourselves to others and their needs. Only God can help us change our way of living.

Yielding to Him in obedience to His Word is a condition of being a child of God—surrendering to God in everything. We must admit our sin and turn from sin before we can receive His salvation. We must acknowledge that we are poor before we can be made rich. We must admit we are destitute before we can belong to Him. When we become aware of the destructive power of our stubborn wills, when we realize our absolute dependence upon the grace of God through faith and nothing more, then we have started on the road to finding fulfillment within and in relationships with others.

The Way Home

"Enter by the narrow gate. . . . Narrow is the gate . . . which leads to life."
MATTHEW 7:13–14

It is unimaginable that anyone would want to board an airplane knowing the pilot would be tolerant of anything that could bring disaster to the passengers. Just one single error by a pilot going through a storm—one flash of broad-mindedness—could cause the death of hundreds.

Once, on a flight from Korea to Japan, a plane flew through a rough snowstorm. The visibility was nearly zero as the plane approached the runway. The pilot had to make an instrument landing. A controller in the tower talked the pilot in safely, and the crew and passengers were glad the pilot and controller hadn't been broad-minded.

When it comes time for life to end on Earth, each person should want to know that they've followed the narrow way—the only way to be welcomed into Heaven, by following Jesus Christ.

Jesus left the glory of Heaven, took on Himself the form of man, and died a shameful death on a cruel cross to purchase our redemption. With the love that was His, He could not be broad-minded about a world held captive by sin. Jesus said, "He who is not with Me is against Me" (Matthew 12:30). The broad, wide, easy, popular way leads to death and destruction. Only the way of the cross leads home.

Not Our Own

If we ask anything according to His will, He hears us.

1 JOHN 5:14

We are called to trust God's promises; He possesses everything. He will supply our needs according to His riches in glory (Philippians 4:19). The Lord gives His Holy Spirit that guides us in prayer, according to His will, for He knows us best. No task is too arduous, no problem is too difficult, and no burden is too heavy for His loving response. The future, with its tears and uncertainties, is fully revealed to Him.

Christ's own promise is that if those of us who belong to Him abide in Him and His words abide in us, we can ask Him and He will answer (John 15:7). However, many people ask with the wrong motive, not knowing what is best for them.

Contrary to what many say, we are not the masters of our own souls. We must not put our will above God's will. We must not insist on our own way or dictate to God. Rather, we must learn the difficult lesson of praying as the sinless Son of God Himself prayed, "Not my will, but thine, be done." The Scripture says that the one mediator between God and man is Jesus Christ. We must know Him, and we must pray in His name. Our prayers must be directed according to the will of God. Let's be thankful to the Lord for hearing us call on His name.

Unchanging God

"I am the Lord, I do not change."
MALACHI 3:6

The Bible declares that God is Spirit, that He is not limited by body. He is not limited to shape; He is not limited to force; He is not limited to boundaries or bonds. He is absolutely immeasurable and indiscernible to eyes that are limited to physical things. The Bible declares that because God has no such limitations, He can be everywhere at the same time.

In the gospel of John, Jesus made a statement about God, simply saying, "God is Spirit" (4:24). Immediately we imagine a sort of cloudy vapor. But this is not a picture of God. Spirit is contrary to body. God is a Spirit—infinite, eternal, and unchangeable. Those three words beautifully describe God. He is infinite—not body-bound. Eternal—He has no beginning and no ending. He is the One forever self-existent. The Bible declares that He never changes.

God sent His Son, Jesus Christ, to this Earth in bodily form to walk among people, to show us the great and deep love of God by dying in our place and being gloriously resurrected. We cannot fathom the infinite nature of God the Father and God the Son and God the Holy Spirit. Our ever-changing minds cannot grasp His never-changing ways. We must ask the Lord to empower our belief and our faith and walk with Him step by step, and worship Him in spirit and truth (John 4:24).

MORE THAN CONQUERORS

We are more than conquerors through Him who loved us.

ROMANS 8:37

The Bible is clear that either the world's inhabitants are under the influence of this world with its cunning, deception, and spell; or they are in Christ and under the direction of the Spirit of God. There is no neutral ground.

The Bible teaches that worldliness is a force that is in opposition and in contradiction to all that is godly and Christian. Its goal is selfish pleasure, material success, and the pride of life. It is ambitious and self-centered. God is not necessarily denied; He is just ignored and forgotten.

Paul wrote to the Ephesians reminding them that in times past they had walked according to the course of the world, according to the prince of the power of the air, the spirit that works in the children of disobedience (Ephesians 2:2–3).

Now the words "course of this world" carry the meaning of current or flow. There is an undertow, a subtle current, that runs against the will and the way of God. Satan employs every device at his command to harass, tempt, thwart, and hurt the people of God.

Paul reminded us, "For we do not wrestle against flesh and blood, but against principalities, against powers, against the rulers of the darkness of this age" (Ephesians 6:12). The Christian is not left defenseless in this conflict. God provides the power to give us victory over Satan.

ANGEL ARMIES

He will command his angels concerning you to guard you in all your ways.
PSALM 91:11 NIV

The great empire of angels is as vast as God's creation. If you believe the Bible, you will believe in their ministry. They crisscross the Old and New Testaments, being mentioned directly or indirectly nearly three hundred times. Some Bible scholars believe that angels can be numbered potentially in the millions since Hebrews 12:22 speaks of "an innumerable [myriads—a great but indefinite number] company of angels."

And angels are not just mentioned in past tense. The Bible says that the Lord Jesus shall be "revealed from heaven with His mighty angels" (2 Thessalonians 1:7). Think of it! Multitudes of angels, indescribably mighty, performing the commands of Heaven as though an extension of the arm of God. Singly or corporately, angels are for real. They are better organized than were the armies of Alexander the Great, Napoleon, or any other mighty world power.

It is important to remember, though, that angels are not to be worshiped. For their powers come straight from God and He commands them at His will.

Just as millions of angels participated in the dazzling show when the morning stars sang together at creation, so will the innumerable hosts of Heaven help bring to pass God's prophetic declarations throughout time and into eternity.

FALSE RELIGIONS

"I am the way, the truth, and the life. No one comes to the Father except through Me."
JOHN 14:6

F ew terms in the language of man have been so distorted and misunderstood as that of *religion*.

Religion has many meanings for many people. It can mean the sadistic symbolism of the occult; it can also suggest quiet meditation within the comforting walls of a church.

Many people say rather proudly, "I'm not very religious," but in spite of some of his own objections, man is a religious being. The Bible, anthropology, sociology, and other sciences teach us that people long for some sort of religious experience.

Religion can be defined as having two magnetic poles, the biblical and the naturalistic. The biblical pole is described in the teachings of the Bible. The naturalistic pole is explained in all the man-made religions. In humanistic systems there are always certain elements of truth. Many of these religions have borrowed from Judeo-Christianity; many use portions and incorporate their own fables. Other religions have in fragments what Christianity has as a whole.

False religions cut away parts of God's revelation, add ideas of their own, and come out with various viewpoints that differ from God's revelation in the Bible. Natural religion does not come from God but from the natural world. God's original design has always had imitators and counterfeits. Anyone who desires God's truth can find it through Jesus Christ, who is Truth.

THE GLORIOUS CROSS

For this purpose the Son of God was manifested, that
He might destroy the works of the devil.
1 JOHN 3:8

In jewelry stores from Fifth Avenue to the airport in Rome, one piece of jewelry is universally displayed—the cross. Clerical robes have this emblem sewn on the front or back. Churches display the cross in wood, bronze, concrete, or brass.

While the cross is under attack today, it hasn't changed people's fascination with this iconic symbol. But many ask, "What does it mean?" If people were stopped on the street and asked to explain this, some would answer that it is the symbol of Christianity. Others might say it is a religious myth. History majors may describe it as an example of Roman justice.

Before the teaching in the Bible about the cross can mean anything to us, the Spirit of God must open our minds. To the "outsider" the cross must appear to be ridiculous. But to those who have experienced its transforming power, it has become the only remedy for the ills of each person, and of the world.

The message of the cross is this: that upon it Jesus was crucified. He died for our sins that we might have life everlasting. God changes men and women by the message of the cross of Christ. God designed the cross to defeat Satan. Through the cross, God not only overpowered Satan but brought Himself and man together. This is glorious news!

THE POWER OF SCRIPTURE

Whatever things were written before were written for our learning.

ROMANS 15:4

Satan is the great discourager. He doesn't want us to read or memorize Scripture because it is the Word of God. When we look into the Bible, we make Satan angry and he will unleash all of his secret weapons. When souls leave his camp and join the family of God, the devil is not happy. But we can overcome everything that he hurls at us with the weapon God has provided—the sword of the Spirit, which is the Word of God.

We must saturate ourselves in His truth. We must read and ask the Spirit of God to clarify what we are reading. The Scriptures are the greatest source of hope we will find in this hopeless world.

Memorize portions of Scripture. "Your word I have hidden in my heart, that I might not sin against You" (Psalm 119:11). Print these portions of Scriptures on small cards and carry them throughout the day, referring to them frequently. Our minds have the capacity to commit them to memory quickly; that brings great blessing.

The Spirit of God takes the Word of God and makes the child of God. He will never lead you contrary to His truth. Our spiritual lives need food. Christ is the Bread of Life for our hungry souls, and the Water of Life for our thirsty hearts. God blesses those who seek Him.

SAVED THROUGH FAITH

*By grace you have been saved through faith, and that not
of yourselves; it is the gift of God, not of works.*
EPHESIANS 2:8–9

Many people decide to join the church because they think getting their names on a church roll is all that is necessary. They perform the rites, pay the money, and think they have done all that is necessary to meet the standard. But worry about eternity nags with doubt; striving to be good seems unattainable.

No matter how much we strive to live according to the precepts of Jesus' message, without Christ living within us it is impossible.

A young college student wrote to his father and said, "I don't believe in God. When I come home I don't want you to cram religion down my throat by taking me to church." His father was brokenhearted. War came. This young man volunteered for the Army Air Corps. One night on his way across the Channel, after having dropped bombs on Berlin, one of the motors in his plane caught fire. He ordered the crew to jump, then he followed. "By the time I hit the silk I was praying to the God who a few months ago I denied existed," he said later. "By the time I hit the water I knew my father's Christ." He went from sinner to saint in a moment's time. What a glorious reality.

CONFESSION IS GOOD FOR THE SOUL

Examine yourselves as to whether you are in the faith.

2 CORINTHIANS 13:5

The Bible says to examine ourselves. God will show us where we are wrong and what is blocking the joy we should experience as Christians. It may be malice, spite, jealousy, or hatred. We may carry a grudge against someone and have unforgiving attitudes. Perhaps we are too easily offended or puffed up with pride. Dishonesty, gossip, criticism, worry, lustful thoughts, unbelief, prayerlessness, neglect of God's Word—any of these things can prevent the joy of salvation from welling up in our souls, hindering the Holy Spirit from taking possession of our lives.

When we confess these things by name, this is the first step to victory. We shouldn't say, "Lord, forgive my sins." Let's define them because God already knows. We must ask Him to give us the power and the strength to overcome. We must take Him at His word.

There are certain sins that have been committed against God alone. This requires private confession. No one except God needs to know anything about them. There are other sins that have been committed against another person. Such transgression should be confessed not only to God but also to the one who has been wronged. There will never be peace until the confession has been made and forgiveness sought. Be reconciled to God and man (Matthew 5:23–24) and the joy of your salvation will be restored.

POWER TO CALM STORMS

Be still, and know that I am God.
PSALM 46:10

An "act of God" is defined as "a natural hazard outside human control for which no person can be held responsible." The key phrase here is "outside of human control."

Mankind takes great pride in being in control. But let a tsunami ravage oceanfronts, and suddenly people resort to silence. Such storms are out of our control. So why do we doubt God's power?

We applaud the power and strength of mankind daily. It is claimed that Caruso, the great opera singer, shattered glass with his powerful voice. It is claimed that one strongman lifted five hundred pounds with his little finger.

But the strong man Jesus Christ did what no man has ever done or will ever do. He spoke "Peace, be still!" and the raging sea quieted and brought relief to a boatload of frightened disciples, who gave glory to the Master of the sea, saying "Even the wind and the sea obey Him!" (Mark 4:39–41).

Invite the Master of the sea into your life. With the power of His gentle voice He can calm the storms.

God takes the weak and makes them strong. He takes the vile and makes them clean. He takes the worthless and makes them worthwhile. He takes the sinful and makes them sinless. Only a gracious and loving God can do this.

REST IN JESUS

"Come to Me, all you who labor and are heavy laden, and I will give you rest."
MATTHEW 11:28

Many people have trouble falling asleep at night. Some take over-the-counter drugs or sleeping pills; others require prescription medication to sleep.

Often sleeplessness is a restless spirit and not a chemical imbalance that keeps us from what our bodies and minds need. It is good for us to remember that the Bible instructs us to lie down in sleep and dwell in safety (Psalm 4:8). One of the best ways we can help ourselves at the close of day is to direct our thoughts toward God, who gives rest in our weariness.

The Psalms are perhaps the most soothing place in Scripture for one to turn to shut out the stresses and troubles of the day. Some of the psalms have been set to music, and listening to them can help soothe the cares of the world.

God desires that we rest in Him. He knows that we need it in order to work effectively while we're awake. So when sleep is difficult, read from the book of Psalms. There is joy in its message and peace in its instruction. We can pray and ask God to give body, mind, and soul restoration. He gives us quiet confidence to live by and rest in.

Take solace in the fact that the Lord will be with us when we are resting in Him.

THE IMPORTANCE OF DISCIPLINE

*I discipline my body and bring it into subjection, lest, when I have
preached to others, I myself should become disqualified.*
1 CORINTHIANS 9:27

One of the greatest needs among Christians today is to exercise discipline. It is one of the great testimonies that points others to Jesus Christ. Just as our country's military academies teach students to live disciplined lives in order to be officers in the armed forces, Christians should do no less. Soldiers are trained for future leadership and service. In order for Christians to serve in the name of the Lord Jesus Christ, obedience to God's instruction should be of utmost importance.

Christians should stand out like sparkling diamonds against a rough and dark background. We should be wholesome and poised, courteous and gracious, industrious and friendly. We should be firm in the things we do or do not do, and we should be able to articulate why we live as we do; we should refuse to allow the world to pull us down.

The Bible says that we should not be conformed to the world so that we can show the world this is God's will for His people (Romans 12:1–2). This should not be burdensome, but we should do this with joy, for God Himself dwells in us and enables us to live in such a way that others see Christ at the center of our lives.

RESENTMENT VERSUS ACCEPTANCE

Count it all joy when you fall into various trials, knowing
that the testing of your faith produces patience.

JAMES 1:2–3

Resentment is a killer. If it doesn't kill physically, it can kill emotionally. Resentment leads to bitterness. Lord Byron and Sir Walter Scott were gifted writers in the eighteenth and early nineteenth centuries. They were both lame. Byron bitterly resented his infirmity and constantly grumbled about it. Scott was never heard to complain about his handicap.

One day Scott received a letter from Byron that said, "I would give my fame to have your happiness." What made the difference in their reactions toward their disabilities? Byron was a man who took pride in his dissolute lifestyle. His moral standards were doubtful. Scott, on the other hand, was a Christian whose courageous life exemplified his values.

Jealousy often leads to bitterness that can strangle a person. The Bible cautions us to refrain from letting the root of bitterness spring up and cause trouble (Hebrews 12:15).

Resentment develops when we persist in resisting what God has allowed to happen to us. We must take our eyes off "self" and look to the Lord.

A muscle becomes weak if it is not used. To become strong, a muscle must push against something—a person must learn how to take advantage of difficulty and give glory to God in all things. It strengthens us for what is ahead.

AWARENESS OF GOD'S PRESENCE

The LORD is near to all who call upon Him, to all who call upon Him in truth.
PSALM 145:18

Charles Spurgeon, often referred to as the "Prince of Preachers," once said that there had never been fifteen minutes in his life when he did not sense the presence of Christ. What strength we would have if we trained for life knowing that Christ walks beside us.

Bestseller *In His Steps*, by Charles Sheldon, told of a pastor's challenge to his people: "Don't do anything without first asking the question, 'What would Jesus do?'"

Do we live our lives with this thought in mind? Do we cultivate the sense of His presence as we go about the daily routine of our lives? Christ must be vitally real to us if we are to remain faithful to Him in the hour of crisis.

Unceasing prayer and Scripture memorization can give us strength through-out the days; they can bring comfort in the lonely nights. There is great power in God's Word. When we experience joy, our memories can bring to mind, "Bless the LORD . . . and forget not all His benefits" (Psalm 103:2). When we feel others are against us, we can call to mind, "[You O Lord] who save those who trust in You from those who rise up against them" (Psalm 17:7). When we need a loving word, we remember, "For His lovingkindness is great toward us" (Psalm 117:2 NASB 1995).

The Work of Our Hands

Whatever your hand finds to do, do it with your might.
ECCLESIASTES 9:10

The Bible teaches that we are to perform our daily tasks and take pride in performing them well. We're given certain work to do, and those who claim to be Christians are taught not only to labor but to labor to the best of their ability.

The Christian ideal certainly does not demand that a person renounce all interest in the affairs of this life, but rather that we seek God's guidance in performing our daily work to the best of our ability and that we keep both our work and our ambitions in subordination to the Lord at all times. We find that Christ offers help in our daily living here on Earth. He inspires us in our talents, helps us in our work, and blesses us as we enjoy all that He has given.

The world's greatest writers have been inspired by Jesus; the greatest artists, musicians, and sculptors have also been illumined by Him. Leaders from the world of business have written books about leadership skills they have learned from Scripture. World leaders have quoted from the Bible in the most memorable speeches recorded.

God's book is filled with promises, and it does not change or get out of date. Each of us has our reference point, and as Christians the reference point by which to measure life and thought is the Bible.

THE PEACE TREATY

Let the peace of God rule in your hearts.
COLOSSIANS 3:15

In the biography of Queen Victoria there is a heart-warming story told. She went into the slums of London and visited the home of an elderly lady. When the queen rose to leave, she asked, "Is there anything I can do for you?" The woman said, "Yes, ma'am, Your Majesty, you can meet me in heaven." The queen turned to her and said softly, "Yes. I'll be there, but only because of the blood that was shed on the cross for you and for me." Queen Victoria, in her day the most powerful woman in the world, had to depend on the blood of Christ for her salvation; and so do we.

The Bible says that God is the Author of peace (1 Corinthians 14:33). God provided salvation through the cross. He made peace by the shedding of His blood. The war that exists between us and God can be over quickly because the peace treaty has been signed in the blood of His Son Jesus Christ. This is the heart of the gospel message that has been proclaimed around the world.

Do not miss the peace of God in your struggles, turmoil, trials, and pressures of life. We can know with certainty the peace of God. God's strength can be yours in your hour of need, and He will grant you faith to believe and follow Him in your hour of decision.

WHERE JOY IS FOUND

You will show me the path of life; in Your presence is fullness of joy.

PSALM 16:11

Doom and dismay have settled upon the hearts of people. There's a specter of hopelessness seen in the headlines and in the deep lines that furrow troubled brows. Humanity searches for fulfillment, yet the purposelessness of living is prevalent, robbing millions of the zest for life.

It doesn't have to be this way. The greatest need in the world is for souls to find rest in Jesus Christ, possessing faith in Him daily no matter the circumstances. This is the ultimate goal—to be conformed to the image of Christ. The Bible says, "For we are His workmanship, created in Christ Jesus for good works, which God prepared beforehand that we should walk in them" (Ephesians 2:10).

Jesus is our example. He will strengthen us in times of difficulty and will be with us when we walk through the trials that come. Jesus walked and talked as a man should. His attitude and approach to life were mature in every sense. He looked with holy eyes upon a sinful world but was not discouraged or depressed by it, but said, "I have come that they may have life, and that they may have it more abundantly" (John 10:10). He has given us the key to living with joy, and that is to know His salvation and obey Him every step of the way.

OUR ONLY HOPE

He made Him who knew no sin to be sin for us, that we might become the righteousness of God in Him.
2 CORINTHIANS 5:21

The world's specialists may employ all the skill at their command, but at best they reach only symptoms. Psychiatrists talk with thousands of people and diagnose their ailments, but a psychiatrist once remarked, "I have a difficult time offering a curative."

The Bible provides the curative—the gospel of the Lord Jesus Christ. God's Word tells us that the human heart is "deceitful above all things, and desperately wicked" (Jeremiah 17:9). Human behavior is warped because of sin.

Many object to the word *sin*, but it is as real as cancer, leprosy, or leukemia. These realities rob us of hope, bring despair, and remind us of death. But sin is curable. Every trace of it can be removed, for God has provided something that can cleanse the vilest sinner and make him or her as pure as fresh-fallen snow.

Everywhere lurk moral entanglements that threaten the soul. We need outside help if we are to find our way to peace of heart and purposeful living. The Bible tells us that there is only one way to God, and that is by the cross! We cannot overcome the difficulties of life without humbling ourselves before almighty God and receiving the salvation offered by His Son Jesus Christ. We must change the direction of our lives. This is mankind's only hope.

Before It's Too Late

Today, if you will hear His voice, do not harden your hearts.

HEBREWS 4:7

When Jesus Christ comes back to this Earth, evil is going to be destroyed. The devil himself is going to be cast into the bottomless pit, and ultimately into the lake of fire. The Bible says that the lake of fire was prepared for the devil and all who follow him. God never wants anyone else to go to Hell.

This is the reason God calls upon people everywhere to follow Him and be obedient to His Word. We must decide if we are going to live for God and serve Him or live for Satan and run after the things of the world.

When Christ returns there will be worldwide justice. Hunger and poverty will be eliminated. Racial hatred will disappear. All the tensions between ethnic groups will be gone. Nature itself is going to be changed. There will be safety and security: "Everyone shall sit under his vine . . . and no one shall make them afraid; for the mouth of the LORD of hosts has spoken" (Micah 4:4). Those who say no to Him now will one day bow at His feet, but then it will be too late to turn to Him and receive His eternal salvation.

Until that time, evil will continue to reign. Salvation now is the answer to evil, and accepting Christ as your personal Savior will bring peace to the heart and strength for the journey until He comes.

No Sin Too Great

In Him we have . . . the forgiveness of sins.
EPHESIANS 1:7

Many see God as able to forgive the small sin but incapable of forgiving the gross sinner. In our own weakness as humans, we tend to grade sins.

The story is told about Hitler and his Third Reich that had gone down in defeat at the hands of the Allies. Many Nazi leaders who committed some of the most infamous crimes known to man were brought to trial in Nuremberg. The world watched as sentences of imprisonment and death were brought against these war criminals. However, an amazing account was given by a prison chaplain who recalled the sincere conversion to faith in Jesus Christ by some of these men who had committed despicable crimes—one of them a former favorite general of Hitler.

At first, the chaplain was very leery of confessions of faith. He said the first time he saw this criminal reading his Bible he thought he was a phony. However, as the chaplain spent time with him he wrote, "But the longer I listened, the more I felt he might be sincere. He insisted he was very glad that a nation which would probably put him to death thought enough of his eternal welfare to provide him with spiritual guidance."

With Bible in hand he said, "I know from this book that God can love a sinner like me." What an amazing love God exhibited for us all at the cross!

Eternity in View

If God is for us, who can be against us?
ROMANS 8:31

I t is wise to be cautious about those who claim to have supernatural abilities to predict the future precisely. At best, such schemes are mere guesswork; at worse, they may be involved in dangerous occult practices. The Bible clearly warns against such things (Deuteronomy 18:9–13). The question, "Who knows what a day may hold?" can be answered by God alone. Only He knows the future.

But we can certainly learn a great deal about the future from the Bible. Over and over through the ages of time, God sent His prophets to the people to warn them of things to come. Rather than be fascinated by man's predictions that fall short, be fascinated about what God has done—and is doing—in the world. Explore the great truths of Scripture.

The greatest discovery we can ever make in life is not someone's prediction but the reality that God loves us and desires that every soul come to salvation in Jesus Christ. For those who repent of sin and trust Him as Savior, they learn to trust the future to Christ. We may not know what is in store for us on Earth, but we can find peace in knowing that eternity for those who believe Christ will be glorious. Live on Earth with eternity in view, and the hope of eternity will guide your steps.

WHY AM I HERE?

"You did not choose Me, but I chose you and appointed you that you should go and bear fruit, and that your fruit should remain."
JOHN 15:16

It is sad to watch someone come to the end of life never having realized the purpose of life. We are not here by chance; God put us here for a purpose, and the most important thing we can do is discover that purpose and commit ourselves to it.

God's purpose for every individual is this: God wants us to know Him personally by giving our lives to Jesus Christ. Then He wants us to discover what it means to live for Him in obedience. "But seek first the kingdom of God and His righteousness, and all these things shall be added to you" (Matthew 6:33).

We must ask this question: What are we living for? Pleasure? Money? Happiness? Security? Success? None of these things will ever fulfill us completely. We were made for a relationship with God, and we will only find true meaning and purpose in Christ. There are those who have made "self" the center of life without even realizing it. How easily this can happen, particularly in today's self-serving world. We must make an about-face and commit ourselves to Jesus Christ by asking Him to come into our hearts as Lord and Savior. He wants to be our counselor and guide. "O LORD . . . show me the path of life" (Psalm 16:5, 11).

WHERE TO TURN IN HARD TIMES

"Blessed are those who mourn, for they shall be comforted."
MATTHEW 5:4

Christians often respond to sickness and death differently because their hope is in what comes after this life—enjoying eternity in Jesus' presence. Believers take Him at His word, that He gives strength to the weary. Living in a sinful world filled with disease and darkness is part of life on Earth.

Death and sickness will always be present until Jesus Christ returns. Many great people of God have spoken of hope in Christ that brings peace in the present life.

As the composer of the great hymn "Rock of Ages" was dying at the age of thirty-eight, he said, "I enjoy heaven already in my soul. My prayers are converted into praises." Those who belong to Jesus rejoice in knowing that He's with us in our trials and waits for us on the other side of life.

When suffering strikes, we have a decision to make. Will we turn away from God, or will we turn toward Him? Turning away leads to doubt, anger, bitterness, and despair. Turning to Him leads to hope, comfort, peace, strength, and joy. Faith in Jesus Christ points us beyond our problems to the hope we have in Christ.

Purpose in Pain

The Lord will fulfill his purpose for me.
PSALM 138:8 ESV

There may not be "simple" answers to why people suffer, but there are many examples of how people survive hardships that come to us in life because they see the bigger picture. In spite of what many people believe, we are put here for one purpose—to glorify God through obedience to Him.

Years ago a woman watched her comfortable world disintegrate in one blinding moment. Without her faith in God, she might have remained hidden in a dark room.

She had been in a hideous accident. While she was spared from burning to death, her beautiful face was disfigured and went through many reconstructive surgeries. One day she had a sun-filled life with beauty, wealth, and an attentive husband; the next day she lost it all.

After six weeks in a coma and seven years of seclusion, she gave her life to Christ and realized it was time to emerge from despair. She knew God had saved her for a reason. She began working at a rehabilitation center. When asked about her greatest joy, she answered, "It's waking up in the morning and knowing that nothing is an accident."

She came to believe that while life can hand us difficulties, the Lord will bring good out of them. We can accept this truth or we can deny it, but our attitude toward the outcome makes all the difference.

A WAY OUT

No temptation has overtaken you except such as is common to man; but God is faithful, who will not allow you to be tempted beyond what you are able, but with the temptation will also make the way of escape, that you may be able to bear it.

1 CORINTHIANS 10:13

Scripture says that mankind is in spiritual warfare and that enemies have power and skill to tempt us (1 Peter 5:8). This is why the Bible warns us to flee temptation and not give Satan a foothold (Ephesians 4:26–27).

Many people believe that when they come to know Christ they will never encounter temptation, but when it comes they are unprepared and in conflict. Sometimes there is a yielding to temptation that leads to discouragement and remorse. The Bible says that God allows Satan to tempt us, but God often uses it as a test to reveal how weak the flesh is. God does not want us to depend on our own strength to flee temptation; He wants us to depend completely on Him.

Spiritual conflict is at work in the heart of every believer. It is true that the Christian possesses a new nature; but the old sin nature is still there, and this is why it is vital to yield to the new nature, which Christ dominates. We can only do this by His power and by calling on His name.

Every believer should commit to memory the wonderful passage above.

THE YIELDED WILL

*"Seek first the kingdom of God and His righteousness,
and all these things shall be added to you."*
MATTHEW 6:33

The story is told of a young man who was having difficulty submitting his will to God. He doubted everything. Emotionally, nothing seemed real to him. Someone gave him some advice: "A man's will is about 'self'—doing what he wants. Your part then is simply to give your will over to God, making up your mind that you will believe what He says and that you will not pay any regard to the feelings that make it seem so impossible. Trust God and He will give you the desire to follow Him." The young man paused a moment and then said, "I will do what you say. I cannot control my emotions, but I can control my will by giving it up to God."

Living life according to the Bible is allowing the power of God's truth to propel our lives with God at the controls. Until we utilize that fuel, we are earthbound, tied down by ego, pride, doubt, and guilt. It often binds people in chains of purposelessness and uncertainty.

Turning all of these things over to God frees mankind from the debt of sin.

Repentance is the absolute step we must take to receive God's forgiveness, opening the way for Him to transform us and strengthen us so that we can live securely in Him and do His will.

APRIL

FIRST BASE

"Not everyone who says to Me, 'Lord, Lord,' shall enter the kingdom of heaven."
MATTHEW 7:21

Years ago in the seventh game of the World Series, the score was tied in the last inning with two outs. The batter came to the plate and hit a home run out of the park. The crowd went wild. For baseball fans, it is about the most exciting thing that can happen. But when the hero crossed home plate to score, the umpire yelled, "Out!" The crowd was stunned. The umpire explained that the batter had not touched first base.

That is the way with many people. They are Christians outwardly; they go to church and talk about being baptized, but they have missed the most important thing: They have not been born again. They haven't touched first base.

Nicodemus was one such man who came to Jesus. Though he was deeply religious, he was not satisfied. He had missed first base—salvation—and then Jesus told Him what it means to be "born again."

There are many who teach that being baptized, going to church, and doing good works will get us to Heaven, but it simply is not true.

We are all born physically, but to get to Heaven, one must be born spiritually. This is the gift of God that only He can give; and He freely gives it when we repent of our sin and come to Him with a humble heart by faith.

WHAT KIND OF PEOPLE SHOULD WE BE?

If our earthly house [body] . . . is destroyed, we have a building from God . . . eternal in the heavens.

2 CORINTHIANS 5:1

One of the Bible's greatest truths is that we were not meant to live only for the here and now. From the beginning, we were meant for Heaven.

The Bible doesn't tell us everything we'd like to know about Heaven, but the Bible does tell us everything we need to know about Heaven while we are here on Earth. We should believe what the Bible says about Heaven and take comfort from its promise that we can spend eternity with Jesus Christ in His heavenly dwelling.

This assurance comes from the Lord Himself because He grants eternal life to all those who will humble themselves in repentance and receive Christ as their Lord and Savior.

The apostle Peter asked the question in his letters to the Christians of the day: What kind of people should we be now as we prepare for Heaven? The answer is found in Scripture that tells us we should live in "holy conduct and godliness, looking for and hastening the coming of the day of God" (2 Peter 3:11–12).

If you are ever going to live for Christ, it should be now. Don't let this life keep you from eternal life with Jesus forever. "This hope we have as an anchor of the soul, both sure and steadfast, and which enters [God's] Presence" (Hebrews 6:19).

No Bargaining

"Strive to enter through the narrow gate."
LUKE 13:24

Jesus spoke of two roads. Every person will have to choose which way they will go. "Enter by the narrow gate; for wide is the gate and broad is the way that leads to destruction, and there are many who go in by it. Because narrow is the gate and difficult is the way which leads to life, and there are few who find it" (Matthew 7:13–14).

This word *narrow* is offensive to many. We live in an age of tolerance, except tolerance for what Jesus commands in Scripture. Society today tells us to "believe anything you want to believe."

Let's apply that principle and see how it works out. Suppose the astronauts blast off in a rocket and get on the wrong path and in the wrong orbit. Would Houston controllers respond, "Oh, that's all right; there are a number of pathways to lead them to their destination." No. The world would never see them again. They must follow precise laws; all nature is governed by them.

People have no authority to lower the standards that have been put in place by the God of the universe and the Savior of men's souls. There is no bargaining with Him.

We cannot work our way to Heaven. We cannot buy our way to Heaven. Heaven is the realm of God, and He desires all people to come to Him.

Slow to Anger

Be swift to hear, slow to speak, slow to wrath.

JAMES 1:19

Every human being is capable of demonstrating anger. Think of a tiny baby who exhibits fits of temper before they can even talk. A toddler can fly into a fit of anger and upset the entire household. Husbands and wives react out of anger before giving any thought to the issue that triggers such a response.

Anger breeds remorse in the heart, discord in the home, bitterness in the community, and confusion in the state. Homes are often destroyed by the swirling tornadoes of heated domestic anger. Business relations are often shattered by fits of violent temper when reason gives way to venomous wrath. Friendships are often broken by the keen knife of indignation.

Anger is condemned by the sacred Scriptures. It murders, assaults, and attacks, causing physical and mental harm.

Jesus said, "Whoever is angry with his brother without a cause shall be in danger of the judgment" (Matthew 5:22). Righteous anger is directed at sinful behavior. The Bible teaches us how to handle anger without doing harm. When anger leads to murder, gossip, etc., it is sinful indeed.

We must not let anger control us, no matter what others do to cause it. We only become guilty of the same sin that afflicts them, and it solves nothing. Don't let the acids of bitterness eat away inside. Look to Christ's example in all things.

An Honest Day's Work

If anyone will not work, neither shall he eat.
2 THESSALONIANS 3:10

It is a great blessing to be able-bodied to work an honest day's job. Laziness is the destroyer of opportunity. It kills the spirit—and many times the body itself. The Bible refers to laziness as "slothful" (Proverbs 18:9). Such a person is like driftwood floating downward with the current. The easy way is the popular way, the broad way, and the way of the crowd.

Many a person has lost their life in an automobile accident, not because they were bad drivers but because they were drivers who had fallen asleep. Likewise, many people are fighting losing battles spiritually because they are drowsy. The Bible says, "Awake, you who sleep, arise from the dead, and Christ will give you light" (Ephesians 5:14).

Jesus spoke a parable about ten virgins. Their sin was not immorality, lying, or cheating—it was pure laziness. They simply neglected to provide themselves with oil for their lamps as they waited for the bridegroom (Matthew 25:1–12). They were judged for laziness and unfaithfulness. Laziness should be judged and faithfulness rewarded.

Laziness is not only attributed to not working, but it can be applied to the neglect of obeying Christ. Many of us would rather catch an extra wink of sleep than to get up and begin the morning reading God's Word to gain strength for the day. Do not refuse what God desires you to have—His way!

BEWARE OF GREED

"You shall not covet your neighbor's house . . . nor his ox, nor his donkey, nor anything that is your neighbor's."

EXODUS 20:17

Greed is an intense and selfish desire for something, often something belonging to another. The Bible speaks of greed as covetousness, as in the Ten Commandments.

Greed seeks more than its own in life. It cheats, robs, and slanders to achieve its desires. The Bible teaches that we are born with the sin of covetousness (Jeremiah 6:13).

Charles Kingsley, a historian, once said, "If you wish to be miserable, think about yourself: about what you want, what you like, what respect people ought to pay you—and then to you, nothing will be pure. You will spoil everything you touch. You will make misery for yourself out of everything good. You will be as wretched as you choose."

Greed is rated with other sins like wickedness and maliciousness in Romans 1:29. Greed is idolatry and not to be confused with riches, if riches have been earned honestly. But if riches choke out spiritual life, then it is sin.

Many people have been blessed by the story of Zacchaeus and challenged to turn from a life of greed to a life of giving—and God's blessing falls on them when they live according to the attributes of Christ. Everything that we see about us that we count as our possessions only comprises a loan from God.

LONELINESS

Let us therefore come boldly to the throne of grace, that we may
obtain mercy and find grace to help in time of need.
HEBREWS 4:16

A few years ago a beautiful young Hollywood star ended her life. She left behind a note with a brief message—she was unbearably lonely. One of the most sought-after box-office draws felt alone.

Then there is the story of Queen Victoria of England. After the death of her husband, she said, "There is no one left to call me Victoria." Even a queen knew what it meant to be lonely.

Then there is the poor person living in a dingy apartment who never receives a phone call or letter or a word of encouragement. There are children isolated in orphanages. The loneliness of solitude affects individuals and whole societies.

The world can be a harsh and sometimes cruel environment, especially when we focus on ourselves. No one can understand loneliness like Jesus Christ. He was "despised and rejected by men, a Man of sorrows and acquainted with grief" (Isaiah 53:3). But Jesus did not only come to identify with mankind's griefs, He came to destroy the grief of sin, the grief of disappointment, and the grief of loneliness. Because Jesus willingly bore the pain and paid the price to redeem our sinful natures, we can have full fellowship with Him forever.

Reach out to others who may have never known acceptance, and great blessing will come.

THE PROBLEM OF SIN

All have sinned and fall short of the glory of God.
ROMANS 3:23

When we look at our own goodness, we tend to get sidetracked by the fact that mankind is weighed down by its own sin. When one does something good for another, that person can take advantage of that goodness because of his or her own sin. It doesn't change the fact that something good was done; it simply highlights the fact that man's heart by nature is evil.

For humans, there is a mystery about sin. But God has revealed answers through the Bible and through Jesus.

We must always start "at the beginning." Man rebelled against God after God had given man a perfect environment. Man said, "I don't need You, God. I can build my world without You." Rebellion against God is sin. When mankind took that position, suffering entered the world.

Remember, Satan is the author of sin. Sin is the reason we have afflictions, including death. This is why Jesus came. To give us new life. For those who belong to the Lord, we have the privilege of demonstrating more than human love. "Love your enemies, do good, and lend, hoping for nothing in return; and your reward will be great" (Luke 6:35). This is a difficult message, but not if we pray first and ask the Lord to guide us in all that we do, that His name may be known.

Be Filled with the Truth

Faith shows the reality of what we hope for; it is the evidence of things we cannot see.
HEBREWS 11:1 NLT

The Bible says, "The entirety of [God's] word is truth" (Psalm 119:160). God calls on mankind to believe His Word, by faith.

Face-to-face, Pontius Pilate confronted Jesus, asking, "Are You a king then?" Jesus answered, "You say rightly that I am a king. For this cause I was born, and for this cause I have come into the world, that I should bear witness to the truth. Everyone who is of the truth hears My voice" (John 18:37). Truth is timeless. Truth does not differ from one age to another, from one person to another, from one geographical location to another.

Even if truth is unpopular, that does not mean that it should not be proclaimed. Humans are emotional beings, but emotions can deceive us. When truth is mixed with error there is always compromise. We need to counter our emotions with the pure truth of God's Word.

If our minds and hearts are not filled with God's truth, something else will take its place: cynicism, occultism, false religions and philosophies, drugs—the list is endless.

It is far better to know God's truth than to be ignorant of it. While Pilate declared that he found no fault in Jesus, neither is there indication that he ever accepted the truth that Jesus proclaimed. Don't make the same mistake.

EMPOWERED

I will see Your face in righteousness; I shall be satisfied when I awake in Your likeness.

PSALM 17:15

All those who know Christ as their personal Lord and Savior will see Him in all His splendor and glory. In His Sermon on the Mount, He said, "Blessed are the pure in heart, for they shall see God" (Matthew 5:8).

What a promise this is. But we do not have to wait to know His power. He gives it to us while we live: a supernatural power to overcome temptations, to smile through tears, to experience joy despite life's burdens. His Spirit raises us up from the mundane, the monotonous, and the hopelessness that we encounter on Earth. He brings us out of spiritual lifelessness and transforms us day by day.

Imagine plugging in to such power as this—the power of the Lord Jesus Christ. He calls us to follow Him and to serve Him, and He does not do that without enabling us. When we work in our own power, we struggle. With Christ, though, all things are possible, and He enables us to do His will. What a reversal there would be in our culture's deteriorating morals. What a lessening of tensions we would see in individuals, groups, and even nations! What a new purpose and power we would experience if we caught the wonder of the biblical truth that Jesus is alive!

Healthy Roots

Your roots will grow down into God's love and keep you strong.
EPHESIANS 3:17 NLT

Some neighbors planted a young plum tree thinking it would shade a corner of their home. Instead, it was struck with blights and would lean until its branches touched the ground in any strong wind. No matter how they staked it, it would not stand tall against the elements. When examined, the tree had never taken root because it had been planted close to a downspout. The roots never stretched beyond its infant root ball to find water.

Contrast this with another sapling planted in a different environment but on the same property. The sapling was able to reach up for sun and out for water and its roots had room to grow—it was not bound by its environment.

After our roots of faith are planted in the fertile ground of truth, we should grow in understanding God's Word with the help of His Spirit, and through prayer and fellowship with other believers. Only with a deep root system can we endure the storms of life. This prepares us for things ahead. If believers stay entrenched in things that pull them down or are motivated to please others, it will stunt their growth and render them ineffective.

We mustn't plant ourselves in an environment that causes us to fall. We must grow in the things of God and apply His truth to everything we do.

GOD'S LOVE FOR SINNERS

He knows the secrets of every heart.

PSALM 44:21 NLT

Sin presents itself in the mind, manifests itself in word and deed, and is hidden in the hearts of everyone. It will overtake the man and woman who refuse to believe it and will conquer them.

The Bible says that the whole world is a prisoner of sin. Sin has crippled human nature, but God has provided the cure. There is no sin that the blood of Jesus Christ cannot cleanse. And that's good news indeed for a culture that still doesn't know what to do with sin.

All the distress, bitterness, heartache, shame, and tragedy can be summed up in the three-letter word *sin*. Its meaning—to fall short of God's standard and to do contrary to God's law—has an impact on every soul.

The world's system claims that the notion of sin is old-fashioned. People "in" the world prove that claim erroneous. A national newspaper quoted a sociologist who admitted, "Secular people still believe there's sin, judgment, and punishment." Sin is definitely "in" and it is "in" every single heart that beats.

The truth is that everyone is born in sin. While some may not think of themselves as sinners, God does. He hears every word we utter; He knows the hidden things. But He loves sinners more than we love sin. There is no greater love than what Jesus offers every person ever born.

THE GIVER OF HOPE

My flesh also will rest in hope.
PSALM 16:9

Good things can come out of bad situations. While it is wise to be realistic, we must be careful not to dampen the spirit of hope due to lack of faith in what God wants to accomplish in each person's life. After all, hope is a gift.

What is hope? Some equate it to a fanciful wish. But the word explodes with confidence to believe in something greater than ourselves. Hope is not found in things but in God who is the Giver of hope.

We know that darkness does not remain, for the sun breaks through the night. God is the Light and creates the light, whether in the flicker of a flame, a sunray, a moonbeam, or the twinkle of the stars. And the flicker of life in the soul is hope.

A contemporary philosopher, the late Richard Rorty, claimed that hope placed in the promise of Jesus Christ returning to Earth has failed because He has not returned. This philosopher believed a new document of promise is needed for hope to exist again. But there is a document of promise that has never grown old. It is new every morning. The Bible says that Jesus is the very hope that lies within. He is our only hope.

Hope is an unseen commodity that pays dividends while we still live. God bless those who live in hope and with hope.

A Spirit of Discernment

"Take heed that no one deceives you."
MATTHEW 24:4

Many years ago a distinguished Methodist minister was preaching on sin. Some deacons approached him afterward and said, "We don't want you to talk so plainly about sin; if you do, our people will more easily become sinners. Call their sin mistakes if you will, but do not call their mistakes sin."

The minister picked up a small bottle and showed it to the group of deacons. The bottle was clearly marked "Poison." "Would you like me to change the label?" the minister asked. "I can mark that this strychnine is the essence of peppermint to make you feel better, but if you take it you will still die. Don't you see that the milder you make the label, the more dangerous you make the poison?"

Satan is the great deceiver. He is crafty and clever, disguising his lies as truth. For his deceptions to be successful, they must be so cunningly devised that his real purpose is concealed. This is manifested even in the spirits of people. We see ourselves as self-sufficient, self-important, and self-sustaining. God sees us as dependent, self-centered, and self-deceived.

One of Satan's greatest feats is to portray evil as good. But it is the people who listen and follow his pathway that will ultimately pay the awful price.

Jesus came to rescue us from Satan's terrible grip. We must pray for God to give the spirit of discernment.

The Search for Freedom

"The Spirit of the Lord GOD is upon Me, because the LORD has anointed Me . . . to proclaim liberty to the captives."
ISAIAH 61:1

People seek freedom in various ways, not realizing that the freedom they seek is often the pathway to bondage. Einstein said, "I feel like a man chained. If only I could be free from the shackles of my intellectual smallness, then I could understand the universe in which I live." My, what insight into a man who is considered one of the most brilliant minds.

Freedom for the scientist, he thinks, is found in seeking truth about the physical universe. The philosopher tries to discover truth about human existence. The psychologist looks for truth about the action and reaction of the human mind. At the end of his life, Buddha said, "I am still searching for truth."

We say we want freedom from prejudice, freedom from ignorance, and freedom from poverty. We even say we're searching for religious freedom; yet even in America there are groups that want to throw out religious symbols. They wish to be free from bondage while throwing away the symbols that speak of true freedom.

Jesus is Truth—all psychological truth, all sociological truth, all scientific truth, all philosophical truth, all religious truth (John 14:6). He came to deliver the most freeing message of all and to rescue mankind from bondage and bring peace and freedom to weary souls.

The Heart of God

O Lord, You have searched me and known me.
PSALM 139:1

The word *heart* is used in different ways all through Scripture. The Bible says that man looks on the outward appearance but God looks at the heart (1 Samuel 16:7). When God looks at man He doesn't look at the color of his skin or what kind of house he lives in. The Bible says simply that God looks upon the heart to see what we are on the inside—the thoughts, motives, and intents of the heart.

The Bible speaks of the heart that is full of evil imaginations. It tells us that our hearts are deceitful and wicked (Jeremiah 17:9). Jesus said in Matthew 15:8 that our hearts are far from Him. The Bible says that our hearts are dark (Romans 1:21) and rebellious (Jeremiah 5:23). God's Word also informs us that our hearts can become hardened (Hebrews 3:15).

That's the bad news. Now here is the good news. God knows our hearts and searches our hearts. When we open our hearts to Him and read His Word, He reveals His heart to us. Christ revealed His heart to us on the cross when He shed His blood to cleanse mankind from the stain and destruction of sin that has darkened the hearts of people. His pure heart, His perfect heart, His glorious heart, His loving heart, His tender heart, His compassionate heart, calls out to us today.

WHERE FULFILLMENT IS FOUND

"Look to Me, and be saved, all you ends of the earth!
For I am God, and there is no other."
ISAIAH 45:22

Mankind is on a great quest from birth. Sometimes many years pass before people realize they are on a constant search for something. Others have felt freed from the need to go on seeking this nameless thing, almost dismissing the quest.

Some find fulfillment in marriage and family living. Others achieve fame and fortune in other parts of the world, while many stay close to home and prosper. At a glance it appears they have found their way, leaving those who don't "find it" forlorn—still asking, seeking, and stumbling along.

No one is alone in this quest. All mankind travels the same road, noticing the emptiness that oppresses the world, crying out for guidance, for comfort, and for peace.

For generations the human race has been on the great quest, trying every pathway. One path is political freedom. When found it still does not achieve a better world. Another hopeful path is education, and many put complete faith in it, since it seems a sensible path to travel. We are the most informed society in the history of civilization, yet the most confused.

The solution to satisfying this great quest is putting faith in the Lord Jesus Christ. This is the blessed hope. Do not cease to seek out the Lord, for you will find Him and be satisfied.

OUR CODEBOOK

In the beginning was the Word, and the Word was with God, and the Word was God.
JOHN 1:1

The authoritative source for mankind is the Holy Bible. Its wisdom is both ancient and relevant, historic and prophetic. Above all, it is the Word of God. It is our codebook and its message is the key to life. The Bible has come down to us through the ages. It has passed through so many hands and survived attacks of every kind. Neither barbaric vandalism nor civilized scholarship has touched it. Neither the burning of fire nor the laughter of skepticism has accomplished its annihilation.

History recounts the true story of the British and Foreign Bible Society during World War II. When the Germans began bombing the city of Old Warsaw, the wife of the director went to the storeroom and carried some two thousand Bibles to the basement. She was trapped by the bombing and later captured by the Germans and put in a prison camp. She managed to escape, and after the war was over she was able to retrieve the Bibles and distribute them to people in need. Warsaw was flattened, but one wall of the Bible Society remained standing. On it were these words, painted in large letters: "Heaven and earth shall pass away, but my words shall not pass away."

Oh, that people would retrieve their Bibles and open their pages of truth. It's the indestructible Book written by God Himself.

Reaching the Lonely

There is a friend who sticks closer than a brother.
PROVERBS 18:24

Loneliness can bring solitude. The sentry standing duty alone at an outpost, the thousands in mental institutions, and those in solitary confinement in prisons and concentration camps know the meaning of the loneliness of solitude.

In his fascinating book *Alone*, Admiral Richard E. Byrd told about the time he spent in bewildering and soul-shattering darkness. He lived alone in a shack buried in the great glacial ice cap that covers the South Pole. The days were as black as the nights. No living creature existed within a hundred miles. The cold was so intense that he could hear his breath freeze and crystallize as the wind blew it past his ears. But he kept his mind challenged by thinking on good things.

There are some who never hear one word of encouragement. Loneliness comes to shut-ins and wealthy society personalities. Some hide behind smiles and others are left with vacant eyes.

We may not be able to go to the lonely, but the joy of the lonely receiving hand-written letters in the mail can be better than a spoonful of medicine, especially when the message tells of a Friend who sticks closer than a brother. Jesus Christ is that Friend who wants to come near and abide in the hearts of those who will receive Him as Savior and Lord. Nothing dissolves loneliness like reading God's love letter, the Bible.

STANDING STRONG

Hold firm to the trustworthy word as taught.

TITUS 1:9 ESV

It's well and good when a person's convictions are based upon the "thou shalts" and "thou shalt nots" of Scripture rather than individual ideas. The Bible tells us to hold fast the faithful Word of God with sound doctrine. His truth becomes the foundation of everything we believe, and to live by His commandment to "love the LORD your God with all your heart, with all your soul, and with all your mind" (Matthew 22:37), He provides the strength to live for Him without compromise, because we're putting Him first in all things.

People generally respect a person of convictions, and many of them wish they had the moral stamina to stand alone. But when a Christian compromises, often the very ones who cause Christians to compromise will despise them for it. Returning to biblical conversion, faith, and conviction would have a great impact on society, and God gives the strength to individuals to do this. When faith in Christ is anchored in Him alone, men and women can withstand peer pressure.

God often gives us an inner conviction or prompting to confirm which way He wants us to go. The prompting comes from the Holy Spirit. When we put Christ first in life, we will be walking with Him every step. May the Lord give added courage for His people to be witnesses for Him, even in hard places.

Our Full Attention

Behold, to obey [the Lord] is better than sacrifice.
1 SAMUEL 15:22

Mankind has always worshiped things: status, fame, popularity, people, money, and security. Anything that comes between God and man is idolatry. Many believe that pagan worship is a thing of the past, but it is ever present. We have just given it a new name: pop culture!

Daily we are called to make choices. When it comes to whom or what we worship, we have two choices: bow to the things of this world and spiritually die, or bow down before the true God and live.

Worship in the truest sense takes place only when our full attention is on God—on His glory, His power, His majesty, His love, His compassion. If people are really honest, this doesn't happen very often, because even in church or in our times of quiet devotion, we get distracted and fail to see God as He truly is. Those who worship God first of all recognize that God is the Lord, the Sovereign and all-powerful God of the universe. Worship is acknowledging God as Creator.

True worship should come from God's people because He has made them part of His family. We must learn to shut out the distractions that keep us from truly worshiping God. We must turn our minds and hearts to Him every day, praising Him for who He is and what He has done to save lost souls.

GUILT AND FORGIVENESS

"I have blotted out, like a thick cloud, your transgressions."
ISAIAH 44:22

Guilt is inescapable. The Bible proclaims that we all have broken God's laws. Therefore, guilt rests upon the entire human race. Some people may feel it more intensely than others, but the guilt is there, whether in the conscious or the subconscious realm. It must be dealt with before we can become fulfilled personalities. This is why Jesus died. He shed His blood to purge our dead consciences. So guilt is not all bad, for without it there is nothing to drive a person toward self-examination and toward God's forgiveness.

The human heart is empty; hearts that are not attuned to God will become catch basins for every device of the devil. Satan has control over multitudes whose hearts have never been captured by Jesus Christ. The devil has hundreds of agents writing pornographic literature and producing immoral movies to pollute human minds. He has intellectuals in high positions teaching a hedonistic and permissive philosophy.

While the culture has had great success in infiltrating people's minds, it is possible to overcome. The Bible is filled with testimonies of those who, by God's grace, were victorious over Satan's power. John Newton was a slave trader. One day in a storm at sea, he met Jesus Christ and it changed his life forever. He will always be remembered for writing the hymn "Amazing Grace." No one is beyond the reach of the loving arms of the Savior.

SPREAD THE WORD

According to His mercy He saved us.
TITUS 3:5

There's a wonderful story about Paul and Silas in Acts 16:16–34, who were thrown in a Philippian prison for preaching. Instead of complaining, they sat in the damp dungeon listening to the groans from others in chains. But the jailer that night heard a strange sound that drowned out the wailing. Paul and Silas were having a song service at midnight, praising the name of their great and mighty God. They used their imprisonment to proclaim the news that Jesus had come to free people from the chains of sin. What was Heaven's response? The prison walls shook on their foundations and crumbled, giving the chance for prisoners to escape. The jailer was about to commit suicide because of a mass escape. Paul glanced in the jailer's direction and said: "Don't kill yourself; we're still here!"

The jailer fell upon his face and said, "Sir, what must I do to be saved?" Paul didn't answer, "Join the church and thou shalt be saved." Oh no! "Live the best you can and thou shalt be saved." Oh no! The answer that rang through the jail that night is the same message that's been ringing down through the centuries: "Believe on the Lord Jesus Christ, and thou shalt be saved" (v. 30–31 KJV).

It is faith placed in Christ alone that assures the soul is saved, and we are surrounded by those who need to know Christ as Savior.

GROUNDED IN TRUTH

Grow in the grace and knowledge of our Lord and Savior Jesus Christ.
2 PETER 3:18

The story's been told of engineers who made plans to construct a suspension bridge over a deep river gorge. The first problem was how to get the heavy steel cables from one side of the gorge to the other. Helicopters hadn't been invented, and the turbulent river below made it too dangerous to transfer the cables by boat. One day, the engineers flew a kite over the gorge and grounded it, which meant the two sides of the river were now linked by a thin kite string. They tied a slightly heavier string to one end of the kite string and carefully hauled it across to the other side. Once it was in place they tied a still stronger cord to the end of that string and pulled it across. They repeated this process several more times until eventually they were able to pull the heavy steel cables across the gorge and construct the bridge. By grounding the kite, their work continued with success.

Spiritual growth is like the construction of that bridge. Becoming a Christian is the work of a moment; being a Christian is the work of a lifetime, and it must be grounded in God's truth.

God's will isn't simply our conversion but our spiritual maturity. Nothing strengthens us more than immersing ourselves in God's Word, fixing our eyes on Christ, and praying for His guidance.

A Consecrated Life

Hold firmly to the word of life.
PHILIPPIANS 2:16 NLT

We live in a hostile world that constantly seeks to pull us away from God, and sometimes its pressures are enormous. Trouble seeks out weak places in our lives.

A dam can hold enormous amounts of water back; it can be 99 percent solid, but if 1 percent is weak, eventually the whole structure may give way. This is why we must fortify ourselves by the Word of God. His promises strengthen us and prepare us for times when the dam breaks, whether through the loss of a loved one, illness, mental anguish, or a host of other calamities that assault us. The Bible tells us to put on the armor of God (Ephesians 6:10–18). It also tells us that when we are weak, our God is strong and shows Himself to us in remarkable ways, strengthening our faith—even though we live in a dark and sinful world (2 Corinthians 12:9–10).

Worldliness is an inner attitude that puts self at the center of life instead of God. God's people should live consecrated, Spirit-filled lives because Christ lives in us and is victorious over the world, the flesh, and the devil. It is the Holy Spirit who goes before us to make our pathway sure. We must lift our eyes above our circumstances and "lay aside . . . the sin which so easily ensnares us . . . looking unto Jesus, the author and finisher of our faith" (Hebrews 12:1–2).

UNITY IN CHRIST

He came and preached peace to you who were afar off and to those who were near.

EPHESIANS 2:17

There are many groups that espouse the brotherhood of man and make appeals on behalf of peace. In times past, mighty leaders such as the Caesars, Constantine, Charlemagne, Napoleon, the czars of the East and the kings of the West each in turn promised peace. But they all failed.

Bold schemes for global unity and brotherhood are still proclaimed. It's always good to work for peace, but true peace will come only when Christ returns to bring lasting peace. He alone transcends the political and social boundaries of the world.

But can we know His peace in our own hearts today? Yes. When we are brought into the family of God through the Fatherhood of God, we enjoy the brotherhood of man. God is not our Father automatically when we are born; He must become our Father spiritually.

The Bible teaches that we can experience unity through the cross of Jesus Christ because of His perfect obedience to His Father in Heaven.

Apart from this, we see only a world filled with bitterness, intolerance, hatred, prejudice, lust, and greed. Within the powerful working of the cross grow love, new life, and true brotherhood. The only human hope for these lies at the cross of Jesus, where all people—no matter what their background of nationality or race—can become one in Christ.

THE POWERFUL SCRIPTURES

The word of God is living and powerful, and sharper than any two-edged sword.
HEBREWS 4:12

When we approach the Bible as history and biography, we approach it in the wrong spirit. We must read and study the Bible as men and women seeking God.

The Old Testament predicted Christ's birth, death, and resurrection, and the New Testament documents the fulfillment of these prophecies, yet many people reject its truth. God has revealed Himself in the pages of Scripture, yet the truth about God, His Son, and the Holy Spirit are often debated and disbelieved.

While the Bible is much more than a book of history, it's interesting to go back through the centuries and consider what others have said about Jesus. Skeptics claim that the Scriptures are not believable, yet testimonies about Jesus' life and resurrection come from historians, philosophers, scientists, churchmen, and yes, even atheists. Evidence is substantiated in scrolls of antiquity, quill-stained parchments, and modern communications. But the most compelling evidence is seen in those whose lives have been transformed by Christ!

God gave the books of the Bible to us because He wants us to know Him and to love and serve Him. Most of all, He gave us His Word with a command to obey it so that we can become more like Christ. The Bible is trustworthy because it points man to the most important events in human history: the life, death, and resurrection of Jesus Christ.

SADNESS INTO JOY

Put on the whole armor of God, that you may be able to stand.

EPHESIANS 6:11

Not one account in the Bible tells us that living for God will be easy. Look at Joseph. He did the right thing and fled from temptation and ended up in prison. Look at the three Hebrews in the book of Daniel. They refused to worship anyone other than almighty God and they were thrown in the fiery furnace by a pagan king. David the shepherd boy stood before the great giant Goliath and said, "I come to you in the name of the Lord" (1 Samuel 17:45). When we encounter difficulties, if we rely on the Lord to strengthen us and teach us, He will be with us through it all and victory will be won.

There is nothing easy about the Christian life. It doesn't mean that Christians cannot have fun times, but for Christians, life is more about living joyfully no matter our circumstances. This is where we have the opportunity to show others that our strength comes from the Lord.

Ask the Lord to change your sadness into joy because He will use everything in your life to make you fit to serve Him faithfully. God can take anything that happens to us—even bad things—and use them to shape us and make us into the person He desires—if we will let Him. Walk with Him and let your light shine.

LIVE SOBERLY

To be carnally minded is death, but to be spiritually minded is life and peace.
ROMANS 8:6

The Bible teaches that sin is transgression of the law (1 John 3:4). This word *transgression* could be translated "lawlessness." Jesus indicated that as men approached the end of history there would be a worldwide rebellion against law and order. Rebellion and lawlessness are present on a scale such as the world's never known. Children rebel against parents until many parents are actually afraid of their children. University students rebel against society. People corrupt themselves by worshiping "self." But most of all, transgression of God's law is sin against Him.

The world today is on an immoral binge much like it was in ancient Rome. Before Rome fell, her standards were abandoned, the family disintegrated, divorce prevailed, and immorality was rampant. We're in a hedonistic society watching human nature expressing itself without God. While we often think of outward rebellion as sin, we fail to look inward.

But God can break the chain of every transgression that binds us if we repent and follow the Savior. "For the grace of God that brings salvation has appeared to all men, teaching us that, denying ungodliness and worldly lusts, we should live soberly, righteously, and godly in the present age, looking for the blessed hope and glorious appearing of our great God and Savior Jesus Christ . . . that He might redeem us from every lawless deed" (Titus 2:11–14).

HE LIVES!

"I am He who lives, and was dead, and behold, I am alive forevermore."
REVELATION 1:18

Alexander the Great's biography was written four hundred years after he died, so its author obviously never knew him. But Alexander's legacy lives on, while people doubt the life of Christ as documented by those who walked with Jesus. Many people down through the centuries never had a record of their own births. Yet the existence of Jesus is still called into question despite the intricate genealogy found in Scripture.

Some question whether Shakespeare wrote the plays that bear his name because none of his original manuscripts survived. Some see Shakespeare as a pseudonym because there are no documents dating his birth. His biography is peppered with suppositions, yet it's said that Shakespeare is the second most quoted writer in the English language—after the various writers of the Bible.

We'll never meet Shakespeare in this life because he's dead. But today every person can meet Jesus Christ in this life because He lives! The marks of His sacrifice on the cross are found in human hearts. Gravestones often bear the words: "Here lie the remains of . . ." But from Christ's tomb came the living words of an angel, declaring: "He is not here, but is risen!" (Luke 24:6). Jesus' tomb is empty. The resurrection of Jesus is an attested fact of history and a fact to be proclaimed as truth. Jesus lives.

May

MAY 1

Directing Our Emotions

A fool vents all his feelings, but a wise man holds them back.
PROVERBS 29:11

God's anger is always just. Even His anger is righteous because it is directed solely against evil. Jesus forcefully drove out from the temple those who were callously making money (Matthew 21:12–13).

In much the same way, when we see children abused, we should speak out and pray that righteous anger will lead to solutions to protect the helpless. We must be careful, however, that our anger is not a cover for lovelessness or self-righteousness. Anger and bitterness (as well as hatred, jealousy, and resentment) aren't identical, but they are closely related. Bitterness is anger gone sour, an attitude of deep discontent that poisons our souls and destroys our peace.

Paul's anger against Christians was replaced with a burning passion to spread the gospel. Peter's anger was channeled into boldness for Christ. Our goal should be to reflect Christ in all that we do.

The heart is the center of our emotions and the seat of decisive action. Our emotions can lie to us, and we need to check our emotions against the Word of God. While we strive to live as Jesus would have us live, He will help us direct our emotions. His great, all-prevailing truth stands for time and eternity.

THE POWER OF PRAYER

In the morning . . . He went out and departed to
a solitary place; and there He prayed.

MARK 1:35

When we have a personal relationship with Jesus Christ, we can be certain that God hears our prayers. He Himself gave us the example of true prayer to the Father in Heaven. The Bible tells us that Jesus prayed hours before breakfast, rising a great while before daybreak. The precious hours of fellowship with His Father meant more to Him than sleep (Luke 6:12). Jesus would leave the great crowds gathered to hear Him preach and go to the wilderness so that He could spend time in prayer (Luke 5). How different our world would be if people were committed to do the same.

God blesses those who commit themselves to prayer. Noah prayed, and God gave him a blueprint to build the ark. Moses prayed, and God delivered the Israelites from bondage. Daniel prayed, and the mouths of the lions were closed. Elijah prayed, and the fire of God consumed the sacrifice in the presence of the prophets of Baal. David prayed, and he defeated Goliath on the Philistine battleground. The disciples prayed, and three thousand people were added to the church in one day.

Remember that the disciples asked Jesus to teach them to pray. We must ask God to help us pray with our hearts and minds centered on Him. This is the power of prayer.

Our Advocate

"When He, the Spirit of truth, has come, He will guide you into all truth."
JOHN 16:13

The Holy Spirit—the Spirit of the living God—has been sent to help those who have been redeemed by Jesus Christ. The Holy Spirit is the third person of the Trinity: God the Father, God the Son, and God the Holy Spirit. He is a great and wonderful gift from almighty God. Jesus promised that He would send "the Helper" so that Christians would not be alone in this world (John 16:5–7).

A friend once said, "I need Jesus Christ for my eternal life, and the Holy Spirit for my internal life." For those who believe in Jesus, His power can change a life, a marriage, a relationship, a church, and a world. Unfortunately, this power has been ignored, misunderstood, and misused. The Holy Spirit is not to be confused with the "spirit world." He is a Person, not to be feared but to be embraced by believers because when someone gives their life to Jesus Christ, God's Holy Spirit comes and indwells the believer with faith to trust, and live for, the Lord.

The Holy Spirit illuminates our minds, makes us yearn for God, and takes spiritual truth and makes it understandable to us. The most important thing that the Spirit of God does for mankind is to show sinners that Jesus is "the way, the truth, and the life" (John 14:6).

TRUE FREEDOM

I know that in me (that is, in my flesh) nothing good dwells.
ROMANS 7:18

*F*lesh is the Bible's word for unperfected human nature. Leaving off the "h" and spelling it in reverse, we have the word "self." Flesh is the self-life: it is what we are when we are left to our own devices. "Self" will show itself to be selfish. Jesus said that "the flesh profits nothing" (John 6:63).

There was once a man who had lived a wild life and became a changed man when the Lord saved Him. His friend said to him, "I feel sorry for you. You're going to church, praying and reading the Bible instead of going to the nightclubs, drinking, and enjoying beautiful women. You can't do anything fun anymore." The man laughed and said, "No, you don't understand. It isn't that I can't; it's that I don't want to. The Lord changed what I want to do by making me a new man!"

When we truly love God, we will "want to" do what pleases Him. The Bible promises that He will give us the desires of our hearts because our minds are "fixed" on Him. This is the work of His Spirit within us.

It is God who makes it possible for us to live apart from fleshy desires while still in our human bodies. "If we live in the Spirit, let us also walk in the Spirit" (Galatians 5:25).

THE EMPTY PLACE

You have made known to me the ways of life.
ACTS 2:28 NIV

We are taught to be independent, to make it on our own. Yet within each of us is a deep-seated frustration: *I ought to be better. I believe I was made for something more; there must be more to life than this. Why am I so empty?*

Such feelings can cause us to struggle toward some unknown, unnamed goal. While we are told to "plan ahead," few really think about the future. A good many people make spontaneous decisions, never considering the consequences. When their world begins to crumble, they begin to feel empty inside. Their emptiness is the absence of God in their lives.

There was once a brilliant young lawyer who did not seem to find a need for God. He began to write about a famous person, hoping to find a surprising secret to his life. In the process of his research, he discovered that the man had a personal relationship with Jesus Christ, which led the young attorney on his own spiritual quest.

The only answer to filling the empty place in the heart is found in God. The most important quest is our personal search for answers concerning life that will lead us to the One who created life. His name is almighty God, and He cares deeply for mankind and proved it by making a way for us to have eternal life and joy unspeakable.

MADE TO WORSHIP

*The god of this age has blinded the minds of unbelievers, so that they
cannot see the light of the gospel that displays the glory of Christ.*

2 CORINTHIANS 4:4 NIV

There is one who works very hard at directing the human race right into Hell. The Bible says, "Your adversary the devil walks about like a roaring lion, seeking whom he may devour. Resist him" (1 Peter 5:8–9). Satan wants to portray himself as God; he disguises himself as an "angel of light" (2 Corinthians 11:14). But the truth is that he is the father of darkness, confusion, and lies.

A remarkable fact for all seekers of God is that belief in some kind of god is universal. Whatever period of history we study, whatever culture we examine, we see all peoples acknowledging a deity. During the past two centuries archaeology has unearthed the ruins of many civilizations, but none has ever been found that did not yield some evidence of a god who was worshiped.

Man has made gods out of his imagination—some people even worship themselves! They find it necessary to fill the vacuum left within them. We must pray for those around us who are searching for the truth. We must ask the Lord "to open their eyes, in order to turn them from darkness to light, and from the power of Satan to God" (Acts 26:18).

THE SKEPTIC

The natural man does not [accept] the things of the Spirit
of God, for they are foolishness to him.
1 CORINTHIANS 2:14

There have always been skeptics who say that believing the Bible is for uneducated people. This is contrary to truth. Understanding the Bible demands the use of the mind, but when the mind is diseased by sin, it is clouded and confused.

Years ago a young man by the name of Joel was a living example of such a person whose mind was under attack. He was thrown in prison for trying to kill a man. When released, he was filled with hatred and did everything he could to show his scorn to society, only to land in San Quentin. There he was diagnosed as "criminally insane." When released eleven years later, his godly mother was there to greet him and said, "Joel, you need the Lord Jesus. You need to ask Him to forgive your sins, to give you a new life."

In time, Joel did just that. His mother's faithful prayers were blessed by God, and Joel's life was transformed. He became a prison chaplain and won many criminals to Christ.

The Bible teaches that sin affects the mind. A person may be intellectually brilliant but spiritually ignorant. An intellectual mind can be turned into a first-class mind when Christ penetrates the very heart of a person. We must never give up praying for others.

THE FIFTH COMMANDMENT

"As I have loved you . . . love one another."
JOHN 13:34

The Bible clearly says, "Honour thy father and thy mother" (Exodus 20:12 KJV). This passage sets no age limit on such honor. It does not say they must be honorable to be honored. This does not necessarily mean that we must "obey" parents who are dishonorable. We must honor them. Honor has many shapes and affections. Yet adult children sometimes say things to their parents that they would never say to their friends.

While every circumstance is different, the Bible says, "In lowliness of mind let each esteem others better than himself. Let each of you look out not only for his own interests, but also for the interests of others" (Philippians 2:3–4). This speaks of "others." How much more should we do so, then, for parents?

Stories of strained relations between mothers and daughters are not unusual, unfortunately. One woman wrote and lamented over difficulties with her mother, but when her mother died, the daughter grieved because she had not tried harder to heal the relationship and said, "I'll never have another chance."

We must be mindful that life is lived only once. One of life's hardest lessons is that we cannot change the past—and this is especially so when death intrudes. It is a bitter lesson that leaves guilt and regret. The only solution is to ask God to open our eyes to things we need to do now.

REVIVAL

It is high time to awake out of sleep.
ROMANS 13:11

The lawlessness, the crime, the immorality that are a stench in the nostrils of God are hastening God's judgment upon this land. The ills, divisions, troubles, and difficulties that beset our nation could be turned around if its people would humble themselves before God in repentance.

This could be changed and transformed by a spiritual awakening to the Word of God. History records the importance that Christian revival has had in paving the way for better conditions around the world. One example is in the story of John Wesley, who began preaching in the fields, churches, barns, on hillsides, in the rain, in the scorching sun—at any place people would gather to hear God's Word proclaimed. Then he took up his pen and wrote against the evils of his day. He opposed everything that he found to be contrary to the commandments of God.

From the heart of this great man had come a message that meant new life to the common man. Indeed, the foundations of the Western way of life had begun to bear fruit and a new consciousness under his ministry. It was the great revival under Wesley that set in motion forces that eventually destroyed slavery around the world.

Never stop praying that God will raise up a generation that will speak God's truth, and pray that hearts and ears will be open to His call.

JESUS' WELCOME

The LORD searches all hearts and understands all the intent of the thoughts. If you seek Him, He will be found by you.

1 CHRONICLES 28:9

If you found yourself wandering around in the forest with no food or water, no compass, and no communication device, would you be content to remain lost? If someone suddenly called out your name, would you remain hidden? It's doubtful. You would run toward the sound of the voice. God is calling lost souls to come to Him. Just as He called out to Adam and Eve, He sends out the rescue call to us. "Incline your ear, and come to Me. Hear, and your soul shall live" (Isaiah 55:3).

The world is filled with lost and wandering souls. It is wise to ask: What preparation have you made for your soul? If you stop and listen with your ears and your heart, you will hear God's voice. If you ignore Him, you are gambling with your eternal future. If you have rebelled against God, please do not turn away from this message until you open your heart to Him.

Jesus has His hand outstretched, waiting for the lost to come to Him. When we start down the road to repentance, He does not cast us off and forsake us. He is there to meet us and welcome us home.

Our Enemy

It is no great thing if [Satan's] ministers also transform
themselves into ministers of righteousness.
2 CORINTHIANS 11:15

Deception is everything opposite the truth. People will stand in roaring ovations for the illusionists, escape artists, and magicians. Much of it, in the form of entertainment, tricks the mind, causing us to think we are seeing something real when truthfully it is fraudulent. Prisons and jails are filled with con artists—and sad to say, so are many churches. We must have discerning spirits to determine right from wrong, and God will give us the power to know truth if we submit wholly to Him.

Some deceivers around us are more obviously in league with Satan than others. Scriptures tell us that Satan himself masquerades as an angel of light. Even when Satan appears to be on the side of good, he is only using it as a mask to deceive us. His real intentions are always evil.

Never underestimate Satan's power, and never underestimate his ability to deceive us and make us think he isn't to be feared. He is not as powerful as God, but he still is a powerful spiritual force who works against God in every way he can. This is why the Bible commands us to put on the full armor of God so that we can withstand his power (Ephesians 6:13).

The most important truth about the devil, however, is that in the end he is a defeated foe!

SIN'S COST

God demonstrates His own love toward us, in that while
we were still sinners, Christ died for us.

ROMANS 5:8

Sin is a terrible and destructive thing, and sometimes we have to pay the consequences for our foolishness and rebellion against God. He doesn't promise that consequences of sin will vanish when we come to Him with repentant hearts and submit ourselves to Him, but He does promise to be with us.

The story of King David is well known. He sinned greatly when he committed adultery with another man's wife. God forgave him when he truly repented, but the child born of that illicit union still died as an act of God's judgment on David.

Now God does not always respond in the same way to the same circumstances, but He is sovereign and will use things in our lives to teach us about Him. There are times when God works in ways that are beyond our human understanding to bring healing and restoration, although none of us can predict when this will be the case or in what fashion. God is able to do immeasurably more than all we ask or imagine, according to His power (Ephesians 3:20).

The best we can do for those who suffer from their past is to tell them about the Savior, Jesus Christ, and show them through Scripture that He is ready to hear their prayer of repentance and be Lord of their lives.

THE BLOODSTAINED CROSS

He humbled Himself and became obedient to the point
of death, even the death of the cross.
PHILIPPIANS 2:8

There is victory in the cross because it represents doom for sin and hope for sinners.

Satan overstepped his bounds, and God turned what seemed to be life's greatest tragedy into history's greatest triumph. The death of Christ, perpetrated by evil men, was thought by them to be the end, but His grave became a doorway to victory.

The ultimate victory of the cross is that it could not hold the Savior of the world. He finished His work for mankind there, but the cross did not finish Him. He triumphed over sin and death, winning salvation for mankind. The resurrection story of Jesus Christ is what gives meaning and power to the cross.

Some believe that Jesus died leaving a legacy of "do good to your neighbor," never believing that He was raised from the dead. Others think the resurrection was a hoax or that Jesus never lived at all.

But the truth is that though the cross repels, it also attracts. It possesses a magnetic quality. It has become the symbol of Christianity because the cross is where Jesus purchased our redemption and provided a righteousness that we could not earn. True believers in Jesus glory in the cross of Christ because He shed His precious blood to cover man's sin; He conquered death so that we might live forever with Him in Glory.

THE WILL OF GOD

Teach me to do Your will.
PSALM 143:10

God's will is for everyone to obey His Word. All through Scripture He tells us what to do and what not to do. He tells us how to live. He gives us the strength to endure hardships, and He brings joy when we walk in His ways.

Many pray, "Lord, show me Your will," and then never open up the Bible. When our hearts are right before Him, He promises to teach us. In teaching us, He gives us understanding. His power is put within us through His Holy Spirit. God's will is revealed in Scripture, and it pleases Him when we desire and do what He instructs. "The world is passing away along with its desires, but whoever does the will of God abides forever" (1 John 2:17 ESV).

To those who truly seek God's will, the key is to become more and more like Christ. If we are ignorant of God's Word, we will always be ignorant of God's will. When we are at a point of decision about choices in life, and it is not contrary to God's Word, start moving in that direction. Ask Him to close doors and open others. What grieves the heart of God is when we deliberately make a choice that is in conflict with His truth. God will never—never—lead us to do something that is contrary to His written Word.

GOD'S STANDARD

Christ also suffered once for sins . . . that He might bring us to God.
1 PETER 3:18

Christians do not set the standard of truth; this is God's exclusive territory. Not only are Christians commanded to obey God's standard; all people are commanded to do so. By God's standard there are two groups of people in the world: believers in Christ and unbelievers, those who reject Jesus Christ as the Lord God.

The Bible says, "For all have sinned and fall short of the glory of God" (Romans 3:23). Good people are measured by human standards. It is when we make the comparison with the holiness of God that we realize that every person falls short and is a sinner before God.

We must acknowledge that there is a defect in human nature that comes from our rebellion against God. "There is none righteous, no, not one" (Romans 3:10).

Our nature and destiny are revealed in the Scriptures. In taking our human nature upon Himself, Jesus showed us what we might become and what God meant us to be. He will give us the power and might to live up to His standard if we will repent of our sin and submit ourselves to Him.

There is no greater joy than knowing that our sins are forgiven and that the Savior wants us to spend eternity with Him.

DRIVEN TO THE LORD

Always be ready to give a defense to everyone who asks
you a reason for the hope that is in you.
1 PETER 3:15

There are many who have enjoyed good health most of their lives. But those who suffer bad health often learn how to help others going through similar valleys of despair. That's why it is wise to be a good listener when others are suffering. There isn't much that can be said to those who are hurting, and we should ask God for wisdom—when to be silent and when to speak. Often it isn't the words we say as much as encouraging others with our presence. Sharing our own experiences can help people to realize that they're not alone in their suffering.

So many testimonials speak of how God spoke to people in sickness and how their personal faith in Him grew stronger. Someone recently said, "I could have never said this before cancer, but now that I have completed my treatment and am on the road to recovery, I praise the Lord that He used it to open the door to tell others why I hope in the Lord!"

No one knows what a day may bring, but Christians can point to the One who sees us through trials. "Through the LORD's mercies we are not consumed, because His compassions fail not. They are new every morning; great is Your faithfulness" (Lamentations 3:22–23).

GOD'S ADVERSARY

Resist the devil and he will flee from you.
JAMES 4:7

Satan is a mighty prince with hosts of demons at his command, and he has set up his kingdom on Earth. His power and position are revealed in the Holy Scriptures. Confusion about the personality of the devil has resulted in large measure from the caricatures of him that became popular during the Middle Ages. To allay their fear of the devil, people pictured him as a foolish, grotesque creature with horns and a long tail. They put a pitchfork in his hand and a feeble-minded leer on his face, and then proclaimed: "Who's afraid of a ridiculous figure like this?"

The truth is that the devil is a creature of intelligence and resourcefulness. He was once a sublime figure who decided to use his divine endowments for his own aims instead of God's. His reasoning is brilliant, his plans ingenious, and his logic well-nigh irrefutable. God's mighty adversary is no bungling creature with horns and tail—he is a prince of lofty stature, able to take advantage of every opportunity that presents itself. He is unrelenting and cruel. The devil is not, however, all-powerful, omniscient, or omnipresent.

The devil has a plan and God has a plan, and each person must decide which plan to follow. Jesus said, "Follow Me," and those who flee the devil and turn to Jesus Christ by faith will know His joy and peace for eternity.

OUTSIDE INTERVENTION

"The Son of Man has come to seek and to save that which was lost."

LUKE 19:10

Who doesn't want to be saved? Some years ago, a man's plane crashed into the ocean. He survived the crash but had blood on his forehead that attracted the sharks. He spent ten hours kicking at the sharks to survive. Finally, he spotted an aircraft and waved his orange life vest. The Coast Guard swooped in and rescued him. The man did not need a new swimming technique in order to be saved; he needed outside intervention.

We all need outside intervention if we're going to live eternally with God in Heaven someday. This is why God sent His Son on a rescue mission.

It isn't narrow-minded to claim that there is only one way of salvation or that the Christian message leads to the right way. Do we fault a pilot for being narrow-minded when he or she follows the instrument panel while landing in a rainstorm? No, we want the pilot to remain narrowly focused! Millions of people today want salvation and the hope of Heaven, but on their own terms. Christians do not proclaim salvation in any other but Jesus Christ. The Christian hope is that everyone will come to know Jesus as their Savior. The greatest act a Christian can perform is to tell others about Him.

THREE TYPES OF PEACE

God is my salvation, I will trust and not be afraid.
ISAIAH 12:2

Most people yearn for one thing more than anything else: inner peace. Without it, they have no lasting joy or security. The word *peace* is used in the Bible in three main ways. First, there is spiritual peace—peace between God and man. Second, there is psychological peace—peace within. Third, there is relational peace—peace among mankind.

The Bible says that sin has destroyed or seriously affected all three of these dimensions of peace. When man was created, he was at peace with God, with himself, and with others. But when he rebelled against God, man lost peace in every way. These dimensions of peace can be restored. We cannot bring this about, but God can, and has.

Jesus Christ, God's only Son, was sent into the world to take away our sins by His death on the cross, therefore making it possible for us to be at peace—with God, within ourselves, and with each other. By His resurrection, Christ showed that God desires that all people know perfect peace.

Christ provides the power to overcome every sin. He can break the ropes, fetters, and chains of sin; but each person must repent, confess, commit, and surrender to Christ first. Right now, it can be settled and we can know peace, joy, and fellowship with God, with ourselves, and with others.

LOVE YOUR NEIGHBOR

As we have opportunity, let us do good to all.
GALATIANS 6:10

It's natural to feel helpless when we read about trouble at home and abroad. We see destruction that threatens the lives of millions and the struggles of those in our neighborhoods.

We cannot solve every problem, but we shouldn't let that stop us from doing something for those who cross our paths. We can use those opportunities to tell others about Jesus Christ.

This is His call to His followers: "Go into all the world and preach the gospel to [everyone]" (Mark 16:15). While everyone cannot travel the whole world, we have been given a command to tell others about Christ, those in our part of the world. We should be careful about comparing our abilities to those of others. As God leads, He equips.

Are we paying attention to those who are in our pathways day in and day out?

One faithful witness is worth more than a thousand professors of religion. We witness by our lives and by His Word. When people in Christ unite in the common bond of the Word of God and prayer, we are strengthened in our life's work—to be salt and light in the midst of darkness. The Spirit of God goes before us, preparing the way, giving us the words and granting us courage. But we must be diligent to live His Word, read His Word, speak His Word, and trust His Word.

GROWTH ESSENTIALS

Walk worthy of the Lord, fully pleasing Him.
COLOSSIANS 1:10

The idea of growing mature in the things of the Lord is similar to babies going through the stages of childhood. Each phase causes children to grow physically and mentally, always learning. The apostle John wrote about becoming mature in the faith. We can never live the Christian life on the highest plane unless we are continually growing and moving forward. Whether a teenager, young adult, career person, or a senior citizen, for those who have been Christians, growing strong in the Lord is never finished.

The Bible says, "As newborn babes, desire the pure milk of the word, that you may grow thereby" (1 Peter 2:2). Read it, study it, think on it, and memorize it! How many things could be more easily solved if we read what God thinks? What we dwell on, we love. "For as [a person] thinks in his heart, so is he" (Proverbs 23:7). The more we dwell on the Word of God, the more we will thirst after it, and the more it will keep us from wandering from its truth.

When coupled with prayer, we have put on the armor of God to help us withstand the evil that is in the world, and we will learn compassion toward those who do not know Him. These disciplines are essential to spiritual growth, and God blesses those that seek after Him.

THE SECOND COMING

Christ . . . will appear a second time . . . to save those who are eagerly waiting for him.

HEBREWS 9:28 ESV

The first coming of Jesus Christ is the greatest event in world history and will climax with His second coming. This is the centerpiece of God fulfilling His promises.

Jesus came the first time in a humble way—as a baby cradled in a manger in Bethlehem. But the next most important event will be the second coming of Jesus as King of kings, when He will set His feet on the Mount of Olives overlooking His beloved city of Jerusalem.

This event will be so revolutionary that it will change every aspect of life on this planet. When Jesus conquers at Armageddon, He will usher in life as it was originally intended. Righteousness will reign. Disease will be arrested. Death will be modified. War will be abolished. Nature will be changed.

What a time to take the world headlines and God's headlines found in His Word and watch the unfolding of the great drama of the ages. History is going somewhere. God will bring beauty from the ashes of world chaos. A new social order will emerge when Christ comes back. The paradise that mankind lost will be regained. For those who have not yet accepted His gift of grace—eternal salvation—today is the time to make Jesus the center of your life.

TRENDY RELIGIONS

In the last times some will turn away from the true faith; they will
follow deceptive spirits and teachings that come from demons.
1 TIMOTHY 4:1 NLT

Professing faith in Christ isn't the same as possessing Christ, who is the Source of faith. "Whatever" has become a mantra for many, a trendy approach to a religion of belonging to self. Some identify as Christians but can't explain it. Others call themselves religiously sympathetic.

News articles have been written about the trend of designer religion: developing a religion that reflects one's desires. When the gospel of Jesus Christ is watered down to a myth, it is no longer the gospel of Christ. The world doesn't object to this kind of religion. But the Bible says, "Woe to those who are wise in their own eyes and clever in their own sight" (Isaiah 5:21 NIV). Society may think itself clever in devising new ways to worship, but the Bible tells us that there is nothing new under the sun (Ecclesiastes 1:9).

Religion is being rebranded as spiritualism and encompasses whatever people want it to be. But true Christianity is distinguished from all the religions of the world by God sending His Son to redeem the human race from sin and empowering them to know and receive the truth of redemption for sin by Christ's death on the cross, and resurrection to life everlasting. He offers this to all who will repent and receive His gift. Christians distinguish themselves by being followers of Jesus Christ and obeying Him.

No Compromise

I have refused to walk on any evil path, so that I may remain obedient to your word.

PSALM 119:101 NLT

Following Christ and growing strong is exercising the freedom to trust in Him and obey His commands. When a soldier submits to the authority of his commanding officer, he obeys what that officer tells him to do. If a patient submits to a doctor's treatment, she follows the instructions. If a football player submits to the direction of his coach, he abides by the coach's plan. When we submit ourselves to the Savior, we obey what He tells us to do because we know His way is right.

How many problems could be avoided if God's people would obey His Word? The Bible gives us principles that will guide our lives. God's Word isn't to be debated or dissected; it is to be done.

God also leads by His Holy Spirit. Sometimes we struggle to know what is right. Many times it's because we don't want to give up something we know we should walk away from. But through prayer, asking God to give us strength, He will enable us to make the hard decisions, and we will find that the joy of obeying Christ fills the void.

When we take a stand for Christ, we may be forsaken by friends, but we must never compromise our faith. The Bible tells us that we should influence others toward God (Jeremiah 15:19).

ETERNITY IN EVERY HEART

God's invisible qualities . . . have been clearly seen . . .
so that people are without excuse.
ROMANS 1:20 NIV

God has put within each of us an inner sense that life on Earth is not all there is. The Bible tells us that God has set eternity in the hearts of the people (Ecclesiastes 3:11).

Many may suppress this truth or even deny it, but the human conscience still speaks. The still small voice of God tells us down deep what is true (1 Kings 19:12). We must never ignore that inner voice but rather check what we believe it is saying alongside Scripture, where God reveals these truths to mankind.

The apostle Paul wrote about this danger of denying God's truth: "What can be known about God is plain to them, because God has shown it to them" (Romans 1:19 ESV).

We are not simply physical beings; we also have a soul (or spirit), and we bear within us the likeness of our Creator. That likeness has been marred and distorted by sin—but it is still there. And just as God is eternal, so we sense in our hearts that we, too, must be eternal.

Death reduces all people to the same rank. Death knows no age limits and no partiality. But death is not without hope.

For those who know Christ Jesus, death is the doorway into His presence, and death is more friend than foe, the beginning rather than the end.

STRADDLING THE FENCE

Watch, stand fast in the faith.
1 CORINTHIANS 16:13

Morality and traditional values have declined in America because its people have forgotten God. Satan has deceived the hearts of the people, persuading us to disobey God. This great deceiver has betrayed our culture and convinced leaders in government, media, the universities—and even many churches—that wrong is right. The reality of daily life shows that biblical morality has little place in the lives of most people. By and large, the secular culture will accept any values, beliefs, and behavior, so long as it is not noticeably Christian.

The Scripture teaches that God hates immorality, but today immorality is glorified and excused while purity is scorned. Secular culture militates against biblical virtues and, sadly, the church often follows close behind. As principles and values are crushed, even some Christian leaders are charmed by sin's allure and have fallen from grace.

The apostle Peter warned of this over two thousand years ago. "Be vigilant; because your adversary the devil walks about like a roaring lion, seeking whom he may devour" (1 Peter 5:8). "Resist him," the Bible tells us in the following verse, and be "steadfast in the faith."

Too many people want to have one foot in the world and one foot in the kingdom of God. It doesn't bring contentment and it's certainly not acceptable to almighty God. When we declare ourselves for God—and obey Him—an inner peace will come.

The Highway of Salvation

He is also able to save to the uttermost those who come to God through Him, since He always lives to make intercession for them.
HEBREWS 7:25

God has provided a great highway of salvation. Many people may be too proud to express their interest in knowing what that is, but in the quiet moments, in times of loneliness or solitude, people often sense in their hearts the need for a Savior and ask, "What must I do to be saved?"

The great highway of God was built by a cross—the cross of Jesus—when Jesus hung on it and died for the sins of mankind. It was there that Christ's blood was shed for the human race. And then—God raised His Son from the dead. The death, burial, and resurrection of Christ is the good news that God has prepared a highway, a way out of the entanglements of life.

The narrow pathway is not hard to find, yet few find it. Many people will profess Christ, go to church, or be baptized. But few find salvation under the lordship of Christ. Why? People reject the narrow way because they are not willing to lay aside self and receive Christ into their lives and make Him Lord of all. The narrow way must be entered through the narrow gate, the Lord Jesus Christ. The narrow way is through the gate of repentance of sin and coming to faith in Jesus alone (John 14:6).

Transformed Hearts

"To you it has been given to know the mysteries of the kingdom of God."
LUKE 8:10

Many people struggle with whether to receive the forgiveness of Christ and accept His salvation. They want Christ to walk with them, but they don't really want to walk with Him.

We cannot live a good enough life to earn salvation, but when we repent of sin before holy God and receive His free gift of eternal life, He transforms our hearts and gives us a desire to live according to His will.

The Bible says it this way: "The mystery . . . has been revealed to His saints. To them God willed to make known what are the riches of the glory. . . . which is Christ in you, the hope of glory . . . that we may present every [one] perfect [complete] in Christ Jesus" (Colossians 1:26–28).

Those who walk according to the ways of the world walk with Satan, and he doesn't go out of his way to bother them. But those who are in Christ will become targets of Satan. This is why it's vital to walk with Christ, His way. Remember Jesus said, "Follow Me" (Luke 18:22). As His people persist in Bible study, prayer, and seeking the fellowship of other believers, we begin to grow and treasure the discipline of living as children of light in a very dark world. Jesus stands ready with open arms to welcome anyone who will put their faith and trust in Him alone.

TRUE LOVE

God is love.
1 JOHN 4:8

The Bible says, "Let us love one another, for love is of God. . . . for God is love. In this the love of God was manifested toward us, that God has sent His only begotten Son into the world, that we might live through Him. . . . He loved us and sent His Son to be the [sacrifice] for our sins" (1 John 4:7–10). Until the good news of Jesus Christ burst onto the human scene, the word *love* was understood mostly in terms of seeking one's own advantage. A loving God reaching down to sinful humans was unthinkable.

The greatest act of love a person can ever perform for people is to tell them about God's love for them. God is the Source of love; He is the demonstration of love, wrapped up in His righteousness, judgment, mercy, and grace. To receive it, we must be willing to listen and obey His Word.

It is also important to understand that true love—God's love—is unchangeable; He knows exactly what we are and loves us anyway. It was God's love that knew mankind was incapable of obeying His law, and it was His love that promised a Redeemer, a Savior, who would save His people from their sins and empower them to live for Him. True love is an act of the will, and anyone who receives Christ as Savior does the will of the Father in Heaven.

Two Lies

He [the devil] is a liar and the father of lies.

JOHN 8:44 NASB

The devil is aptly named the "father of lies." From the beginning, he's deceived people of every age. An old Scottish clergyman said the devil has two lies, which he uses at two different stages. Before we commit a sin, he tells us that one little sin doesn't matter; it's a trifle, and we can easily recover ourselves. The second lie is this: after we've sinned, he tells us it is hopeless, we're given over to sin and shouldn't attempt to overcome. Both are terrible lies.

We've all fallen, and God doesn't consider this a trifle. Judgment hangs over the whole human race because of our rebellion and disobedience. The Scripture tells us that sin entered the world through one man, and through Adam sin brought death; all people are sinners (Romans 5:12). However, because Jesus Christ came and died on the cross and rose from the dead, we're not in hopelessness. We're in a position to be reconciled to God.

Man has always been dexterous at confusing evil with good. That was the problem Adam and Eve had, and it's our problem today. If evil were not made to appear attractive, there'd be no such thing as temptation. It's in the close similarity between good and evil, right and wrong, that the danger lies. Belonging to Christ and feeding on His Word will keep us close to Him.

Now Is the Time

He who does not believe the Son shall not see life.
JOHN 3:36

There is life after death, and every individual must make the decision to repent of sin and receive Jesus Christ as Lord and Savior to inherit eternal life. Our eternity is determined while we live.

Some say that people in Hell will make restitution and then be allowed into Heaven. Others counsel that perhaps the Hell-bound will eventually be annihilated, put out of the misery of having to face the fact that they took the wrong road. "Hell," some say, "is what Christians have used to scare people into converting to Christ." But is this really true? Did Jesus use scare tactics? No. Every word that proceeds out of the mouth of God is truth. Jesus spoke the truth because of His deep love for us. If the truth scares us, it is the guilty conscience reacting to Truth.

There are two roads to the afterlife: one leads to Heaven, the other to Hell. It is unbelief in the Lord Jesus Christ that shuts the door to Heaven and opens it to Hell. It is unbelief that rejects the Word of God and refuses Christ as Savior. It is unbelief that causes people to turn a deaf ear to the gospel. Receive Him and the afterlife will be in the glorious presence of God.

The Bible admonishes all people to settle things with Christ as we live.

JUNE

Our Generous God

Their trust should be in God, who richly gives us all we need for our enjoyment.
1 TIMOTHY 6:17 NLT

God delights in giving—even to those who have more than they need. Everything good comes from God. Whatever material things we enjoy come from God. We may work hard for them, but God is the Provider and He gives them to remind us of His goodness and our constant dependence on God. The bread and the blessings are from Him.

Everything that we count as our possessions only comprises a loan from God, and it is when we lose sight of this all-pervading truth that we become greedy and covetous, thinking that what we have is to our own credit. God owns all we have, and it is our responsibility to manage everything in an acceptable way that brings glory to Him.

But the most important thing we should remember is that we are God's possession and He wants to fill us with His truth. We should bless Him by living lives that point others to His goodness.

Whether in a season of need or plenty, we must keep our eyes on the Lord. All of God's generosity should drive us to thanksgiving—it should be a daily part of life. Envy and greed starve on a steady diet of thanksgiving! The Bible tells us to give thanks always, in all circumstances, because it pleases Jesus Christ (1 Thessalonians 5:18).

A Deadly Disease

Who will deliver me from this body of death? I thank
God—through Jesus Christ our Lord!
ROMANS 7:24-25

Sin is the most serious thing man will ever deal with. Sin is a spiritual virus that invades our whole being. It makes us morally and spiritually weak. It's a deadly disease that infects every part of us: our bodies, our minds, our emotions, our relationships, our motives. We don't have the strength on our own to overcome its power.

But when we come to Christ, the Holy Spirit comes and dwells in us. When this happens, any sin that comes in begins to fester, and God's Spirit reveals it to us. The Holy Spirit tugs at our souls to get our attention, telling us that we are not right with God.

The cause of trouble, the root of all sorrow, the dread of every man lies in this one small word—*sin*. We all have this terminal disease and it's far worse than the flu or even cancer. It has crippled the nature of man and has caused man to be caught in the devil's trap!

Sin is the great clogger, and the blood of Christ is the great cleanser. We don't need to be crippled any longer by the disease of sin because God has provided the cure. "The blood of Jesus Christ . . . cleanses us from all sin" (1 John 1:7), and He will give us the power to turn from sin.

THE BREVITY OF LIFE

Turn away my eyes from looking at worthless things.
PSALM 119:37

Many today find the idea of reincarnation attractive—the belief that after we die we come back to Earth. Some people are influenced by other religions; others simply like the thought of being able to live out multiple experiences.

The Bible is clear: reincarnation isn't true, and the life we're leading now is the only one we'll ever live. Once we die, we go into eternity—either to Heaven to be with God forever, or to that place the Bible calls Hell, where we will be eternally separated from God and His blessings.

What difference should this make? First, it gives urgency to our lives right now.

God's plan for each person is one life. There is no chance after death to do life over again. One life is all we have, and it is gone in the blink of an eye.

Sometimes we get tired of the burdens of life and wish we could start all over again. We can, with God. He desires that we walk His way through the one life He has granted us.

The Bible has much to say about the brevity of life and the necessity of preparing for eternity. Only when a person is prepared to die is he or she also prepared to live. Oh, that we would pray to the Lord to turn our eyes from worthless things and receive the life God wants us to live.

Our Security

*[Take] the shield of faith with which you will be able to
quench all the fiery darts of the wicked one.*

EPHESIANS 6:16

The devil and his demons know God exists. The demon world also believes in the facts of Jesus' birth, life, death, and resurrection. But their belief is not a saving belief because it does not lead them to turn to God in repentance.

A saving belief in God is what happens when sinners turn from sin to Christ and put their trust and faith in Him. It involves not only an intellectual acceptance of certain facts about God and Jesus. It involves complete surrender and committing to living an obedient life according to God's Word. This means to turn away from the former life and walk in new life with Him. Jesus Christ gives us this ability, but we must follow.

The Bible tells us over and over again of God's love and warns us constantly of the devil who wants to come between us and God. Satan is ever waiting to ensnare our souls. But when our minds are on the things of God, Satan has little room to maneuver.

Satan does not care how much we theorize about Christianity or how much we profess to know about Christ. What he opposes vigorously is the way we live for Christ. We must not give Satan a foothold but discipline ourselves to stay close to God. He alone is our security.

We Will See Him As He Is

It is the God who commanded light to shine out of
darkness, who has shone in our hearts.
2 CORINTHIANS 4:6

The Bible does not tell us what Jesus looked like. There have never been accurate paintings or drawings made of Him during His lifetime. Artists throughout the centuries have tried to imagine what He must have looked like, but the truth is, we don't know.

God knew that if we had an accurate portrait of Jesus in human form, we would be tempted to worship the picture instead of Jesus Himself. But someday we will know what the risen Christ looks like, for someday we'll enter into His very presence forever. For Christians, the Bible says, "we shall be like him; for we shall see him as he is" (1 John 3:2 kjv).

When we pray to the Lord Jesus Christ, may we have in our minds and hearts the sacrifice He made for us on the cross. May we hold in our hearts the gift of His wonderful grace and bow to Him with our eyes fixed upon the nail prints in His hands, giving Him praise and glory for overcoming death and the grave so that we can live with Him for eternity.

When we look at Jesus, may we see the light of His glory. This comes through knowledge of Him that comes through reading and studying His Word, for He is the Word of truth.

GOD'S LOVE LETTER

"I have loved you with an everlasting love . . .
with lovingkindness I have drawn you."

JEREMIAH 31:3

Often people make judgments about the Bible without ever picking it up and reading it. These judgments are passed on to others and believed. It is man, and not the Bible, that needs correcting. We must discover the Bible for ourselves.

There is a great deal of inaccurate teaching about the Bible, portraying a different God in the Old and New Testaments. Too many people talk about the God of wrath in the Old Testament and a God of love and peace in the New Testament. But God is the same throughout the Bible.

The Old Testament tells us that God is holy and pure, and He punishes those who rebel against Him. But the New Testament tells us the same thing. In fact, some of the strongest warnings about judgment in the Bible come from the lips of Jesus in the New Testament (Matthew 7:14).

The New Testament certainly stresses God's love and mercy. In fact, it gives us the greatest proof that God loves us: He sent His Son, the Lord Jesus Christ, to die in our place, and by His grace we can receive His salvation. But the Old Testament also tells us repeatedly about God's love for us.

The Bible will always be the center of controversy, but it is still God's love letter to us.

No Room for Doubt

"Greater love has no one than this, than to lay down one's life for his friends."
JOHN 15:13

No matter how terrible our sins, God loves us. Were it not for the love of God, none of us would ever have a chance in the future life. The Bible tells us that while we were yet sinners, Christ died for us. What a statement!

The promises of God's love and forgiveness are real because His Word is real. The human language cannot adequately describe something so wonderful, but God's Word is absolute.

Until you actually accept God's love and forgiveness, until you actually possess true peace with God, no one can describe its wonders to you. It's not something that you do with your mind. Your finite mind isn't capable of dealing with anything as great as the love of God. Our minds have difficulty explaining how a black cow can eat green grass and give white milk—but we drink and are nourished by it. We can't understand radio, but we listen. The mind can't explain the electricity that creates light—but we know it's there.

God's love must be received by putting faith in Him completely, accepting His forgiveness of sin totally. When that happens, there isn't any room for doubt. You cannot do this on anyone else's word. Put the Lord first in life and you will know His love.

THE TRAGIC SNARL

For as in Adam all die, even so in Christ all shall be made alive.

1 CORINTHIANS 15:22

Adam was the fountainhead of the human race. He sprang up by the hand of God like a crystal-clear spring from the ground. Adam was permitted to choose whether he would become a river running through pleasant green pastures or a muddy torrent.

God isn't to blame for the tragic snarl in which the world has so long found itself. The fault lies squarely with Adam—Adam who chose to listen to the lies of the tempter Satan rather than the truth of God!

The history of the human race from that day has been the story of mankind's futile effort to gain back the position that was lost by Adam's fall.

Mankind attempts to excuse away sin, believing somehow it can improve itself by improving its environment. Yet the first sin was committed in God's perfect environment. Think of the cold, dark river that runs at the bottom of the deep, dreary gorge. Why doesn't this river make its way back up to the warm, pleasant fields that lie above it? Because it can't; it has no power within itself.

In despair, we turn against God and blame Him—finding fault with His mercy and love. Humanity is called to be humble before God, who will forgive and grant salvation.

The Fight Against Aging

Though our bodies are dying, our spirits are being renewed every day.
2 CORINTHIANS 4:16 NLT

From the moment a child is born, the fight against aging and death begins. The mother devotes years to protecting her child. In spite of her loving care, the child has already begun to die. The tangible signs of aging happen. Glasses will be needed to help improve our fading vision. Skin will wrinkle and sag; shoulders will droop and steps become slower and less sure. The brittleness of the bones increases and energy fades.

Everyone living today will be dead a hundred years from now, or very close to death. So we are faced with the question: Is old age only a cruel burden that grows heavier as the years go by, or can there be something more?

Someday life will be over, no matter how much attention is given to staying fit and healthy. More important than keeping the body healthy is to prepare the soul for eternity with the Lord Jesus Christ. Too many nourish the body and starve the soul.

God has conquered death for us through His finished work on the cross. But He requires each person to confess and renounce sin and turn by faith to His Son, Jesus Christ. When this happens, a soul is born again, and in spite of the body that grows old, the soul is filled with hope and eternal joy.

THE KINGDOM WITHIN US

He who is in you is greater than he who is in the world.

1 JOHN 4:4

Believers in Jesus are members of God's kingdom. The Bible says that the kingdom of God is within them. While good citizens (many who are believers in Christ) give allegiance to their country, Christians also give ultimate allegiance to the highest authority—almighty God—while still living in an alien world as pilgrims and strangers.

The world as it is known is under the rule and reign of the prince of this world—Satan. But from the cross of Christ, Jesus has conquered Satan, and all those who have accepted Jesus as Lord have been reconciled to God.

Jesus dwells within the believer through His Holy Spirit, and He desires that all people know the joy of His great salvation. The crucified and risen King has all authority, and His indwelling Spirit is greater than Satan and his demon powers.

The signs of the kingdom are not political, although they may have political implications. Jesus' signs were given to lead people to faith in Him, not to political reform. Jesus, by His Spirit, draws sinners to the cross, leading men and women to reconciliation with God, which then produces peace in the hearts of those who believe in Him.

His kingdom will one day come to this Earth. In the meantime, God reigns supreme over the world, leading it providentially toward His perfect will.

OUR TRUE HOME

Here we have no continuing city, but we seek the one to come.
HEBREWS 13:14

The Bible assures us that Heaven is a definite place. Jesus said, "In My Father's house are many mansions; if it were not so, I would have told you. I go to prepare a place for you. And if I go and prepare a place for you, I will come again and receive you to Myself; that where I am, there you may be also" (John 14:2–3). But we all have to be saved in Christ to be assured of a heavenly home someday.

Today homeless people can be found just about everywhere throughout the world. During cold spells many street people suffer and some die. Those of us who have comfortable homes may want to help those who are less fortunate, but deep inside we may think, *I'm just glad I have a bed tonight, a warm house, and food to eat.*

In some ways, Christians are homeless. Our true home is waiting for us, prepared by the Lord Jesus Christ. If we look at the beauty He has created on Earth, can we comprehend what He has furnished for us in Heaven? How is this hope attained? By repenting of sin and looking to the Savior of the world for forgiveness.

No Boundaries

"Before they call, I will answer; and while they are still speaking, I will hear."

ISAIAH 65:24

Before the great flood of Noah's time, people communicated in one language. After the flood, another crisis emerged when the people again revolted against God. Defiant of God's laws and provisions, they wanted to reach into the heavens by building a tower designed to rise above everything else in the world. Judgment fell upon the human race, and God confused the languages. The name of the place was called Babel, which means "to confuse." The Bible records that the Lord scattered them over all the Earth, and because of mankind's rebellion against Him, we experience difficult communications among the nations even today.

But God's Word is not limited by language or culture. With the invention of the printing press and the tremendous advances in learning linguistics, God's Word is readily available in hundreds of languages around the world.

Likewise, prayers have no boundaries. God can hear and understand the prayers of those who earnestly seek Him. For those who have never accepted Christ as personal Savior and Lord, the Bible says: "If you confess with your mouth the Lord Jesus and believe in your heart that God has raised Him from the dead, you will be saved" (Romans 10:9). To those who walk with Him, the Lord declares that His ear is not "dull, that it cannot hear" (Isaiah 59:1 ESV).

THE HIGHEST BELIEF

The law was our guardian until Christ came, in
order that we might be justified by faith.
GALATIANS 3:24 ESV

The Ten Commandments are founded on God's great love for us and are designed to help us live obedient lives. They are just as valid today as they were when God gave them. They reflect the moral character of God, and they also provide the foundation of right living with others.

Obedience to God's commandments doesn't flow naturally out of a heart of love for God. We may trick ourselves into believing we keep all the commandments, but the truth is, people violate them every day.

The Bible tells us that the first and greatest commandment is to love the Lord "with all your heart, with all your soul, and with all your mind" (Matthew 22:37). Violating this command is what constitutes the worst sin.

God's standard is His own standard of perfection and righteousness, and because men and women have rebelled against Him, He devised a way to bring us back to Him by sending His only Son, Jesus Christ, to die for our sin and bring us back into fellowship with our Creator. Faith in this truth that He is the Redeemer of human souls is the highest belief people can have in this world.

Believers in Christ owe God a life of undivided devotion, obedience, and service; this is what it means to love the Lord your God with completeness.

THE ONE WHO BRINGS FREEDOM

"He who believes in the Son has everlasting life."
JOHN 3:36

No one belonging to the human race is capable of bringing any kind of lasting peace to the world. The flaw in human nature is too great. History gives account to the social order called communism that emerged as one of the most powerful ideologies of all time. It challenged every concept man had ever held and threatened the whole world. Only one Man that is not of this world can bring hope for a better future.

While some countries have won freedom from bondage, others are in danger of exchanging freedom for bondage. We have seen freedom of speech give license to spewing hate and tolerance, skewing right and wrong. Some freedom-lovers value laws based on moral standards while others fight for laws that uphold the debasement of immorality. Some want to change what God has defined as evil and define it as good.

Who is the Man of hope who brings true freedom? His name is Jesus Christ. Hope rests in Him alone, and He is going to return to Earth someday in judgment. No government can prevent it, no individual can escape it, and those who refuse to embrace its reality will never change its certainty. Mankind may not be looking for Him, but all mankind will come face-to-face with the One who desires every soul to come to Him; salvation is found in no one else.

A High Calling

"You are the light of the world."
MATTHEW 5:14

God wants us to consult Him above all. When we read the Bible and commit every decision to prayer in the name of the Lord Jesus, asking for His direction, He will lead through the illumination of the Holy Spirit in our hearts.

Many people believe that service to God can only be done in the church or in a Christian organization. While this is a worthy calling, it does not necessarily mean that God doesn't call many others to serve Him in other vocations. It is a high calling to live the Christian life in the midst of those who do not know Jesus. We are called to serve Christ in our sphere of influence.

Consider Joseph, who was sold into slavery but lived a godly life in the midst of a pagan kingdom and was used by God to bring salvation to his own nation. Daniel and his three Hebrew friends did the same when they were exiled to Babylon.

The biblical principle of Christians being salt and light speaks of the influence they can have for the good of society as they live according to God's truth.

Christians at work in the world are the only real spiritual light in the midst of great spiritual darkness. This places a tremendous responsibility on us, but it is also a great privilege to live for Christ.

FAITH AND WORKS

Fulfill all the good pleasure of His goodness and the work of faith with power.
2 THESSALONIANS 1:11

There is always debate about the doctrines of faith and works—and which should come first. Which carries the most weight with God?

Jesus Christ did not offer us a choice of faith or works. The Scripture teaches that works without faith have no meaning to God, because we cannot work our way to Heaven. Those who seek to testify of what they think is their goodness often talk about paying their taxes on time, never defrauding anyone, being faithful to their spouse, and giving to charity. But God is clear that our righteousness is like a filthy rag. There is nothing we can do to measure up to God's standard.

Once we are saved, however, God expects us not to be hearers of the Word only but doers as well. Works, when we are in Christ, are an extension of Christ's ministry. In fact, works are not ends in themselves, but they demonstrate God's love toward others so that they will know God loves them, and so that they will desire to learn about God's provision for every need.

The Bible says a man in a ditch is not helped if we pass by him, wish him well, and tell him of God's love (Luke 10:25–37). No, God's love is demonstrated by attending to the man's physical needs and helping him out of the ditch.

Beware of Being Misled

"Beware of false prophets."
MATTHEW 7:15

Almost since the dawn of the human race, people have tried to discern the future. Millions of people read their horoscopes daily, trying to find some guidance.

Only God knows the future. Many look to the stars, the tea leaves, or the lines on the palm of the hand to find confidence in the future. Some of these attempts to learn what the future holds are merely foolish or useless, but others involve occult practices that can bring people into contact with spiritual forces that are not from God but Satan.

This is one reason the Bible tells us to avoid any practice that may be linked with the occult. Astrology can never provide the answers to life's deepest questions.

If our minds are not filled with God's truth, something else will take His place: cynicism, occultism, false religions and philosophies. It's Satan's purpose to steal the seed of truth from our hearts by sending distracting thoughts, clever deceptions. People have always been caught up in whatever appears to be the most bizarre, looking for truth and settling for folly. The occult is clever in reaching seekers who want to experience a rush of any kind.

Jesus told us not to be misled by the voices of strangers; there are so many strange voices being heard in the world. He is the embodiment of all truth. The only answer to man's search is found in Him.

CHRIST'S SACRIFICE

Surely He has borne our griefs and carried our sorrows.

ISAIAH 53:4

God did not exclude himself from human suffering. He became man—the Person of Christ.

We've read stories, seen paintings, and sat through numerous Christmas pageants about the birth of Jesus, focusing on the sweetness of it all, but Jesus' life was in peril from the time He uttered His first cry. The most illustrious Child ever born was hated by many while He lay in a manger.

We don't know much about His life as a child, but His entire life was one of humiliation. He came not as a conquering king but as a humble servant. When He was an adult, the leaders were suspicious of this carpenter from Nazareth, because He was a threat to them. They scorned Him and treated Him with contempt. They said He broke God's law, that He was an unholy person—a drunkard and one who made friends with the scum of society. He had the label of "guilt by association" stamped upon Him by self-righteous men. At the beginning of His ministry, His own "townsfolk" at Nazareth tried to throw Him off a cliff. Religious and political leaders often conspired to seize and kill Him.

He knew the path of pain He would experience, yet He went to the cross for us. Oh, what love, mercy, and salvation! No man has ever endured—or will endure—what Christ did voluntarily for us.

BLESSED HOPE

"They will see the Son of Man coming in a cloud with power and great glory."
LUKE 21:27

The Bible says the state of the world will grow darker as we near the end of the age. This is evident when even news reporters ask the question: "What is the world coming to?"

The Bible gives the answers. The end of the world as we know it will culminate with Jesus Christ coming again as the King triumphant. For those who don't settle the state of their souls in light of this truth, their future is dark indeed.

The Bible says that the god of this age (Satan) has blinded the eyes of those who don't believe God's truth so that the light of the gospel of the Lord Jesus Christ will have no impact (2 Corinthians 4:4). They have more faith in mankind's empty promises than the God who created them and holds the future in His hands.

There's coming a time when the Antichrist will take the world by storm, promising peace. His popularity will lure hearts and deceive minds. The human race will be caught up in exhilaration, believing the Antichrist alone will solve their dilemmas and bring global tranquility. This is why God's Word proclaims: "Be saved from this perverse generation" (Acts 2:40). But when the King of glory breaks through the storm clouds, He will reveal to the world the great deceiver and gather to Himself all those who belong to Him.

FORGIVE ONE ANOTHER

"Do to others as you would have them do to you."

LUKE 6:31 NIV

*F*orgiveness is one of the most beautiful words in the human vocabulary and is best illustrated by God's forgiveness of sin. When someone sins against us, they bear a terrible guilt. Likewise, when we refuse to forgive a wrong, we become part of the problem. When God's people practice forgiveness, sweetness replaces harshness.

We cannot force another to have a spirit of forgiveness, but we can demonstrate it by how we react. It is not always possible to mend a broken relationship. Some people refuse to accept responsibility for what they have done, always blaming someone else for what happened. Be willing to go the extra mile in an effort to be reconciled with someone who has turned against you, and remember always to pray for them. Remember to treat others as you would like to be treated.

A marvelous example of this is revealed in the life of Joseph. His brothers were jealous of him and sold him into slavery. But as the Old Testament story unfolds in Genesis 50, we see that Joseph did not hold it against them. The Lord used Joseph to save his family, and even a whole nation. Because of Joseph's forgiveness, he was blessed of God. If we cannot find it in our hearts to forgive within our own family, we will never exhibit this attribute of Christ with others and know God's blessings.

Judged by the Law

The law is holy, and the commandment holy and just and good.
ROMANS 7:12

Many people advocate doing away with all law until it begins to impact their own lives. What would happen if travelers got out on the roadways of the world without signposts, speed limits, rights-of-way, and stoplights? What would happen if planes took to the skies without air traffic control? Who would enjoy sports without rules or boundaries? Basic laws are necessary, just like rules of the game are necessary.

When the guilty are judged by the law, there are consequences. Likewise, there is a penalty to pay when we transgress the laws of God. When we violate His perfect law, it proves we do not measure up and sin overtakes us.

So what are we to do? God gives us the answer. He sent His only Son, the Lord Jesus Christ, to pay the penalty of breaking God's law. Jesus alone paid the price to redeem us from our guilt and shame. Through the shed blood of Christ on the cross, He said to the world, "I forgive you." The question is whether we are willing to admit our sin and turn from it and believe that Christ is the answer to fulfilling the law of God. He will bring peace to our hearts and give us a new pathway to walk. "[God] condemned sin . . . that the righteous requirement of the law might be fulfilled" (Romans 8:3–4).

Strength to Flee Temptation

"Pray that you may not enter into temptation."

LUKE 22:40

An important lesson can be learned by experimenting with magnets. Children often do this, placing two magnets a distance apart and then moving just one toward the other. One magnet will draw the other closer until they adhere, making it difficult to pull them apart.

Temptation is something like that, and it often begins with giving in to peer pressure. The more we dwell on what we are being tempted to do, the more likely it is that we will succumb. Giving in to temptation brings about sin. The Bible says, "No temptation has overtaken you except such as is common to man; but God is faithful, who will not allow you to be tempted beyond what you are able, but with the temptation will also make the way of escape" (1 Corinthians 10:13).

This is what God promises. Now what is our responsibility? We must not toy with such things in our minds. The Bible says to flee.

Joseph is an example. When he was tempted by his master's wife, he said, "How then can I do this great wickedness, and sin against God?" (Genesis 39:9). Joseph recognized the temptation and fled. When we sin we not only hurt ourselves and others, but most importantly we sin against God. But what gave Joseph the strength to flee? The Bible says, "The LORD was with him" (Genesis 39:3).

An Illuminated Mind

God has not given us a spirit of fear, but of power
and of love and of a sound mind.
2 TIMOTHY 1:7

The mind is the devil's favorite avenue of attack, always striving to put doubt in people's minds that leads to doubting God and His creation. We must trust God our Maker, submit wholly to Him, and not allow Satan to bring confusion as he did to Eve.

If we are not under the loving care of Jesus Christ, we will be influenced by Satan, who thrashes about in people's lives hoping to capture as many souls as possible before his inevitable end. Don't be caught in his trap.

The Bible teaches that Satan is the author of sin. Sin is the reason we have afflictions and wrong affections. The demons that serve him are busy writing pornographic literature and producing sexual materials that pollute the mind. He has infiltrated our education system, teaching hedonistic and permissive philosophy. The culture is bombarded by a sexual tempest.

Table talk these days centers not only on sexual perversion but every sinful thought and deed. It is true that society has become so obsessed with sex that it seeps from all the pores of our national life.

The converted person will love the good he once hated, and hate the sin he once loved. Be filled with the Spirit of God, which illuminates the minds of people, causing us to yearn for God.

THE NEW NATURE

Make no provision for the flesh.
ROMANS 13:14

S o many people react with disappointment when they learn that someone they have loved and respected ended up with a regretful past. When we come to respect someone, there are usually good reasons for it, and we must reconcile the fact that people can change and be converted. This is actually the truth about what salvation in Jesus Christ has done for mankind. Every person has a past of sin, but when Christ comes into our lives and cleanses our sinful hearts, a transformation takes place.

The Bible is filled with such testimonies. Saul, the Pharisee, sought and killed Christians until he was transformed by Christ and spent the rest of his life serving God and proclaiming the gospel. He became known as the apostle Paul.

Most of all, we must remember that we, too, are sinners. Those who repent and turn from sin and surrender their past to the Lord Jesus will experience the amazing love of God that turns darkness to light and despair to joy.

The greatest need in the world is the transformation of human nature. We all need a new heart. We must feed the new nature on a steady diet of the Word of God. We must starve the old nature, our sinful past, and no longer make provision for such things. The Lord will empower us to turn away from sin and look to Him.

A WARNING LIGHT

Keep your conscience clear.
1 TIMOTHY 1:19 NLT

And the LORD God formed man . . . and man became a living soul" (Genesis 2:7 KJV). Likewise, the "conscience also bear[s] witness" (Romans 2:15). God has put within us something that cries against us; it bears witness whenever we do that which we know to be wrong (Romans 1:19, 2:15). The conscience is the detective that watches the direction of our steps and decries every conscious transgression. It's not imagination but rather a vigilant eye before which each imagination, thought, and act is held up for either censure or approval.

Every human being is a living soul with a conscience: a warning light to go on inside when we do wrong; this is our conscience. It wants to steer us away from evil and toward good. Even when the conscience is dulled or darkened by sin, it can still bear witness to the reality of good and evil, and to the holiness of God. Immanuel Kant, a German philosopher, once stated that there were two things that filled him with awe—the starry heavens above and the human conscience within.

Continual sin can dull or even silence our conscience. On the other hand, continual attention to God's Word will sharpen our conscience and make us more sensitive to moral and spiritual danger. We are instructed to "cleanse" our conscience, "not with fleshly wisdom but by the grace of God" (Hebrews 9:14 NIV; 2 Corinthians 1:12).

THE ETERNAL NAME

For thus says the High and Lofty One who inhabits eternity, whose name is Holy.
ISAIAH 57:15

The names of politicians, sports figures, inventors, and others from all walks of life come and go. While their names may continue in history, their impact is not lasting. Only one name is eternal and worthy of our praise and attention; the name of the Lord God, Jesus Christ. The prophet Daniel who served the king of the dominant power in the world declared: "Blessed be the name of God forever and ever, for wisdom and might are His" (Daniel 2:20).

The strength of nations is not found in the names and personalities of men and women, but in God alone who is sovereign. No form of government has been able to establish righteousness, justice, and peace, the three elements without which we can never have continued national prosperity or international peace.

Our government is certainly going to fall like a rope of sand if unsupported by the moral fabric of God's Word. The moral structure in our country grew from Judeo-Christian roots. When those values are applied, they produce moral fruits. Our government needs prayer. Our leaders need prayer. Our schools need prayer. Our families need prayer. We must be people of prayer and express thankfulness for the blood of Christ that purchased men for God from "every tribe and language and people and nation" (Revelation 5:9 NIV).

GOSPEL MANDATE

The gospel is bearing fruit.
COLOSSIANS 1:6 NIV

There's a familiar passage often quoted that motivates humanitarian work found in Matthew 25:40: "Inasmuch as you did it to one of the least of these My brethren, you did it to Me." Meeting the needs of others is much more than just meeting physical needs. The work of the Lord Jesus Christ is wrapped up in this: "How beautiful upon the mountains are the feet of him who brings good news, who proclaims peace . . . who proclaims salvation" (Isaiah 52:7).

Meeting just the outward needs has no lasting effect if we do not preach God's truth. The Word of God is the all-important action. Meeting people's needs without the message is known as the "social gospel," but there is no such thing as a "social gospel." There is only one gospel. "If anyone preaches any other gospel to you . . . let him be accursed" (Galatians 1:9). The gospel, not humanitarian aid, is the Christian's mandate.

Reaching out to others with the gospel shows people their emptiness and bestows on them love. It shows them their bondage and supplies the hammer to knock away their chains. It shows them their nakedness and provides them the garments of purity. It shows them their poverty and pours into their lives the wealth of Heaven. It shows them their sins and points them to the Savior. This is the heart of Christ and the reason why His followers reach out to others.

OUR FRIEND IN GRIEF

He will be with you, He will not leave you nor forsake you.
DEUTERONOMY 31:8

Grief can kill a person emotionally and physically. An onslaught of grief can cause people to think they're losing their minds. The grief-stricken person can lose the ability to concentrate, which adds to panic. This may lead, then, to emotional paralysis. Guilt, anger, resentment, and panic are some of the faces of grief.

Like soldiers going into battle, we need to be prepared for grief, but the culture of today does not prepare us for it. What we need more than anything else during times of grief is a friend who stands with us. Jesus is that Friend. The Lord prepares us to weather life's storms. He tells us to have faith in Him. He has told us that He will be with us always and "never leave [us] nor forsake [us]" (Hebrews 13:5). Often it takes that "knife in our heart" to drive us to Him. Our faith is dependent upon God, and when we enter the valley of grief, we need His help.

When we belong to Christ, He offers forgiveness and strengthens us to overcome our failures and sin. We can take our cares to Him and He'll see us through. The Bible says to fill our minds with things that are true, honorable, pure, and lovely and "His peace will guard your hearts and minds as you live in Christ Jesus" (Philippians 4:7 NLT).

FAITH ROOTED IN THE WORD

May the God of hope fill you with all joy and peace in believing.
ROMANS 15:13

Faith not rooted in the truth of God's Word has no power. Power comes from the Source of faith, and that is in Christ Jesus the Lord. The Bible says, "Your faith should not be in the wisdom of men but in the power of God" (1 Corinthians 2:5). How do we get that power? When we humble ourselves before God, He gives us the gift of faith to believe.

Faith is belief in someone greater than ourselves, and it is Jesus Christ and Him alone. The Bible teaches that faith is the only approach we have to God. No one has sins forgiven, no one goes to Heaven, no one has assurance of peace and contentment until we exhibit faith in Jesus Christ.

"But without faith it is impossible to please Him, for he who comes to God must believe that He is, and that He is a rewarder of those who diligently seek Him" (Hebrews 11:6).

What does this mean? It means that we are convinced that Jesus is who He claims to be—God in human flesh, sent to save us from our sins. "Let us lay aside every weight, and the sin which so easily ensnares us, and let us run with endurance the race that is set before us, looking unto Jesus, the author and finisher of our faith" (Hebrews 12:1–2).

Not My Will

You ask and do not receive, because you ask amiss,
that you may spend it on your pleasures.

JAMES 4:3

When we become God's obedient children, He helps us walk with Him every mile of our life's journey. God commands that we first submit our lives to Him. He equips us to carry out His plan for our lives.

God also puts His desires down in our hearts and minds. If a person excels in mathematics or biology, there is nothing wrong with going into finance or medicine, for instance. When a person begins pursuing such a pathway, the Lord will open and shut doors as a way of guiding. God doesn't expect us to be paralyzed when it comes to making decisions about our futures. Neither does He give us what we always want, because it may not be for our good or according to His will.

We mustn't ask for our will to be done but for God's will to be done (Matthew 6:10). He reveals His wisdom to us through the reading of His Word and through prayer. Some people pray they will pass a test without studying. Others fail to pray about their choice of college or their career or their future spouse and do what pleases them. Many pray only when they face a crisis. The Bible tells us to pray about everything (Philippians 4:6). God is concerned about every detail of our lives, both big and small.

JULY

THE GOD OF ALL COMFORT

"I . . . am He who comforts you."
ISAIAH 51:12

Personal pain has been with us since God told Eve she would have pain in childbirth. Suffering comes in all forms—physical, emotional, spiritual. Some people have their share of pain more than others, but all experience it.

Every generation sees their era as filled with the greatest despair. We are plummeting into a world where, in spite of wonder drugs and medical breakthroughs, suffering intensifies.

Without God's guidance, our response to suffering is a futile attempt to find solutions to conditions that cannot be solved. Some who refuse to turn their hearts toward God search for Utopia and come up empty. Apart from the Bible there are no solutions.

While individual suffering has no respite and the collective suffering of our world continues, there are those who have found a refuge in the midst of the rubble. What is the difference between the paraplegic woman with the smile that lights a room and the millionaire with a suicide wish? Or what makes one person accept and keep his balance during a painful time and another become a self-pitying whiner?

We cannot avoid suffering, but we can determine our response to it. God is not blind to our troubles and He waits to comfort us. He is the Father of compassion and the God of all comfort in our troubles (2 Corinthians 1:3–4), and we should do likewise—reach out to others in need.

A Plan for Deliverance

Christ has redeemed us from the curse of the law.
GALATIANS 3:13

Once, a man was standing on top of a mountain and noticed two cars in the distance heading toward each other on a dangerously winding road. Neither driver could see the other approaching. The man at the top of the mountain shouted a warning, even though he was too far away to be heard. The crash was fatal and several people were killed.

God does not stand on a mountaintop watching the disasters that befall mankind. He left the highest Heaven and came down to Earth in the Person of His Son Jesus Christ. He intervened on behalf of the human race by demonstrating so deep a love for His creation to extend salvation to all who would receive Him.

From the beginning of man's journey, God had a plan for his deliverance. The plan is so fantastic that it ultimately lifts each person far above even the angels.

God is at work to get us to stop our downward plunge into sin. Evil forces building up in our world are so overwhelming that people everywhere should cry out, "What must I do to be saved?" (see Acts 2:37).

The answer is found all through Scripture. Repent of sin and turn from it, confess that Jesus is Lord, and make Him the Master of your life, and your journey will take on new meaning.

The Dangers of Self-Reliance

He has . . . conveyed us into the kingdom of the Son of His love.
COLOSSIANS 1:13

Our modern philosophy of self-reliance and self-sufficiency has caused many to believe that man can make the grade without God. "Religion," they argue, "may be all right for certain emotional people, but you can't beat a man who believes in himself."

The Austrian neurologist and founder of psychoanalysis, Dr. Sigmund Freud, said that religion is the universal obsessional neurosis. But a self-confident generation has produced more alcoholics, more drug addicts, more criminals, more wars, more broken homes, more assaults, more embezzlements, more murders, and more suicides than any other generation that ever lived. It is time all of us begin to take stock of our failures, blunders—and yes, sin. It is time we put our trust in almighty God.

But while our problems are enormous, our problems are not new. The young man in the Bible, often called the Rich Young Ruler, approached Jesus with his piety, his riches, and his greed. He wanted assurance of Heaven, but when Jesus told him he would have to "sell out" and follow Him, the rich man revolted. He found it impossible to give up what he had accumulated. He had a lofty estimate of his own importance (Mark 10).

All around us are arrogance, pride, and selfishness. These are the result of sin. But Jesus calls us out of that and into His realm, where we can find mercy and grace.

Prayer: A Way of Life

Pray without ceasing.
1 THESSALONIANS 5:17

Prayer is more than a wish; it is the voice of faith directed to God. Prayer should not be merely an act; it is a way of life. We must learn to shut out the distractions that come from Satan. He wants to break the fellowship with the Master of our lives so that we become ineffective.

Life is busy for most, but still we generally find time for the things we truly want to do. Prayer is for every moment of our lives. It is an attitude, an acknowledgment, that God knows our thoughts and sees our deeds. But do we actually ever share our hearts with Him?

One of the best ways to prepare ourselves for prayer is to read the Word of God. When we keep our eyes fixed on God's promises, we are encouraged. He has spoken to us on every subject that concerns us. How wonderful it is to make the Bible central in our lives—not to just know it but obey it.

We cannot afford to be too busy to pray. In the Bible God speaks to us; in prayer we speak to God. Both are essential. Most Bibles remain unopened and unread and then we panic when our lives begin to falter. If we cling to this Guidebook, it will lead us to the Guide, the Lord Jesus Christ, and His Spirit will "teach us to pray" (Luke 11:1).

CLEANSING AND REFRESHMENT

May the LORD give strength to his people!
PSALM 29:11 ESV

Science has confirmed what the Bible taught centuries ago: There is a close relationship between our minds and bodies. Proverbs puts it this way: "A merry heart does good, like medicine, but a broken spirit dries the bones" (17:22).

But there is also a close relationship between our mental and physical health and the health of our spiritual lives. Guilt, fear, jealousy, bitterness, futility, escapism—these and a host of other problems are spiritual ills, brought about by the disease of sin. Like poison, they can sicken us in mind and body. There are many things that cause depression, but anxiety is certainly one culprit, and the more you feed anxious thoughts, the more they grow.

But when Christ comes into our lives, He removes our guilt and takes away our fears. He gives us love for others and a new purpose in life. His joy and peace neutralize sin's poison—and that promotes emotional and physical health.

Does that mean our emotional and physical problems will vanish? Not necessarily. But like a spring of pure water, God's peace in our hearts brings cleansing and refreshment to our whole being.

The Bible is filled with passages that bring comfort and joy. Read them and dwell on them. If you want comfort in sorrow, light in darkness, peace in turmoil, and rest in weariness, the Lord offers it all through His Word.

REFINED BY FIRE

Blessed is the one who perseveres under trial.
JAMES 1:12 NIV

When Job, of the Old Testament, considered the wonders of God in the midst of his trials and hardships, he proclaimed: "When He has tested me, I shall come forth as gold" (Job 23:10).

Anyone who goes through difficulties while keeping their eyes on the Lord and trusting Him for the result will come forth victoriously.

A bar of raw steel may be purchased for a few dollars. But when it has been thrust into the fires and processed, when it has been tempered and forged and made into tiny watch springs for expensive watches, it is turned into something worth thousands of dollars.

Just as the sun by its heat and light performs a thousand miracles a day in the plant kingdom, God, through the refining fire of His Spirit, performs a thousand miracles a day in the spiritual realm. His regenerating power can take the dull and ordinary things of our lives—even the burned-out ashes of our past—and forge them into something useful, even beautiful, for His purposes.

The apostle Peter wrote concerning trials: "In this you greatly rejoice, though now for a little while, if need be, you have been grieved by various trials, that the genuineness of your faith, being much more precious than gold that perishes, though it is tested by fire, may be found to [glorify Jesus Christ]" (1 Peter 1:6–7).

UNLIMITED GOD

"Did I not say to you that if you would believe you would see the glory of God?"
JOHN 11:40

If God can be fully proved by the human mind, then He's no greater than the mind that proves Him. Humans are limited in every way, and that's why it takes faith in "Someone" more powerful than mankind to set our hearts right. His name is almighty God.

There's no limit to God. There's no limit to His wisdom. There's no limit to His power. There's no limit to His love. There's no limit to His mercy. We cannot confine God or measure His works; that would be like trying to measure the water in the ocean.

Most of us know "about" God, but that's quite different from knowing God. He hasn't only revealed Himself to the human race from the beginning of time; He cared so much for our suffering that He sent His only Son to walk among us.

Every word that Jesus spoke is historically true. Every word that He spoke was scientifically true. Every word that He spoke was ethically true. His ethical vision was wholly correct in the age in which He walked on Earth, and correct in every age that has followed.

If you want to know God, take a look at Jesus Christ. He is the great Gift God has given to the world to prove the reality of His love.

FROM MYTH TO TRUTH

You were bought at a price.
1 CORINTHIANS 6:20

The apostle Paul appeared before King Agrippa and presented the truth of Jesus Christ, but the king said, "You almost persuade me to become a Christian" (Acts 26:28), but not even Paul could convince him. Our job as Christians is to tell others about Jesus Christ and the hope we have because of His death on the cross for our sins. God sent His Son, who gave everything to purchase the souls of men, women, and children for the kingdom of Heaven. Jesus rose from the grave by the power of God to confirm Heaven's reality. Believing in Christ settles the question about Heaven.

Many young people are convinced that life after death is just a myth, and because of it they live in darkness and despair, without hope. While young people may not give life after death serious thought because they are young, healthy, and energetic, it doesn't mean that life after death is not a reality. They fool themselves.

The greatest discovery we will ever make is to know the love of God, which was fully demonstrated by His Son's sacrifice on the cross for us. This is the power that transforms man's myth into Christ's truth. Jesus did not die on the cross for people's sin so that we would believe in Heaven—but that we would believe in Him. Heaven does not save souls—it collects them.

Turn Your Eyes Upon Jesus

"He who abides in Me, and I in him, bears much fruit."
JOHN 15:5

No one who is a Christian is perfect, but there are people who claim to follow Jesus yet are far from His teaching. At the same time, it is dangerous for others to let what they perceive as hypocrisy in others divert them from Christ. Christians will sometimes falter in their walk with Christ, but Christ never falters. We must not put our trust in people. The object of our faith is in Christ alone.

Christ never brings disappointment. We grow in Christ not by following other people but by following God's Word. Understand His teaching and examine His life. We must not get sidetracked with disappointment in others. We must live our lives consistently. We must always ask ourselves if our life reflects the things of Christ: His love, joy, and peace.

Jesus Christ is the complete fulfillment, example, and demonstration of perfection. While we will never attain perfection in this life, we are told to walk in His footsteps and strive to please Him in everything we do. This is only possible when we stay connected to the Source of all things good. When a true believer stumbles and sins, God's Holy Spirit brings conviction and turns the individual to repentance. This is what restores our souls and clears the way for fellowship with Him. We must never put our eyes on people but on God.

HUMANISM

[They] worshiped and served the creature rather than the Creator.
ROMANS 1:25

Humanism is the worship of man. It has taken on the form of religion, glorifying self and taking God out of His rightful place. This has always been prevalent in the world and is called by many different names.

Humanism has become for many a polite name for a vocal and aggressive movement against God's truth to advance its own brand of social influence. Humanism is not new; it emerged in the Garden of Eden. It is the yielding to Satan's first temptation of Adam and Eve. He told them they could be gods (Genesis 3:5).

Mankind continually rejects the revelation of the Bible concerning the true and living God, substituting gods of its own making. Many intellectuals have come to believe that the human mind can understand everything eventually. This is nothing but total rebellion toward God, and Satan is behind it all. The underlying principle of all the devil's tactics is deception.

The Bible warns, "The devil walks about like a roaring lion, seeking whom he may devour. Resist him" (1 Peter 5:8–9). The Lord will help us stand strong in the face of deception if we will stay in the Word of God and pray that He will give us discerning minds. The important thing for all of Christ's followers is to live "in Christ" as the Bible teaches (2 Timothy 1:1).

THE CHURCH

Know how . . . to conduct yourself in the house of God,
which is the church of the living God.
1 TIMOTHY 3:15

Going to church doesn't make one a Christian, nor does every church building represent Jesus Christ. Satan often invades Sunday school and Bible classes, and even the pulpit. Many people sit in some churches week after week without hearing the whole gospel and learning what it is to be born again.

The true church on Earth is made up of individuals who have repented of sin.

Jesus established the church for the purpose of fellowship and instruction on how to live in obedience to God and His Word. The Lord didn't design the church to cater to people's needs, establish community programs, or blend into the community by embracing what the world enjoys. When this happens, the world's ideas and interests infiltrate the church. The Bible warns of this: "For certain [people] have crept in unnoticed . . . who turn the grace of our God into lewdness and deny the only Lord God and our Lord Jesus Christ" (Jude 4).

The Lord breathed life into the church to proclaim His truths. The church is a storehouse of spiritual food whereby the inner man is fed, nourished, and developed into maturity. If it fails in this, it is not fulfilling its purpose.

We must pray that the Lord will lead every believer into fellowship with others who desire to glorify God in everything we do.

A BETTER WAY

With my whole heart I have sought You.

PSALM 119:10

Attaining success in life is not wrong, but if we go about it without obedience to God's Word, it can lead us down the wrong path. The Bible tells us that God's thoughts are different from our thoughts.

The psalmist's pen presents a view of life that is the exact opposite of what the world around us promotes. "Live for yourself," the world proclaims. "Have a good time; indulge your senses; pursue every pleasure; strive for success. And if you do," these voices add, "then you'll be happy and blessed."

But God calls us to another way—His way. The Bible says, "Blessed are those who keep [the Lord's] testimonies, who seek Him with the whole heart!" (Psalm 119:2). Blessing, He says, comes only from following Him. Every other way promises what it cannot deliver—and delivers exactly the opposite of what it promised. Some of the most miserable people are those who are highly successful in the eyes of the world.

Don't fall into the world's trap. It can happen without you even being aware of it. Our job in life is not to be successful but to be faithful. Regardless of our cleverness, our achievements, and our gadgets and devices, we are spiritual paupers without God. Make sure Christ is first in your life, and make it your goal to live according to His Word. For then you will know true contentment.

Learning Patience

The fruit of the Spirit is . . . self-control.
GALATIANS 5:22-23

Learning patience is not easy for most. The Bible calls patience an attribute of God, and we are to pray for it and practice it with the strength that God gives us. While it is important to consider the needs and thoughts of others, it doesn't mean that people should let others take advantage of them. But we must also guard against selfishness. Patience is not simply "teeth-clenched" endurance. It is an attitude of expectation.

The Bible says, "Be patient. . . . See how the farmer waits for the precious fruit of the earth. . . . You also be patient. Establish your hearts, for the coming of the Lord is at hand" (James 5:7–8). The farmer patiently watches his barren ground because he knows there will be results. As we strive to live for the Lord, we must exhibit patience, knowing that our obedience to Him will result in good fruits that He will accept in eternity.

Patience also speaks of a person's steadfastness when irritated or experiencing conflict. Enduring ill treatment without anger or retaliation is a fruit of the Spirit, referred to in Scripture as self-control. Our lives are to be characterized by patience, for it is important in developing stable character and integrity. This is why God allows difficulties, inconveniences, trials, and even suffering to come our way: they help develop the right attitude for the growth of patience in our lives.

THE GIFT OF ANIMALS

Let everything that has breath praise the LORD.

PSALM 150:6

God's creation story is the first miraculous account in the Bible, which includes His creation of animals. While the Bible does not specifically answer the question of animals in Heaven, no one can miss God's creative work in the animal kingdom. His written Word provides us with a snapshot of His original handiwork: "Let the earth bring forth the living creature according to its kind: cattle. . . . and everything . . . on the earth. . . . And God saw that it was good" (Genesis 1:24–25).

Animals are fascinating creatures, and the variety seems endless. We know that God gave them to us for a purpose, because in the days of Noah, before the great flood, God preserved every species—male and female—on the ark so they would inhabit the land again. Animals are among God's many diverse gifts to man. Who doesn't smile while watching chimpanzees mimic one another, or marvel at the monstrous whales in the ocean, or be inspired to watch swans gracefully move through the waters?

Scripture speaks of the future messianic kingdom that captivates our imaginations: "The wolf will live with the lamb, the leopard will lie down with the goat, the calf and the lion and the yearling together; and a little child will lead them" (Isaiah 11:6 NIV). One day perfect peace will reign, and everything that has breath, including animals, will praise the Lord.

PARDONED

Return to the LORD . . . for He will abundantly pardon.
ISAIAH 55:7

A young boy joined the British army, but when the shots began to fly, he deserted. In time he became a great astronomer and discovered a new planet. He was sent for by King George, but the man recognized his guilt and his unworthiness to be in the presence of the king. Before the king allowed the man to appear before him, the man was sent an envelope and requested to open it. When he did, he discovered a royal pardon. He was brought before the king, who said, "Now we can talk, and you shall come up and live at Windsor Castle." The name of the pardoned man was Sir William Herschel.

Herschel was guilty and did not deny it! But King George had mercy on him and made him a member of the royal household. That is what God promises to do for us. He has extended His mercy to all who will receive His pardon, bringing those who accept His gift of forgiveness into fellowship with Him in His heavenly kingdom.

God's forgiveness is the complete blotting out of all dirt and degradation of our past, present, and future. There have been people who have extended forgiveness to others; there have been those in authority to extend pardons. How much more does a loving God grant mercy to those who humble themselves before Him and receive His great love?

IDOL WORSHIP

Therefore, my beloved, flee from idolatry.
1 CORINTHIANS 10:14

The apostle Paul stood before the people of the city of Athens and directed their attention to the unknown God. He had been walking through the city, observing the customs of the people.

This pagan society had a niche for every god in the world, yet their moral corruption was revealed by the hundreds of idols at a place called Mars Hill in ancient Greece. Paul spoke with power before this congregation and acknowledged all their gods and even the unknown God, who is none other than God's Son, the Lord Jesus Christ.

Paul said, "Men of Athens, I perceive that in all things you are very religious; for as I was . . . considering the objects of your worship, I even found an altar with this inscription: TO THE UNKNOWN GOD. Therefore, the One whom you worship without knowing, Him I proclaim to you" (Acts 17:22–23).

Our culture is saturated with the worship of sports, sex, and pleasure. While we are busy humanizing God, we are deifying man. Our idols are not statues of gold and marble; our idols come from the things we love the most: celebrities, behaviors, etc. One who truly follows Him will have a hunger to worship Him and His Word. Life does not have to be filled with such emptiness, but we can fill our minds and hearts with the things that bring glory to the Lord Jesus Christ.

THE TRANSFORMING WORK OF GOD

The garment of praise for the spirit of heaviness.
ISAIAH 61:3

People cannot change their past. But with God's help, they can change the future. This should bring comfort to every hopeless heart. The future doesn't need to be a copy of the past, nor does God want it to be. No matter what life has been like so far, God wants to set our feet on a new path—His path. His path holds promises far beyond anything imaginable.

But this doesn't just happen. An architect draws up plans for a new building—but it still has to be built. A composer writes a new piece of music—but it still has to be played. A chef devises a new recipe—but the ingredients still have to be cooked.

In the same way, God has given us a blueprint for living—but we must know what it is and then put it into action, and God does not leave us to do it alone. He wants to be with us every step of the way, guiding and helping us (and even correcting us when necessary) to keep us walking right.

No matter what age a person may be, it is never too late to turn to God. When we come before Him with a humble spirit and in truth, admitting our sin and our willingness to turn from sin with His help, He will do a transforming work in our lives.

THREE GREAT TRUTHS

In the way of righteousness is life.
PROVERBS 12:28

There are three great truths about our journey through life.

First, God put us on the journey of life. We were not put on Earth by chance or by accident.

Second, God wants to be with us on our journey through life. We must never assume that God is not interested in us.

Third, God calls us to a new journey—the path of faith and trust in Him.

Imagine we hike a path never traveled and come to a fork in the trail. Which path is right? Both lead somewhere—but which one will lead to the right destination? One path appears wider and easier to travel and apparently is used by more people, who conclude it must be the right way. Then another hiker approaches and we may ask, which road would he or she take? Without hesitation the hiker points to the lesser path traveled and waves us onward. "I'll lead you to your destination." Then we ask: "How do you know this is right?" The hiker answers: "Because I cut this pathway from start to finish. In fact, I'm headed that way myself, and I'll walk with you so you won't get lost."

Which path would we choose? We would likely follow the one who had created that path. This is what Christ says: "Follow Me. I will lead you along the path of righteousness."

GOD HAS REVEALED HIMSELF TO US

He has put eternity in their hearts.
ECCLESIASTES 3:11

Down inside, we all sense there is Someone greater than ourselves. We also sense that death is not the end, that there must be something beyond the grave. The Bible says that God has set eternity in the hearts of people (Ecclesiastes 3:11).

Some picture God as a kindly old grandfather with a long white beard and a vague smile. Others see Him as a stern policeman, always ready to punish us if we get out of line. Still others conclude that God must be like their own father might have been, indifferent or cold or never satisfied, because we always fall short of what He demands. And some believe God is only an impersonal force, or they conclude we can't know anything for certain about Him. Your guess about God, they say, is just as good (or bad) as mine. And some people, of course, reject the whole idea of God.

Some say that it is just too narrow to believe in only one God and one way. Sadly, most speculations about God miss one very important truth. God wants us to know Him. We don't have to guess about who He is because He has revealed Himself to us. His footprints are everywhere. His very image is in our DNA. The Bible tells us that God has not left Himself without testimony.

CREATED FOR FRIENDSHIP

The LORD is a friend to those who fear him.

PSALM 25:14 NLT

God created us to have a personal relationship with Him. When Adam and Eve were first created, the purpose had its origin in the love of God. It was, however, a friendship with a difference. On a human level, we usually choose friends who are similar to us. But God and Adam were not equals. God is the Sovereign Ruler of the universe, the all-powerful Creator, who not only made everything but also controls and sustains it, from the largest galaxy to the smallest glimmer of light.

God is also everywhere at the same time. He is the all-knowing Lord who sees everything that happens, including every detail of our lives.

Adam was none of these. God was the Creator; Adam was the creature. God was limitless; Adam was limited. God was independent; Adam was dependent. But in spite of the vast difference between them, God still wanted Adam and Eve to be His friends. This was why they were created, and this was how they lived until sin entered the world and destroyed that perfect friendship.

In the beginning, God was Adam's perfect Friend, and Adam was God's perfect friend. God's plan for Adam and Eve is also true for us. God has not changed and neither has His purpose. But we must give ourselves completely to Him and accept His perfect gift of salvation.

WHAT IS A DISCIPLE?

"If you abide in My word, you are My disciples indeed."
JOHN 8:31

People in Jesus' day knew what the word *disciple* meant. John the Baptist had a band of disciples around him, and so did the Pharisees (a group of religious leaders). But Jesus expanded its meaning by saying that everyone who truly believes in Him is called to be a disciple.

What is a disciple? First, a disciple is a learner or a student. The Twelve whom Jesus called to be His closest companions were with Him day and night. They had a personal relationship with Him, walking with Him, eating with Him, sharing in His conversation, observing the way He lived, listening to Him preach to the crowds. But they weren't following Jesus just to enjoy His presence. They had a purpose: to learn from Him. And this was true for all His disciples, not just the Twelve.

What keeps us from being the right kind of disciple? One factor may be laziness (or a lack of discipline). Or we may not realize how much we need to know and be guided by God's truth. The psalmist was right when he wrote that the words of God give light and understanding (Psalm 119:130).

Our journey through life is filled with all kinds of pitfalls and temptations, and unless we allow our minds and hearts to be shaped by Christ's truth, we risk falling into all kinds of errors and dangers.

THE DIFFERENCE

You are not in the flesh but in the Spirit, if indeed the Spirit of God dwells in you.

ROMANS 8:9

One Christian might say he is different from his non-Christian friends because he belongs to a church. Another might reply that she is different because she knows she has been forgiven of her sins and is going to Heaven. Someone else might say Christians are different because of what they believe: that the Bible is the Word of God and Jesus was the divine Son of God who died for our sins. Still others might suggest that what makes Christians different is the way they live.

The complete answer is that the difference in Christians—followers of Jesus Christ—is that God Himself lives within them by His Holy Spirit, who does a transforming work in the life of every true believer.

When we come to Christ and give our lives to Him, God actually takes up residence within us. We may not always feel different or be aware of His presence, but Jesus' promise to His disciples was fulfilled; for He sent a Counselor to be with us forever, and that is God's Holy Spirit (John 14:16–17).

The Bible clearly tells us that if we have given our lives to Jesus Christ by receiving His forgiveness of sins and accepting His salvation, He now lives in us through His Spirit.

The Secret of Domestic Happiness

As for me and my family, we will serve the Lord.
JOSHUA 24:15 NLT

God designed marriage, family, and home as sacred institutions. These are falling away for one reason: God has been left out of the domestic picture. With the breakdown of discipline in the home, the home has been battered and scarred.

Restoring these gifts God has given to mankind takes humbling ourselves before God and asking forgiveness for being reckless and distracted. Many homes today have become little more than dormitories, where the members of the family eat and sleep but otherwise have little communication or interaction with each other. Family life has disintegrated and children are growing up insecure, never knowing the stability of a happy family.

The secret of domestic happiness is to set aside self-fulfillment and let God have His rightful place in the home. We cannot undo what has been done in the past, but we can change the things that lend to the breakdown. God can restore broken marriages, families, and homes.

God ordained monogamous marriage and the sanctity of what is known as the traditional family. He has given clear instruction on making Him the center of home life: "Lay up these words of mine. . . . teach them to your children, speaking of them when you sit in your house, when you walk by the way, when you lie down, and when you rise up. . . . write them on the doorposts of your house and on your gates" (Deuteronomy 11:18–20).

RESENTMENT TOWARD GOD

"My strength is made perfect in weakness."
2 CORINTHIANS 12:9

How does resentment develop? It develops within the climate of resistance to God's will for our lives. Christians who are strong in faith grow as they accept whatever God allows to enter their lives. They bow to His good and perfect will and become more mature. In a true sense, Christian character is growth, not a gift.

Alexander Maclaren, a distinguished preacher (1826–1910), wrote, "What disturbs us in this world is not trouble, but our opposition to trouble. The true source of all that frets and irritates and wears away our lives is not in external things but in the resistance of our wills to the will of God expressed by eternal things."

To resist God's disciplining hand is to miss one of the greatest spiritual blessings we Christians can realize this side of Heaven.

Whatever it is, we haven't "learned Christ" until we have discovered that God's grace is sufficient for every test.

The attitude, which can overcome resentment, is expressed by the writer to the Hebrews—that no discipline seems pleasant at the time; it is painful. But later on, it produces a harvest of peace for those who have been trained by it (Hebrews 12:11).

True Christian victory does not lie along the path of mere resignation. Instead, the growing Christian sees that though God may wound us (or allow us to be wounded), His hand also heals (Job 5:18).

God's Unchanging Care

God is our refuge and strength.
PSALM 46:1

Many changes have taken place in our world. In fact, it is no longer the same world; it is totally different. There are new generations—young people who have grown up in a new society and are challenged by new ideas. But it isn't "entirely" new because every generation experiences change.

But one thing is certain. God has not changed, for He said, "I the LORD do not change" (Malachi 3:6 ESV). This is an immeasurable comfort to the believer in times of change.

John Bunyan tells us, "Afflictions are governed by God, both as to time, number, nature, and measure. Our times, and our conditions in these times, are in the hand of God, yea, and so are our souls and bodies, to be kept and preserved from the evil while the rod of God is upon us."

God is interested in, and concerned about, every aspect of our lives—physical, mental, emotional, and spiritual. The Bible makes it clear that nothing that concerns us is beneath His concern.

It would be impossible to list all the Bible's promises. Some estimate there are anywhere from eight thousand to thirty thousand promises of God.

Our God is in the arena of life. He goes with His people into the scene of difficulty and onto the platform of pain, not necessarily to deliver us from them but to sustain us in the midst of them.

ATONING SACRIFICE

This Man, after He had offered one sacrifice for sins
forever, sat down at the right hand of God.

HEBREWS 10:12

When we look into God's Word, we see what true righteousness is. The Ten Commandments describe the life that pleases God. If we are separated from God by sin, the law exposes our sin and shows us our true spiritual condition.

Sin had to be paid for, so in the beginning God instituted the sacrificial system by which we finally could be brought into a right relationship with God. In Old Testament times, those who had sinned brought sacrifices of animals and offered them to God. This foreshadowed the Great Sacrifice yet to come.

What is the significance? It was an atonement for mankind in regard to sin. The sacrifices were visual aids to show sinners that there was hope because the punishment for sin could be transferred to another. However, this symbolically demonstrated that God could forgive them in the light of what He would one day do at the cross.

God did not initiate the sacrifices because He was bloodthirsty or unjust. He wanted us to zero in on two things: first, the loathsomeness of sin, and second, the cross on which God Himself would satisfy forever the demands of His justice.

No Worries

"Do not worry about your life."
MATTHEW 6:25

If we trust in our worry more than we trust God, we are sinning by our lack of faith in Him who has given us the richness of His constant abiding presence, for those who put their faith in Him. Counter your worry by thinking about the things you do not worry about. Perhaps you never worry about whether you will be able to get water out of the faucet in your kitchen, or maybe you do not worry about a tree falling on your house. You may be a worrier by nature, but even the worst worrier in the world doesn't worry about some things!

Ask yourself why you do not worry about some things. Is it because, in the case of running water, it has always been there when you wanted it? Or that a tree has never fallen on your house before? Certainty breeds trust, doesn't it?

We can be just as certain and worry-free about God's love and protection. What is the evidence? It is the cross, where God fully expressed His love for us. Since Jesus overcame death, can He not help us overcome worry about things that will probably never happen? We should turn worry into gratitude for all the times He has seen us through difficulties. Worries flee before a spirit of gratitude, and the Lord is pleased when we trust Him (1 Peter 5:7).

THE GREATEST FRIEND

Turn to me and be gracious to me, for I am lonely and afflicted.

PSALM 25:16 ESV

Loneliness often comes to the busiest people. Loneliness can also be self-inflicted through self-isolation. Some long for togetherness; others demand privacy and independence. The kind of society we live in today can contribute to loneliness. It is difficult for some to maintain strong relationships. Mobility and constant change tend to make some individuals feel rootless and disconnected.

In spite of the multitudes that claim to have millions of friends, loneliness is the predominant attitude in our culture. A person can be lonely in the midst of a party; he can be lonely in a crowd. Loneliness may be experienced by the rich and famous or the poor and unknown. And surveys indicated that there are millions of very lonely faces peering into computer screens. Social media today has given people a way to search for total strangers as friends and gain listening ears.

There is a listening ear that waits patiently to hear from us. His name is Jesus Christ. Some of the greatest Christians I know have led quiet yet full lives because they were in tune with God. When we pray to Him, we are in touch with the greatest Friend mankind will ever know. We must learn to set aside some of our busyness and make Christ the focus of life, and loneliness will be replaced by His compassionate love.

THE UNPARDONABLE SIN

"Every sin and blasphemy can be forgiven—except blasphemy against the Holy Spirit."
MATTHEW 12:31 NLT

When people cannot explain the unpardonable sin, it is unlikely that they have committed it; their feelings of guilt seem to support this conclusion.

The unpardonable sin involves the total and irrevocable rejection of Jesus Christ. It is void of guilt. Resisting the Holy Spirit of God is a sin committed by unbelievers that, when carried on long enough, leads to eternal doom. Only certain judgment remains for those who resist the Holy Spirit that is sent by God to draw us to Himself.

It is not unusual for people to wonder if they have committed a deed that cannot be forgiven, such as murder, incest, abortion, or even something that may not seem quite so serious. Such people often develop obsessive guilt.

It seems that no one has committed this sin who continues to be under the disturbing, convicting, and drawing power of the Holy Spirit. So long as the Spirit strives with a person, he or she has not committed the unpardonable sin. But when a person has so resisted the Spirit of God that He strives with him or her no more, then there is eternal danger.

What is the answer, then, to this overwhelming guilt? Each of us must humble ourselves before God and admit our sin. Cry out, "God, be merciful to me a sinner!" (Luke 18:13). God is in the business of forgiving sin.

CALLED TO BE SET APART

"I will give you a new heart and put a new spirit within you."
EZEKIEL 36:26

When Rome was at the height of her glory and power, there appeared a disturbing sect called Christians. Because of a fire that burned within them, realizing their sins had been forgiven by Jesus Christ, they dared to be different so that their lives would reflect that they were sinners forgiven by Jesus Christ, who died for them and rose again to give new life.

In an era when immortality prevailed, Christians refused to be defiled by the sensual practices of a disintegrating civilization. In a period when human life was cheap, they put a high value upon human beings, their souls, and their destinies. These Christians refused to be absorbed into the godless society of Rome. The Roman high tribunal initiated a drive to stamp out Christianity as a disturber of pagan unity.

The Romans had a false notion that a person's conscience could be controlled by law, so they made it illegal to be different. But the early Christians learned from Scripture that they were called to live according to God's standard. Christians are called to be a holy people—separated from the moral evils of the world.

NONCONFORMIST

Do you not know that friendship with the world is enmity with God?
JAMES 4:4

Jesus dined with sinners, but He did not allow the social group to conform Him to its ways. He seized every opportunity to present a spiritual truth and to lead souls from death to life. Our social contacts should not only be pleasant, they should be opportunities to share our faith with those who do not yet know Christ.

No nation was ever more religious than Israel in the days of the prophet Isaiah. The temple was filled and prayer was heard in the house of God. But there was a lack of true devotion. The nation was deteriorating morally. Speaking as God commanded, His servant Isaiah said, "Bring no more futile sacrifices; incense is an abomination to Me. The New Moons, the Sabbaths, and the calling of assemblies—I cannot endure iniquity and the sacred meeting" (Isaiah 1:13).

Then Isaiah told them how they could be cleansed from their sin. "Wash yourselves . . . put away the evil of your doings from before My eyes. Cease to do evil. . . . 'Come now, and let us reason together,' says the LORD, 'though your sins are like scarlet, they shall be as white as snow'" (vv. 16, 18).

There are multitudes of people who do not give themselves to Jesus Christ, because they have conformed to this world. They are afraid of being called fanatic and pious. A true Christian is a nonconformist.

AUGUST

THE GREATEST DOCUMENT

Such things were written in the Scriptures long ago to teach us.
ROMANS 15:4 NLT

The Bible's message is straightforward. No writer changed the message to put himself or his friends in a better light. The sins of mankind are frankly admitted, and life is presented as it actually was.

Critics claim the Bible's full of forgery, fiction, and unfulfilled prophecy; but the findings of archaeology have corroborated rather than denied the biblical data.

The Christian faith is not dependent upon human knowledge and scientific advancement. The inability to comprehend fully the mysteries of God doesn't in any way curtail the Christian faith but enhances it. The Bible is the greatest document of the human race and remains a bulwark of national, personal, and spiritual freedom.

A well-known quote by Yale educator William Lyon Phelps, once called the most beloved professor in America, stated, "I thoroughly believe in a university education for both men and women, but I believe a knowledge of the Bible without a college course is more valuable than a college course without the Bible." The world has a multitude of people who agree with the famed professor.

The first requirement placed upon the critic is that he or she read every page of the Bible. The critic should also know something of the Bible's history and the miracle of its writing. Biblical history is fascinating and makes us appreciate the Book, which has been preserved for us to this day.

SOLD OUT FOR GOD

We should live in this evil world with wisdom, righteousness, and devotion to God.

TITUS 2:12 NLT

The world appreciates and understands emotion and enthusiasm, unless it is religious; then immediately it is suspect. It's strange that the world accepts enthusiasm in every realm except the spiritual.

People can don political buttons, hats, and T-shirts and be accepted as "all in." They can go crazy over the World Series or the Super Bowl. Young people can scream until they're hoarse amid the hype of a rock concert. But bring the same excitement into living a life for Christ and the world thinks Christians have lost their minds. This is what people thought about the disciples after Jesus was crucified and resurrected, but they didn't allow what others thought to deter them from what they believed, and they turned the world upside down (Acts 17:6).

Commitment to Christ means burning the bridges of sin and its influence. There's a high price to commitment. Jesus expects His followers to clean up their lives, and that's why He sent His Spirit to help. He gives power and encouragement to live for Him, "purify[ing] for Himself His own special people" (Titus 2:14). Christians should be so filled with righteous living that nothing could ever quench their passion. While most of the crowd will turn their backs on Christianity, there will be some who may be impacted by the strong testimony of another that brings conviction to their own souls.

God Our Judge

Every one of Your righteous judgments endures forever.
PSALM 119:160

A Bible professor once said, "Never preach Hell without tears in your eyes." Proclaiming the love of Christ cannot be fully preached without first establishing that God the Father will judge the human race for its disobedience to Him.

Because God is righteous, He wants to spare us from the awful reality of Hell. He devised a way to rescue us and save us from His judgment, and so He sent His one and only Son to pay the penalty for our sin. He judged sin at the cross and extended His forgiveness to those who would accept His gift of salvation. For those who reject what Christ did at Calvary, He will judge the world.

None of us deserves God's love. All of us deserve His righteous judgment and wrath (John 3:18; Romans 3:9–12). It is easy to think of evil and depraved people deserving divine judgment, but the kind people that we know will also be judged if they refuse God's offer of mercy and forgiveness.

God judges mankind by the standard of the only God-man who ever lived, Jesus Christ. Jesus, the innocent Lamb of God, stands between our sin and the judgment of God the Father.

The cross shows us the seriousness of the judgment of sin—but the cross also shows us the immeasurable love of God. Receive Him without delay.

God's Law

The Lord is our Lawgiver.
ISAIAH 33:22

The world has come to understand at exactly what temperature water boils and at what temperature it freezes. Since God is so precise about His natural laws, why should He be haphazard about His spiritual and moral laws?

Many people say, "I believe there's a Heaven and I hope I'll go there when I die, because I'm a pretty good person." Why do people hope to believe it when they can know for certain what their eternal destiny is?

God's law enables us to see ourselves as morally dirty and in need of cleansing. The cross that His Son, Jesus Christ, died upon shows the seriousness of our sin—it also shows us the immeasurable love of God. The cross is the only way to salvation, and what Jesus did on the cross gives us a new purpose to life. He opened Heaven's door for us by His death and resurrection, pointing the way for our sins to be forgiven and offering eternity with Him in Heaven.

Christianity is being compared with other religions as never before. Some even advocate the working out of a system of morals, ethics, and religion that would bring all the religions of the world together. It cannot be done.

God desires that all people be saved. Believe in Jesus Christ and receive His sacrificial gift to have sins forgiven and know Him as Savior and Lord.

LIVING WITH INTEGRITY

He who walks with integrity walks securely.
PROVERBS 10:9

Many people, regardless of spirituality, tend to talk one way and live another, and it is something to guard against. Not too many years ago, honesty was the hallmark of a person's character. But it seems it has been set aside for an "It's all right if you don't get caught" philosophy. But the Bible says, "Be sure your sin will find you out" (Numbers 32:23).

A manager told about a religious convention held in his hotel. When the people returned to their rooms, they turned on pay TV; 75 percent turned to the R-rated programming. What a difference there is sometimes between the way we talk and the way we live. One of the real tests of Christian character is revealed in the lives we live from day to day.

Consistency is vital in having integrity, which means that if our private lives were suddenly exposed, we'd have no reason to be ashamed or embarrassed. It means that our outward lives are consistent with our inner convictions. What young people want to see in leaders is integrity, honesty, truthfulness, and faith. What they hate most of all is hypocrisy and phoniness. People of integrity can be trusted and are the same whether alone a thousand miles away or at home. The Bible tells us how to do this. "Joyful are people of integrity, who follow the instructions of the LORD" (Psalm 119:1 NLT).

Spiritual Maturity

We are His workmanship, created in Christ Jesus.
EPHESIANS 2:10

The greatest need in the world today is for spiritually mature Christians who are not only professing their faith in Christ but who are living it in their daily lives. The moment a person receives Jesus as Savior and Lord, the new life He promises begins. The ultimate goal is that the Christian be conformed to the image of Christ.

Each new believer in Christ may immediately face complications, dilemmas, and problems never before encountered. A complete transformation has taken place inside, and adjusting to a new life is not always easy. But Christians do not make this adjustment alone. We are told in the Scriptures that God's Spirit immediately takes up residence within us to help us.

Still, some people have received Christ but have never matured. They may have gone to church but never grown in faith. They know very little of God's Word, they have little desire to pray, and they bear few marks of a Christian in their daily lives.

Jesus is the only Person who ever revealed absolute spiritual maturity. His attitude and approach in life were mature in every sense of the word. He looked with holy eyes upon a sinful world but was not discouraged or depressed by it. He said to a despairing world, "I have come that they may have life, and that they may have it more abundantly" (John 10:10).

The Fruit of the Spirit

The fruit of the righteous is a tree of life.
PROVERBS 11:30

Of all the passages in the Bible that sketch the character of Christ and the fruit that His Spirit brings to our lives, none is more compact than Galatians 5:22–23: "The fruit of the Spirit is love, joy, peace, longsuffering, kindness, goodness, faithfulness, gentleness, self-control."

These nine words can be divided into three clusters. The first is love, joy, and peace—these speak of our Godward relationship. The second cluster is longsuffering (patience), kindness, and goodness—especially seen in our relationship with others. The third cluster of faithfulness, gentleness, and self-control are especially seen in our inward relationship—the attitudes and actions of the inner self.

These three "clusters" are all related to each other, and all will characterize our lives when we abide in Christ and allow the Holy Spirit to do His work in us.

No matter how else we bear our testimony for the Lord, the absence of love nullifies it all. There should be no more distinctive mark of the Christian than love.

God's greatest demonstration of love was at the cross where He sent His Son, Jesus Christ, to die for our sins. Since we are to love as God does, His children should demonstrate such love by sharing this good news that Jesus came to save the lost. Love is, therefore, an act of the will.

No Other Gods

"Behold! The Lamb of God who takes away the sin of the world!"

JOHN 1:29

At the center of Christianity is the Person of the Lord Jesus Christ, not the practice of religion. Jesus, the Son of God, is the central figure. Many voices make other claims. Atheists say there is no God. Polytheism may allow that Jesus is one of many gods. When people are saved from sin by the sacrifice Jesus Christ made on the cross, the heart must turn from all other gods and turn to the one true living God as revealed in the Scriptures.

As believers in Jesus the Savior, we as ambassadors for Christ boldly echo the ringing conviction of the apostle Peter when he affirmed, "You are the Christ, the Son of the living God" (Matthew 16:16). The title Christ means "anointed one." It is the term in the Greek language for the ancient Hebrew word *Messiah*—the anointed one whom God would send to save His people.

As world leaders struggle with insurmountable problems, as storm clouds gather around the globe, they accentuate the brightness of the One who proclaimed, "I am the light of the world. He who follows Me shall not walk in darkness, but have the light of life" (John 8:12). He is the promised Messiah of ancient Israel. He is the hope of the hopeless, helpless Gentiles—which includes most of the population of the world. What a glorious Savior He is!

POWER OVER SIN

Whatever is born of God overcomes the world.
1 JOHN 5:4

All authority in Heaven and on Earth has been given to Jesus Christ. However, the present evil world system does not yet acknowledge His lordship; it is still under the deceiving power of the prince of this world, Satan. But those whom Jesus indwells have authority over the evil one and all his demons.

In spite of our human limitations and even our failures, the Lord is sovereignly directing His own work of redemption. We are linked to the vast resources of His power so that we don't merely "get by" in our lives, but "in all these things we are more than conquerors through Him" (Romans 8:37). And as the context of that inspiring and reassuring passage promises, nothing "shall be able to separate us from the love of God which is in Christ Jesus our Lord" (v. 39). God can turn the greatest tragedies into that which is for our good and for His glory, for "we know that all things work together for good to those who love God, to those who are called according to His purpose" (v. 28).

Because Jesus is Savior, because He is Lord, He, by His Holy Spirit, gives us power over sin as we daily walk with Him. And some future day He will take us to be with Him, far from the very presence of sin.

Three Enemies

Walk in the Spirit.
GALATIANS 5:16

The Bible mentions three enemies: the world, the flesh, and the devil. They combine to form a powerful foe to defeat and frustrate God's plan and purpose in the lives of His people.

The word *flesh* is the biblical word for our old nature, the nature of sin. The apostle Peter knew a great deal about the struggle with the flesh and said, "Abstain from fleshly lusts which war against the soul" (1 Peter 2:11).

We have two natures in conflict, and each one is striving for the victory. The Bible teaches, "For the flesh lusts against the Spirit, and the Spirit against the flesh" (Galatians 5:17). The flesh is the enemy—the infiltrator—the battle between the self-life and the Christ-life. The old nature cannot please God. It cannot be patched up. However, Scripture does give great hope for us in this conflict, because when Christ died He took us with Him to the cross.

The apostle Paul said that he had no confidence in the flesh (Philippians 3:3). He also said, "Make no provision for the flesh" (Romans 13:14). On yet another occasion he said, "I discipline my body and bring it into subjection" (1 Corinthians 9:27). We are to yield completely and surrender ourselves to God. The old nature can be made inoperative, and we can by faith reckon to be dead to sin but alive in Christ (Romans 6:11). Victory can be obtained.

THE HUMAN DILEMMA

Who warned you to flee from the wrath to come?
MATTHEW 3:7

Everywhere we look, we find people who are unethical—sinful. From the moment we are born, we have a tendency to sin. Our moral universe is out of focus, and we won't get it back into focus until we come to Christ. We accept lies as truth and truth as lies. We don't know what is right and what is wrong. It's as if we are driving down the highway of life with our eyes shut. We act as though we have no soul, as though we are not accountable to anyone. We are a violent society—a wicked society.

What is the answer to this human dilemma? Can we get out of this pit? The answer is yes! Jesus said that He was the truth and the truth will set us free (John 8:32). Jesus declared: "I am . . . truth" (John 14:6). He is the embodiment of all truth. He has given warning to the people of the Earth that judgment is coming. The Scriptures teach that man can heed the warnings from Heaven or ignore them, but those who ignore God's truthful warnings will suffer the consequences eternally.

Jesus told the truth about judgment. He warned people to flee the wrath to come. He also told the truth about love. He said that God so loved the world (John 3:16). Those who believe His truth, and act on it, can be saved.

THE HEART OF THE GOOD NEWS

No one is righteous—not even one.
ROMANS 3:10 NLT

What stirs God most is not physical suffering but sin. All too often, we're more afraid of physical pain than of moral wrong. Many people have distorted the meaning of salvation, saying that it means only political, social, and economic liberation in this life. Certainly, Christians are concerned about injustice and do what they can to promote a more just world. But lasting and complete liberation from social injustice will come only when Jesus Christ returns to establish His kingdom. Biblical salvation is far deeper, because it gets to the root of our problem—the problem of sin.

What then is the heart of the good news?

First, all are sinners and stand under the judgment of God (Romans 3:23). We might believe that we're good enough to win God's favor or that we can perform religious acts to counterbalance our bad deeds, but the Bible says that no one is righteous.

Second, we need to understand what Christ has done to make our salvation possible. He died on the cross as the complete sacrifice for our sins (Romans 5:8). He took upon Himself the judgment that we deserve.

Third, we need to respond to God's call to repent of sin and come to Him. We must turn from our practice of sin and obey His Word. His grace offers forgiveness and the gift of eternal life.

TRUE CHRISTIANITY

Do not believe every spirit, but test the spirits [to see] whether they are of God.
1 JOHN 4:1

There are clear marks between cults and faith in the one true God, Jesus Christ. True Christianity is when Christ alone is worshiped as Lord and Savior. Some cults dismiss Christ completely or suggest that He was only a great teacher; others claim salvation is not to be found in Christ, and still others deny that He rose from the grave. The Bible says that salvation is found in no one else (Acts 4:12; 1 Peter 3:18).

True Christianity is founded on God's Word and central, as the one true guide, to faith and practice. Cults and false religions often ignore or even deny the full inspiration and authority of the Bible as the Word of God. They often add or substitute a set of man-made teachings (doctrine) not found in Scripture. We must even be cautious of translations of Scripture that twist the meaning of the Bible's clear teaching.

True Christianity is centered in a Bible-believing church where Jesus Christ is worshiped and obeyed. While the church is not perfect, God's Word is.

Truth is timeless; it doesn't differ from one age to another. God imparts His wisdom to those who submit to Him, making it possible to decipher between truth and lies. God will always lead people to His truth.

THE GREAT DECEIVER

The way of transgressors is hard.
PROVERBS 13:15 KJV

Scripture teaches that the more sins we commit, the easier it becomes to sin. When people indulge in sin, they weaken the strength of resistance, which prepares the way for more frequent assaults of temptation. The apostle Paul wrote about unbelievers taking pleasure in sin. They became wise in doing evil and fell so deep in sin that they began to call evil good.

Satan is the great deceiver. When he approaches to tempt, he does not carry a sign warning, "I am the devil." He comes in a thousand subtle forms, with delusions and lying wonders.

A young golf pro had high ideals in his youth, but he fell prey to the same delusion when his pals insisted that he conform to their way of life. He began to do the things the gang did until he became an alcoholic. He fell victim to the age-old delusion that the way to a full life is to break God's law. Sin pays—but it pays off in remorse, regret, and failure.

Many people think that it's clever to follow the crowd and that real fun is found in conforming to this world, living a life of unrestrained appetite and pleasure. Following the crowd is devastating. What is the solution? Putting faith in Jesus brings forgiveness of sins and fills the heart with the joy of following Christ every day.

KING AND LORD OF ALL

The government will be upon His shoulder.
ISAIAH 9:6

The risen Christ is big enough to cope with the tyranny of man over man. Not only can He save the individual, but His power has worldwide implications. He has not abdicated His sovereignty in the affairs of men. He is still the Lord of history.

When He was crucified, the Bible describes the inscription written over Him in letters of Greek, Latin, and Hebrew, "THIS IS THE KING OF THE JEWS" (Luke 23:38). He was then, and still is, King and Lord over all. One of our failures is not seeing Christ as King of the physical and material as well as the spiritual, of the mind as well as the soul, of the government as well as the heart.

Christ cannot be separated from anything that pertains to life, for He "is all and in all" (Colossians 3:11). He is the Master of our business on Monday as well as our religious life on Sunday. Secularism grows when God is taken out of the realms of economics, politics, and science. We think that the world's problems could be solved by diplomacy, by scientific advancement, by economic progress.

The world today offers many saviors, but none of them saves. When Christ's forgiveness and love dominate in the human heart, peace and joy are victorious; and when this material world comes to a close, every knee will bow and confess that Jesus is Lord.

DEATH IS INEVITABLE

It is appointed for men to die once.
HEBREWS 9:27

The Bible teaches that all of mankind is rushing toward death. Even though wars rage around the globe, it does not increase death because death comes to every generation. Everybody dies.

God's Word teaches that everything has a beginning and an ending. The day begins with a sunrise; but the sun sets, the shadows gather, and that calendar day is crossed out, never to appear again. We will never be able to repeat today. It's gone forever.

Nations and civilizations rise, flourish for a time, and then decay. Each comes to an end. This, because of sin, is the decree of history and the way of life on this planet. Scripture tells us that the world system as we know it will also come to a close someday.

All of nature is in the process of dying. Yet most people are living as if they will never die. How gracious is the Lord to give us time to consider life and what happens when we draw our last breath. Every soul should settle this with Jesus Christ now. The Bible says that today is the day of salvation. Do not let another hour go by without receiving Christ and humbly accepting Him as Savior. He waits with loving arms outstretched, ready to receive every repentant heart, with His promise to the redeemed souls of eternity in His presence.

THE ETERNAL SOUL

The reward for humility and fear of the LORD is riches and honor and life.
PROVERBS 22:4 ESV

Millions of people are depressed that life has not turned out the way they had hoped. Some people turn to drugs and alcohol to escape. And tragically, more and more people are committing suicide. Too many people believe that if things would go their way, they would live happily.

Yet war, poverty, disease, loneliness, boredom, racism, and starvation still run rampant. Life is not meant to be lived according to man's ways but God's ways. The Bible teaches that every person has a soul—the part of us that lives forever. If a person commits suicide, they will still exist into eternity. Death merely ends the life of the body, but the soul lives on forever.

No one can prove that God exists, but that doesn't mean that He is not real. God reveals Himself to us in nature, in conscience, and in the Scriptures. He also reveals Himself in the Person of Jesus Christ. The Bible says, "In these last days [God] has spoken to us by his Son, whom he appointed heir of all things, and through whom he also made the universe" (Hebrews 1:2 NIV).

God is a holy God, and the Lord is righteous in all His ways—loving toward all He has made (Psalm 145:17). If we will trust Him today, He will meet our needs according to His Word.

THE PRAYER LIFE

"Call to Me, and I will answer you."
JEREMIAH 33:3

Prayer should not be merely an act but an attitude of life. When people have a genuine personal relationship with Jesus Christ as their Savior, they can be assured that God hears their prayers. The wonderful name of Jesus has opened the door to Heaven for us. The phrase "in Jesus' name" isn't a magic formula we add in order to make God answer our prayers. God answers our prayers solely because of His Son, Jesus Christ.

When we pray, we seek God's will. This pleases Him because He wants to show us the way to life, the way to peace, the way to Him. We gain access to the Lord by faith in Him, which brings us into His marvelous grace.

We should never cease to thank God for the wonderful privilege of prayer. It should be an integral part of our lives, as we see from the example of His followers who gave themselves "continually to prayer" (Acts 6:4).

When Jesus walked on this Earth, Scripture shows us that He demonstrated the power of prayer as He prayed to His Father in Heaven. Nothing can replace a daily time spent alone with God in prayer. In the morning, prayer is the key that opens to us the treasures of God's mercies and blessings. In the evening, it's the key that envelops us under His protection and safeguard.

THE MINOR PROPHETS

"Return to the LORD your God."
JOEL 2:13

The Minor Prophets are not so named because they are of less value than prophets such as Isaiah or Ezekiel. Nor are the twelve books minor in message. They are minor in terms of brevity only; but they are power-packed messages from men whom God appointed and called to deliver His warnings of judgment and His ever-faithful invitation to Israel and its neighbors, saying, "Return to Me." They provide an important study for those who truly desire to understand the end times. These prophecies will be fulfilled when the Eternal One comes back to Earth.

In the last twelve books of the Old Testament, we see the name and voice of almighty God and His message to the world of the last days. Studying names and numbers in Scripture is boring to some, but they carry great significance. The number twelve in Scripture is an eternal number.

From Genesis to Revelation, we learn of the 12 patriarchs, 12 sons, 12 tribes of Israel, 12 judges, 12 gates, 12 stones, 12 fruits, 12 angels, 12 apostles, 12 stars, and a heavenly city 12,000 furlongs square. The Bible tells us that after Jesus' birth, nothing more is revealed about Him until He reached the age of 12, when His first words on Earth were recorded. This number is also foreshadowed when 12,000 from each of the 12 tribes of Israel will be saved and evangelize the world in the last days.

NO BOASTING IN HEAVEN

"Lay up for yourselves treasures in heaven."
MATTHEW 6:20

There will be no egos in Heaven. "Nothing impure will ever enter [Heaven], nor will anyone who does what is shameful or deceitful" (Revelation 21:27 NIV).

When we reach Heaven, there will be no opportunity to brag of our exploits, our ambitions, or the joys of our pleasure; but we will have eternity to rejoice in how the Lord blessed our lives in the midst of hardship and blessing. We will fully understand that it was Christ who lived in us and glorified Himself in our weaknesses. We will be blessed to serve our Lord and Savior.

Moses gave up all earthly glory and possessions to identify with God's people. He was the adopted child of an Egyptian princess, but he gave up the kingdom and crown of Egypt to be a child of God. He was educated in the finest schools, but he gave up the prestige to learn the wisdom of God. He gave up the royal scepter to be rich in God's law. The prophet was known as a shepherd, a leader, a deliverer, a lawgiver, and a judge. But Moses said, "O my Lord, I am . . . Your servant" (Exodus 4:10); and when he died, God spoke of him as "Moses My servant" (Joshua 1:2).

While the Bible teaches us to store up treasures in Heaven, the greatest treasure is in knowing that we will be rewarded by His very presence—forevermore.

REPENTANCE

Do not use your freedom to indulge the flesh.
GALATIANS 5:13 NIV

The Bible asks, "Shall we go on sinning so that grace may increase?" (Romans 6:1 NIV). It is dangerous to be so flippant about sin as though God turns His eyes away. God's forgiveness is always connected to the sinner's repentance.

Repentance involves a recognition on our part that what we are doing is wrong, and it also involves a deliberate turning from sin as well. It is not enough to know that what we are doing is wrong in God's eyes. We also are commanded to turn from it.

Jesus declared that He came to Earth to call sinners to repentance (Luke 5:32). Paul stated that God commands all people everywhere to repent (Acts 17:30). Many other verses could be quoted.

We make a mockery of God's forgiveness when we deliberately engage in sin because we think He will forgive it later. People deceive themselves while believing that they will find true happiness while sinning. Rejecting God is embracing a life of sin. The Bible warns that wickedness is like a tossing sea, restless and casting up mire and mud (Isaiah 57:20–21).

For the Christian, the most powerful thing to do on behalf of those steeped in sin is to pray that God's Holy Spirit will infiltrate their minds and hearts and respond in repentance, desiring to do God's will and live according to His Word.

TRUE BELIEVERS

Christ is all and in all.
COLOSSIANS 3:11

Many people who call themselves Christians actually doubt the authority of the Scriptures, believing in a god of their own imagination. Jesus Christ has been robbed of His deity. There are prominent preachers that suggest large passages of God's Word be eliminated. Beware! The truth of Jesus the Christ can be a disturbing thought. He did not come the first time to bring peace, though He will return as the Prince of Peace. He came to show mankind our sin against Him. He came to take our place for the penalty of sin. What a Savior!

Scripture warns that multitudes will reject that message, and we see that happening today. There is a cost to being a Christian, and the cost for many is too great because they must forsake the lure of materialism and secular pleasure.

There is a sense in which Christ cannot be separated from anything that pertains to life. True Christianity is dependent on a personal relationship with God, not on externals.

No pagan philosophy, no atheistic ideology, no deep sorrow can dislodge the joy of living as a true believer in the Lord Jesus Christ. He is big enough to cope with the gigantic social problems of the ages. In himself, man does not have the capacity to do this, but Christ provides all that we need to live in this sin-sick world with victory.

Keep God's Word at the Center

The fear of the Lord, that is wisdom.
JOB 28:28

Science is learning to control just about everything but man. More important than electricity, technology, and medicine are the issues of the heart. Solve the problems of hate, lust, greed, and prejudice and the world would be a different place. Our future is threatened by many dangers, but they all stem from the heart.

Greater than the enemy outside is the enemy within—sin. No matter how advanced their progress, civilizations that neglect their spiritual and moral lives will eventually disintegrate. This is the history of mankind, and it is our problem still today. Science cannot change the seasons, the rising of the sun, or the setting of the moon. Nor can man's knowledge change human nature. When doubt reigns, faith cannot abide. Where hatred rules, love is crowded out.

Much of the world in search of knowledge ignores God. Today we have more knowledge than at any other time in history. In seconds, our computers can call up information about a topic that took years to collect. We are the most informed people in the history of civilization—and yet the most confused.

Though our heads are crammed with knowledge, our hearts are empty. But where man has failed, God has succeeded. Keep His Word at the center of life and remember what the Bible says, "The fear [reverence] of the LORD is the beginning of knowledge" (Proverbs 1:7).

THE SOURCE OF ALL THINGS

God has said, "Never will I leave you; never will I forsake you."
HEBREWS 13:5 NIV

A person's self-esteem is often tied to his or her work. Losing a job can be very traumatic. When someone is laid off or fired, it can have a serious psychological effect. In our culture, men and women often define themselves by the jobs they hold. If you listen closely, you'll hear people be introduced by their name, followed closely by their job title. This usually happens when their work is in a field that is highly visible or exciting. But a person's job tells you nothing about a person's character or value.

It is wise to help others understand that personal worth is not tied to a job. Many people have lost one job only to find that this was God's way of redirecting their lives. Be an encourager by pointing to God, acknowledging His provision for those who will look to Him as the Source of all things.

This can also be an important time for spiritual growth. If a person is not a believer in Christ, losing a job could be God's way of getting one's attention, opening the way to consider the need for salvation and for God's direction in life. For those who know the Lord, pray that they will rely on the Lord to reveal the next step in life, because He promises never to leave nor forsake us.

BE OF GOOD COURAGE

This hope we have as an anchor of the soul, both sure and steadfast.
HEBREWS 6:19

There is a longing in our hearts for happiness. The human spirit also groans for something new. We run after hope as though it has magical power. We trick ourselves into believing that if everything lines up just right, we'll gain hope and success. But true hope is a sure thing, and it is only found with certainty in the man Jesus Christ.

The history of mankind has been a continuous series of half successes and total failures. Prosperity exists for a time, only to be followed by war and depression. Civilizations have come and gone. Success is worshiped, and God is disdained. Pleasure takes precedence over purity, and gain has priority over God. People still battle with the same problems over and over again. One day, the fluctuations of time, the swinging of the pendulum from war to peace, from starvation to plenty, from chaos to order, will end forever because the Bible says, "And of His kingdom there will be no end" (Luke 1:33).

Determination is only part of realizing hope. True hope is not dependent upon us but rather where our hope is anchored. "Be of good courage, and he shall strengthen your heart, all [you] that hope in the LORD" (Psalm 31:24 KJV). We can walk in the "newness of life" (Romans 6:4). Place your trust in the God of hope.

JOYFUL OBEDIENCE

"I have come . . . not to do My own will, but the will of Him who sent Me."
JOHN 6:38

Just to say "believe in Jesus" can produce a false assurance of salvation because even the devil "believes in Jesus." To believe in Jesus is to turn from a life of sin, receive Him as Savior, and follow Him as Lord by obeying His Word. When this happens, a person's desires change.

When Jesus traveled the countryside, great crowds sought Him. But He knew the people desired to see His great miracles more than hear His words, so He told them: "For which of you, intending to build a tower, does not sit down first and count the cost?" (Luke 14:28). When He began to tell them that He would soon die and be raised to life again, many people left Him and "walked with Him no more" (John 6:66). They didn't want to follow someone who promised eternal life if it meant the cruelty of death. They were disciples in name only—and they walked away from the truth because their faith was insincere. Jesus paid the cost of our salvation with His blood, but there is a cost to following this wonderful Savior.

Do not miss the glory of walking with the One who loves you and cares about everything that happens in your life. Those who truly believe in Him will want to obey Him with joy, no matter the cost.

BLESSINGS FROM GOD

Children are a gift from the LORD.
PSALM 127:3 NLT

A study of world history reveals that there isn't a single time when conditions were ideal or the future was not unstable. Even when social and political circumstances have been reasonably good, the world has been ravaged by natural disasters, plagues, and war. While modern medicine has removed many of the things that threatened life only a generation or two ago, modern technology has developed weapons of mass destruction that can wipe out entire civilizations. But thankfully, God is in control of the future.

The Bible gives many examples of harsh times. The Jewish people were carried away into captivity and faced a dismal future because of their disobedience, but Jeremiah told them, "Marry and have sons and daughters. . . . 'For I know the plans I have for you,' declares the LORD, 'plans to . . . give you hope and a future'" (Jeremiah 29:6, 11 NIV).

This does not mean everything will be easy in life. But our responsibility is clear: if God gives children to us, we should do whatever we can to strengthen them spiritually so that they, too, can face the future with a confident hope in God and be an example to others. Children, indeed, are a blessing from the Lord, and parents should raise them up to love Him, obey Him, and become witnesses for the Lord who brings peace and joy to families.

A HEALTHY CHURCH

We are both God's workers. And you are God's field. You are God's building.

1 CORINTHIANS 3:9 NLT

The word *church* comes from a Greek word, *ecclesia*, which means "to call out." The church is composed of all those true believers from Pentecost onward who are united together in Christ. The Bible teaches that we are the body of Christ, of which He is the Head (Ephesians 1:22–23).

Within the vast complexities, bureaucracies, organizations, and institutions of Christendom there exists the true body of Christ. They are the ones who have their names written in the Lamb's Book of Life (Revelation 21:27). They are scattered in all denominations, and many are in no denomination at all. This is the church against which Christ promised the gates of Hell would never prevail (Matthew 16:18).

The church needs to be called back to biblical authority. The Protestant church today is possibly as far from the authority of the Scriptures as was the Roman church in the sixteenth century. We desperately need a new reformation within the Protestant church.

Only a healthy church can help a sick world. Much social action today is nothing but sheer humanism. True members of the church are those who have been transformed by the power of Christ.

The changing of people's hearts is the primary mission of the church. To proclaim the entire gospel of Christ is the only answer to mankind's deepest needs.

Take a Stand

Speak each man the truth to his neighbor.
ZECHARIAH 8:16

Christians understand that the world is embroiled in the great battle between right and wrong, just as the Bible says. "Woe to those who call evil good, and good evil; who put darkness for light, and light for darkness" (Isaiah 5:20).

Christian responsibility is to speak truth in the midst of an unbelieving world. When God's people speak the truth from Scripture, it does offend. Some Christians may do this in the wrong spirit, but God's truth remains and God Himself will fight our battles. But this does not mean that Christians are to be silent when society assaults the Word of God. We must take a stand in light of truth—God's truth.

It is important to understand that "we do not wrestle against flesh and blood, but against principalities, against powers, against the rulers of the darkness of this age, against spiritual hosts of wickedness in the heavenly places" (Ephesians 6:12).

The battles on Earth are far less than what is taking place in the heavenly realm known to God. But on Earth, He empowers His people to be strong and to put on the armor of God. We need to take up the shield of faith and stand on biblical truth and be the light of Christ.

God's people ought to fight for His truth because it is the only hope that mankind has to live in freedom for eternity.

Our Christian Witness

Him we proclaim, warning everyone and teaching everyone with all wisdom.
COLOSSIANS 1:28 ESV

All Christians are witnesses; they are either sharing what Christ has done in their lives by word and deed, or they are not. Some are negative witnesses; others keep silent about their faith, and others are quick to proclaim that Christ saves from sin. Every believer should desire to share this great news.

There is no substitute for the witness of the facts of the gospel—the Holy Scriptures. The apostle Paul gave an example of such witness: "I declare to you the gospel which I preached to you. . . . that Christ died for our sins according to the Scriptures, and that He was buried, and that He rose again the third day" (1 Corinthians 15:1, 3–4).

For those who fear to speak out, let the Word of God speak for you. Satan will do everything he can to make you fearful, but he cowers at the spoken and written Word of God because he knows its power. Quoting Scripture is the one thing the devil cannot stand; it defeats him every time. When we witness, the Spirit of God goes before us, preparing the way, giving us the words, and granting us courage. But this does not come without knowing God's Word. It is our responsibility to read the Bible and declare its great truths. It is the greatest honor a Christian has: to speak the very words of God.

WHEN DOUBT STRIKES

Let him ask of God. . . . in faith, with no doubting.
JAMES 1:5-6

Doubts can be debilitating. When sincere Christians hear critics attack the Bible, there may be increased temptation to doubt God's Word. When confronted with the reality of doubt, people may question, "Am I really saved?"

Satan will do everything he can to cause doubt about our salvation in Christ and destroy our witness. When we find ourselves doubting what Christ has done for us, it is often because we open our ears and minds to what others say. This is the story of Eve. She "listened" to the serpent, Satan. He twisted God's Word, which brought confusion to Eve (Genesis 3). Instead of listening to him, she should have repeated God's command and taken to heart His words of truth. Christians often respond like Eve.

Many unbelievers are skilled at twisting God's Word and distorting its truth to accommodate the destructive morals and secular behavior that they are not willing to give up. Doubt can be an effective tool for Satan.

Doubt can also be planted within us by the Holy Spirit to cause us to examine ourselves. If there is not a time we can remember of confessing our sins to God and accepting His forgiveness, doubt can be a blessing that will bring us to faith in Him.

It is God who gives us faith to believe Him, and it is Christ who brings assurance to our souls.

September

Jesus' Divine Nature

The Lord is . . . not willing that any should perish
but that all should come to repentance.
2 PETER 3:9

Humans do not decide who Jesus is. Jesus Himself said that He was divine. Faith in Him is believing this truth. He said, "I and My Father are one" (John 10:30). His miracles back up His claim, as did His assertion that He could forgive sins—something only God can do (Luke 5:20–25).

Repeatedly, the gospel writers pointed out the way He fulfilled the Old Testament's prophecies concerning the Messiah. But Jesus' divinity was demonstrated most of all by His resurrection from the dead and His ascension into Heaven—events that were witnessed by hundreds.

What difference does it make? Only a sinless, divine Savior could save us, for only He could become the perfect and final sacrifice for our sins. This is truth that has stood the test of time. We should thank Him daily for leaving Heaven's glory and coming to Earth for us. He walked the dusty ground of Earth and suffered unimaginable pain, and He did it because of His love for mankind.

God could not consistently love mankind if He had not provided for the judgment of evildoers. But there is one thing that God cannot do; He cannot forgive unrepentant sinners. His desire is for all people to find His redeeming love. Let Christ occupy every area of our lives that others may see Jesus in us.

VICTIMS OF DELUSION

[They] exchanged the truth of God for the lie.

ROMANS 1:25

The Bible plainly teaches that one of the characteristics of the end of this age is that people will develop a capacity for delusion rather than the truth. The scientific revolution has produced an overemphasis on the secular but a decline of faith and principle. Sin is explained away by psychological terminology.

Many people are enamored and deluded by philosophies that destroy lives and nations. Surely we are living in the day of which the apostle Paul said, "They did not receive the love of the truth, that they might be saved. And for this reason God will send them strong delusion, that they should believe the lie" (2 Thessalonians 2:10–11).

What a candid picture of society today. The Bible is clear that those who reject the truth are victims of a great delusion.

Today many are worshiping everything but God, thus the propensity for delusion. We see it in our gullibility for false advertising. We see this capacity for delusion in politics. Where a person has deviated from the eternal truths of God, there is darkness. When God's truth is rejected, people are opened up to Satan's deception. This is the importance of Christians living out their faith in God; to shine the light on the gospel—carrying a testimony of hope to those living in darkness, that they might come to know God's truth and receive His salvation.

EQUIPPED WITH GOD'S PROMISES

All the promises of God in Him are Yes, and in Him
Amen, to the glory of God through us.
2 CORINTHIANS 1:20

The Bible is a book of many promises, and unlike the books of men, it doesn't change or get out of date. The Bible makes it clear that no problems in our lives are too great or too small for God's concern. He cares about everything that affects those who belong to Him.

God has given us the entirety of His Word of truth, and we must search it out, for there is great blessing in doing so. From one end of the Bible to the other, God assures us that He will never go back on His promises.

But the greatest of His promises given to all mankind is found in perhaps the best-known passage, John 3:16: "For God so loved the world that He gave His only begotten Son, that whoever believes in Him should not perish but have everlasting life." God has given His promise of eternal salvation and says, "If you confess with your mouth the Lord Jesus and believe in your heart that God has raised Him from the dead, you will be saved" (Romans 10:9).

God stands ready to fill us with His words; for there is no greater armor, no greater strength, and no greater assurance that He is with us, and in us. When we walk with Him through this life He will equip and nourish us by His instruction and will help us stand firm on His promises.

THE INFECTION AND THE CURE

"Because lawlessness will abound, the love of many will grow cold."
MATTHEW 24:12

A sense of doom has settled upon the hearts of people today. No matter where they travel, there's a specter of hopelessness. It's seen boldly in the headlines. It's sensed in humanity's futile search for fulfillment. The very atmosphere seems impregnated with a stifling hopelessness that's robbed millions of the zest for living.

What keeps world powers at each other's throats? Why is there so much intolerance? Why do world leaders gamble with the lives of millions and keep the world dangling on the precipice of war? What diabolical force drives people to crime, lust, and unbridled living? What power is it that breaks up homes? What is it that causes people to pour their futures out of a bottle and trade all that others hold dear for a few sparkling drops from the vine?

Such dilemmas cause many psychiatrists to say, "It's difficult to offer a cure." The Bible says that the human heart is desperately wicked (Jeremiah 17:9). Human nature behaves in evil ways because of sin. But the Bible provides a cure. It's found in someone called Jesus, and the remedy is His gospel.

The entire human race is infected with sin and every trace of it can be removed. The cross of Christ is the bridge over which all must pass in order to stand with Jesus for eternity in Heaven.

DENYING YOURSELF

He died for all, that those who live should live no longer for themselves, but for Him who died for them and rose again.
2 CORINTHIANS 5:15

Selfishness is part of human nature. A child says, "It's mine." A teenager centers on his insecurities. An adult proclaims, "Look out for number one." Today, advertising and "pop" psychology have raised self-centeredness to state-of-the-art levels.

Two conflicting forces cannot exist in one human heart. Where selfishness rules, love cannot dwell. When Christ fills our hearts, it puts selfishness on the run. Our personalities, our intelligence, and our capabilities are gifts from God's own bountiful hand. If we divert their use for our own profit, we become guilty of selfishness.

People are conscious of "self," and it's important to have a right understanding of our value—that God loved us so much that He died to bring salvation to the human race. Each person develops best when he or she begins to see themselves as God sees them, as people who are so valuable to Him that He wants to cleanse them of sin and make them children of God. Jesus said, "If anyone desires to come after Me, let him deny himself, and take up his cross, and follow Me" (Matthew 16:24).

THE REAL JOY OF LIVING

"I have come that they may have life, and that
they may have it more abundantly."

JOHN 10:10

We will never be free from discouragement and despondency until we know and walk with the very fountainhead of joy—Jesus Christ. We have to be tuned to God. Joy is not surface; joy runs deep. The ability to rejoice in any situation is a sign of spiritual maturity. Without dark clouds in our lives, we would never know the joy of sunshine.

Suffering can give us opportunities to testify of God's love. The world is a gigantic hospital; nowhere is there a greater chance to see the peace and joy of the Lord than when the journey through life is in the darkest valley. The Bible teaches that we are to be patient in suffering. Tears become telescopes to Heaven, bringing eternity a little closer. The important thing is to be prepared to meet God when this life is over and give account to how we've spent our lives while on Earth.

Whoever reads these words right now can be settled and know the peace and fellowship of Jesus. When Christ transforms our hearts, it brings a glow to the face, puts a spring in our steps, and joy in our souls. Christianity flings open the windows to the real joy of living. Those who have truly been converted to Jesus Christ know the meaning of abundant living, even in the midst of trouble.

The Christian's Privilege

He said to them, "Go into all the world and preach the gospel to every creature."
MARK 16:15

Every believer in Jesus Christ should do the work of evangelizing because we possess the greatest message of all time—Jesus loves the world and came to redeem the world from sin. An evangelist carries a message to others, to tell people simply and clearly what God says concerning His Son, Jesus Christ, and what He has done for all. This is done with urgency because the souls of people are at stake. While some are called to do this as their life's work, all believers have a part in spreading the gospel, and what a privilege it is.

A messenger conveys a message to another. He or she may not enjoy doing it if the message contains bad news, but the messenger should be faithful to deliver it. This is the duty of the evangelist. God has given the message, and those who convey it should be faithful to every word recorded in Scripture.

God's Word alone is the authority, and it is more powerful than human personality or natural speaking ability. The Bible is always living, active, and relevant (Hebrews 4:12).

Doing the work of evangelism is not a calling just for the clergy. There's a mighty army around the world of those who follow Jesus with a vision to reach their own people for Christ.

FULLY GOD AND FULLY MAN

*God sent forth His Son, born of a woman, born under the
law, to redeem those who were under the law.*

GALATIANS 4:4–5

Jesus Christ was not just a great teacher or a holy religious leader but God Himself
in human flesh—fully God and fully man. Jesus is not only the Christ; He is
also God, our Lord and Savior. This is an almost incomprehensible truth: God
Himself came down to this planet in the Person of His only Son. The incarnation
and the full deity of Jesus are the cornerstones of the Christian faith.

This great truth is underscored throughout the New Testament. The Bible says,
"He is the image of the invisible God, the firstborn over all creation. For by Him all
things were created. . . . For it pleased the Father that in Him all the fullness should
dwell" (Colossians 1:15–16, 19). Matthew told us of the birth of Jesus and stated,
"All this was done that it might be fulfilled which was spoken by the Lord through
the prophet, saying: 'Behold, the virgin shall be with child, and bear a Son, and
they shall call His name Immanuel,' which is translated, 'God with us'" (Matthew
1:22–23).

Furthermore, He demonstrated the power to do things that only God can do,
such as forgive sins.

Christ is alive! His resurrection is a fact. His tomb is empty—and this is the
compelling and central proof of His unique divine nature.

BRIGHT FUTURE

God saw everything that he had made, and behold, it was very good.
GENESIS 1:31 ESV

After God created the world, He said it was perfect, because He had made it exactly the way He wanted it to be. He pronounced His creation very good before Satan tempted Adam and Eve and before the world was invaded by sin. Adam and Eve chose to believe Satan's lies instead of God's truth. God had given them everything they needed. They enjoyed fellowship with the Creator; they walked in perfect harmony with Him. But when they turned their backs on Him and listened to Satan's lies, sin took root in the human heart.

We do not live in an ideal world but in a world dominated by sinful, selfish desires. What we see taking place around the globe, rebellion and protest against God, is a revolt in the human heart concerning His truth.

Many have fallen into the world's trap, following its self-indulgent goals and driven by its self-centered motives. We must make sure that Christ is first in our lives, and make it our goal to live according to God's Word.

The history is grim, but the future is bright. Why? Because the Bible tells us that this sin-sick, fallen world will not last forever. At the end of time God will intervene, and the new Heaven and the new Earth He creates will be free from all evil and pain.

THE GOD OF THIS AGE

"The devil comes and takes away the word out of their
hearts, lest they should believe and be saved."

LUKE 8:12

The same Book that tells us of God's love warns us constantly of the devil, who would come between us and God. Some of Satan's favorite tricks are persuading others to ignore or deny God's truth.

The devil is real and he is an enemy. The devil is out to defeat the Christian in his or her walk with Christ and bring doubt to God's Word. He well knows that the child of God is a dangerous enemy to his cause. He made every effort to tempt and defeat Christ, and today he concentrates on Christ's followers. He is the commander-in-chief of the powers of evil and launches attacks against those who have taken sides with Christ and His righteousness.

What the Bible says about Satan and his minions is true because it's God's Word. The devil harasses, accuses, tempts, deceives, and lies in his dealings with Christians. He works through his allies, the world, and the flesh. The devil uses worldliness to wreak havoc among God's people, to hinder the progress of righteousness. The devil is a powerful foe who is called "the god of this age" (2 Corinthians 4:4). When we are filled with the Spirit of God and handle His Word with wisdom, the Word of God will defeat Satan every time.

SAFE IN THE MIDST OF THE STORM

You will keep in perfect peace all who trust in you,
all whose thoughts are fixed on you!
ISAIAH 26:3 NLT

In spite of modern innovations to bring ease, man has not found the cure for the plague of worry. When people are polled, it is not unusual to see that worry often tops the list of things that plague them. Cardiac specialists say that it's one of the causes of heart trouble. Psychiatrists tell us that worry breeds nervous breakdowns and mental disorders. It's disastrous to health, robs life of its zest, crowds out constructive and creative thinking, and cripples the soul.

What's the answer? Bickersteth, a hymn writer, wrote, "Peace, perfect peace, in this dark world of sin. The blood of Jesus whispers peace within." In Christ, we are relaxed and at peace in the midst of the confusions, bewilderments, and perplexities of this life. The storm rages, but our hearts are at rest. We have found peace because we have learned to trust our living God.

Whenever the story is told about the little bird in the midst of the storm, peace falls upon the soul. As the sea waters beat against the rocks in dashing waves, the lightning flashed, thunder roared, and the wind blew fierce, but in the crevice of the rock a little bird was asleep, its head serenely tucked under its wing in peace. Being secure in Christ Jesus brings that perfect peace.

THE COST OF DISCIPLESHIP

What things were gain to me, these I have counted loss for Christ.

PHILIPPIANS 3:7

God has paid the greatest debt we will ever incur, and once we understand the incredible sacrifice He has made for us, we will be compelled to turn to Him in obedience and love. Many people want the benefits of their faith, but they hesitate at the cost of discipleship. To be a disciple of Jesus means to learn from Him, to follow Him. The cost may be high. A person must determine to leave sin behind. Living a disciplined life for Christ helps condition believers for a life of usefulness. Our minds must be set to do the will of the Lord, which is walking in obedience to God's commands.

Jesus does not call us to a life of selfish comfort and ease—He calls us to a battle! He calls us to give up our own plans and to follow Him without reserve. Yes, it costs to follow Christ. But it also costs not to follow Christ.

Saving faith is a commitment to Jesus as Savior and Lord. It is more than assent to historical or theological truth given to us in God's Word. It is faith in the promises of God that all who trust in Christ will not perish but have eternal life. Jesus didn't use gimmicks to gain followers. He laid out tough demands of discipleship—total commitment to His Word.

SERIOUS BUSINESS

This light momentary affliction is preparing for us an
eternal weight of glory beyond all comparison.
2 CORINTHIANS 4:17 ESV

Becoming a believer in Christ is a wonderful new beginning, but it isn't the end of pain or problems. It is the beginning of facing up to them. Being a Christian involves a lifetime of hard work, dedicated study, and difficult decisions. We must beware of any belief system that claims "happy-ever-after" endings on Earth.

The Christian life is not to be lived flippantly. It's serious business. If we have our eyes upon ourselves, our problems, and our pain, we cannot lift our eyes upward. Just as a child looks up to a parent as they walk together, so are we to look up to Christ and follow Him. The majority of difficulties believers experience can be traced to a lack of Bible study and praying to the Lord for direction, correction, comfort, and assurance that He is with us every step of the way.

Christianity is not an insurance policy against life's ills and troubles; it is about glorifying Him in the midst of them. He may not take away trials or make detours for us, but He strengthens us through them. This becomes part of our testimony to the unbelieving world. We must learn to let the Word of God feed and strengthen us in living out Christ's message to the world as we depend upon the Holy Spirit to teach us.

STRONG IN THE LORD

When I am weak, then I am strong.
2 CORINTHIANS 12:10

When we seek the promises of God's Word, His truth will uphold us daily, no matter what we go through. We must turn constantly to Him in prayer, confident not only that He hears us but remembering that even now Jesus intercedes for us. When we focus our thoughts on Christ and maintain our connection, His very words encourage us and keep us pressing onward.

The Bible's words are true: "Neither death nor life, nor angels nor principalities nor powers, nor things present nor things to come, nor height nor depth, nor any other created thing, shall be able to separate us from the love of God which is in Christ Jesus our Lord" (Romans 8:38–39).

True joy is derived from depending on the Lord Jesus. He is the One who supplies our strength in weakness, for when we are weak, He is strong (2 Corinthians 12:10). Strength is found in the wisdom of God, and that is at our disposal whether young or old. We do not have to let the world hold us captive as we work and live in this world; our freedom is in Christ. When faith begins to fade, we must ask the Lord to stir it up by considering all He has done for us, and be strong, for the Bible declares, "My Spirit remains among you; do not fear!" (Haggai 2:5).

FRUITFUL LIVES

"He who abides in Me, and I in him, bears much fruit."
JOHN 15:5

It is hard to understand the Christian life without understanding the Person and the work of God's Spirit, but what a marvelous picture we have in the New Testament book of Galatians, chapter 5.

"The fruit of the Spirit is love, joy, peace, longsuffering, kindness, goodness, faithfulness, gentleness, self-control. . . . If we live in the Spirit, let us also walk in the Spirit" (vv. 22–23, 25). We cannot do this on our own, but as children of God He gives us the gift of His Spirit that resides within us and helps us live according to His example and His loving commands.

This cluster of fruit should characterize the life of every child of God. We're to be filled with love, joy, and peace. We're to exhibit patience and extend gentleness and kindness to those we meet. We're to be filled with goodness, meekness, and temperance. As we grow in Christ and put Him on the throne of our lives, God's Spirit becomes dominant in our thinking and in our actions.

God intends for Christians to live on the highest plane, bearing the fruit of His Spirit because it's His Spirit that empowers us. When we're praying daily for the Lord to empower us, our desire for immorality, dishonesty, jealousy, and all these other things that beset man can no longer find a place in our lives to dwell.

ANIMALS IN HEAVEN?

"The kingdom of heaven is like treasure hidden in a field, which a man found and hid; and for joy over it he goes and sells all that he has and buys that field."

MATTHEW 13:44

God's creation story includes His creative work in the animal kingdom. "Let the earth bring forth the living creature according to its kind: cattle . . . and everything . . . on the earth. . . . And God saw that it was good" (Genesis 1:24–25). All of this took place before sin entered the world.

We know that God gave animals to mankind for a purpose, because before the great Flood, God preserved every species—male and female—on the ark so they would inhabit the land again. Animals are among God's many diverse gifts to man.

It's important, though, to understand that Jesus Christ died for our souls to give us life eternal in Heaven. While we can enjoy the many things God has created for us on earth, we have a responsibility toward other people. He calls us to love one another and gives us His own example of love toward us. It is hard for us to love others if we do not first love the Lord Jesus Christ.

Do not miss Heaven. Even when we allow our imaginations to run wild on the joys of Heaven, we will not really know the realities until we are there, but one thing is certain, nothing will compare to being in the eternal presence of the Lord Jesus Christ. What a thrilling future for those who know that someday we will populate the kingdom of God.

OBEDIENT CHANNELS

Beloved, let us love one another.
1 JOHN 4:7

Visualize a triangle with God at the highest point and the two lower points are "You" and "Others." This is a diagram of a relationship with God and man. Our lives before accepting Christ as Savior are represented by a single dot of self-centeredness, but in salvation, we now make contact with two worlds. Truth flows from God to the believer and out to others who cross our paths. We become obedient channels of His truth and love. To say we love God but care nothing for others is to deny God's Word. Personal faith in Jesus Christ is what makes us able to reach out to others and become a testimony for Him.

Once a cartoonist depicted a man rowing a boat toward a golden shore labeled "Heaven." All around him were people struggling in vain to reach the shore, but he was heedless of their peril. He was singing, "I am bound for Heaven, hallelujah!" This is not an adequate picture of the Christian life. When we have the Lord in our hearts, He gives us peace with Him and with our fellow man. This is our calling, to be His light in a dark world.

"In this the love of God was manifested toward us, that God has sent His only begotten Son into the world, that we might live through Him" (1 John 4:8–9).

By Wisdom and Understanding

Through wisdom a house is built, and by understanding it is established.

PROVERBS 24:3

The family is the most important institution in the world. It was God's plan; He ordained it. It wasn't the idea of sociologists. Families and homes existed before cities and governments, written language, nations, temples, or churches.

God intended for the home to be a family's foundation, a place of security. God meant for the home to be a place where character and attitudes were formed, integrity born, and values made clear.

Instead, we see rubbish everywhere—rubbish on our televisions, on digital devices, in literature, and in magazines that poke fun at the idea of traditional home experience. The institution of the home once fortified society. A popular personality was asked about the institution of marriage and home. She responded, "Who wants to live in an institution?" This is typical of the ridicule that has been heaped on the home.

Satan's attacking the family as never before. What should our defenses against such attacks be? If families would return to God and make Him the focus of the home and the heart of the family, reading the Bible that brings comfort in turmoil and light to dark pathways, the nation would begin to rebuild on a sure foundation.

DELIGHTING IN GOD'S WORD

Your word I have hidden in my heart, that I might not sin against You.
PSALM 119:11

For the Christian, learning to enjoy the Bible is to open the Word of God and read His truth. Almighty God communicates with His people through prayer and the richness of His Word; this is the secret to learning how to walk with the Lord every day. It becomes a joy to wake up in the morning and know He is with us, no matter what the day has in store.

The Christian finds joy in looking back at the end of the day to marvel at how God guided and directed. Then to think about God's love and mercy and to dwell upon all the good things He has done, brings us to the point of thankfulness and praise. Even when circumstances have been hard or the way unclear, we know that God has surrounded us with His fellowship and comfort.

Turning to the Bible every day brings strength and wisdom. Its words have seen believers in Christ through good times and bad.

For those who are new to the Christian faith, turning to the book of John in the New Testament is a good place to start. "In the beginning was the Word, and the Word was with God, and the Word was God. He was in the beginning with God" (John 1:1–2). He—Jesus Christ—is the Word, and those who read His truths will be blessed.

ANTIDOTE TO LONELINESS

"It is not good that man should be alone."
GENESIS 2:18

Loneliness is the predominant attitude in our culture. It may be experienced by the rich and famous or the poor and unknown. The kind of society we live in can contribute to loneliness. Mobility and constant change tend to make some individuals feel rootless and disconnected. Many withdraw from everyday life.

The Bible has a great deal to say about this. God said it was not good for man to be alone, so He made a suitable companion for him. From the book of Ecclesiastes, it states that two people are better off than one, for if one falls, another can reach out and help. If one is attacked, another can defend him (4:9–12).

The Bible also speaks of showing hospitality to others. This is something that has been lost in today's culture.

But there are times when being alone can bring advantages. The Bible tells us that the Lord Himself withdrew from others in order to spend time in prayer to His Father in Heaven, and this is an example that we, too, should follow. We need the fellowship of others, but especially God. With Christ as our Savior and constant companion, we never really need to be lonely. Nothing dissolves loneliness like a session with God in Bible reading and prayer. For those who are lonely today, seek Christ and know the fellowship that He brings to the human heart.

SHINING IN THE DARKNESS

"Blessed are the peacemakers, for they shall be called sons of God."
MATTHEW 5:9

While life can be filled with negatives, for those who know the Lord and have a personal relationship with Him, there are opportunities to demonstrate the peace of God in the midst of trouble.

Isn't it interesting to consider something like a simple battery that has power to illuminate a flashlight? The battery has a positive end, marked by a plus sign, and a negative end, marked with a minus sign. If we don't put the correct end into the flashlight first, the battery will provide no power at all. Both the positive and negative connections must be made.

Faith in God is like a battery in that to tap into the power of God, we must be connected in the right way, by loving and obeying Him and feeding on His Word. We must also love our neighbors. Our personal faith in Christ is useless unless we also love others and do good toward them.

If we belong to Jesus, we have peace with God and the peace of God—and our lives will become more than a flash of momentary light. The Bible tells us to put aside the negative (works of darkness) and instead put on the armor of light (Romans 13:12), for His people are the light of the world, and this light is found in all that is good, right, and true (Ephesians 5:8–9).

WHERE OUR HEARTS ARE

God loves a cheerful giver.
2 CORINTHIANS 9:7

There are many compassionate organizations reaching out to those in need, and people often ask the question, "What can my little amount do when the needs are so great? Why bother to give?"

God looks at our finances differently than we do. He knows that our giving is a measure of something far more important. When we reach out to others with gifts of compassion, we demonstrate God's compassion. We should not give to impress others, but we should give because it expresses concern and compassion. Responsible giving is important, and it is important to ask God to help us make the right choices in our giving.

The Bible tells us to give joyfully and not out of a grudging obligation; God loves a cheerful giver.

God does not need our money, but He wants us to discover where our hearts are, and when we give to bless others, it pleases the heart of God.

God is able to take what we give and use it in ways we never could imagine. The extra dollar, when given in His name, is multiplied in ways we will never know. What a testimony it is when someone receives a gift knowing that God has put it on our hearts to give it. By His hand, He gives the increase.

ASSURANCE OF HIS PRESENCE

"The wind blows where it wishes."
JOHN 3:8

On a windy day, a boy went out to fly his kite. The sky was filled with puffy clouds and a gentle breeze. As the boy lengthened the string, the kite went up and up, until it was hidden by the clouds.

"What are you doing?" a man asked the boy.

"I'm flying my kite," the boy replied.

"Flying a kite?" asked the man. "How can you be sure? You can't see the kite."

"No," the boy said. "I can't see it, but I can feel it tug, so I know for sure it's there!"

God is real. We must not let other people's doubts cast a shadow of disbelief over us. His presence is just as sure as the tug on the boy's kite. And His love is just like the wind that carries the kite high into the sky. You can't see the wind, but you know for sure it is there.

When we invite the Lord Jesus into our lives, He gives us assurance His ever-present Spirit is with us to guide and direct our steps. The Bible tells us that God's Spirit bears witness with our spirit (Romans 8:16).

But we must seek Him every day, asking for His help. This happens when we pray and listen to Him speak to us through His Word. The warm tug on our hearts brings peace that He truly watches over those who belong to Him.

INFORMATION OVERLOAD

Lay up these words of mine in your heart and in your soul.

DEUTERONOMY 11:18

Think about the incredible number of messages that surround us every day. Information that comes to us through television, radio, websites, magazines, song lyrics, movies, conversations with friends—the list is almost endless.

This is sometimes called "information overload," and it goes into the mind and remains. Images, words, and persuasions become part of who we are, and much of it is harmful. The mind is the devil's favorite avenue of attack. Our minds are molded in many different ways—often in ways we are not aware of at the time.

What the world calls valuable, God calls worthless. What the world looks down on, God praises. Our thoughts are not God's thoughts (Isaiah 55:8). When we fill our minds with the things of God, it begins to affect our thinking and our decisions in the right way. The very practice of reading the Bible will have a purifying effect upon the mind and heart. The truth is, God wants our minds to be shaped by Him so that our thoughts and actions reflect Christ.

The Scripture goes on to instruct us to dwell on His words when we rise up and when we go to bed at night, and when we walk along the way of life (Deuteronomy 11:19). It simply means to think of these things continually. His words are truth and they will shape us.

LEAP OF FAITH

The things which are seen are temporary, but the things which are not seen are eternal.
2 CORINTHIANS 4:18

The *Saturday Evening Post* once published a landmark interview with the great physicist and mathematician Albert Einstein. His response to questions of Jesus as a historical figure are breathtaking. He stated, "I am enthralled by the luminous figure of the Nazarene. . . . No one can read the Gospels without feeling the actual presence of Jesus. His personality pulsates in every word. No myth is filled with such life."

No one knows whether Einstein ever received Christ as Savior, but near the end of life he said, "If you ask me to prove what I believe, I can't. . . . The mind can proceed only so far upon what it knows and can prove. There comes a point where the mind takes a leap . . . and comes out upon a higher plane of knowledge, but can never prove how it got there. All great discoveries have involved such a leap."

But we can't rely on the testimony of others over the testimony of Christ Himself, who said, "Most assuredly, I say to you, before Abraham was, I AM" (John 8:58). This leap of faith is given when we speak the name of Jesus in sincere truth, realizing that we're bound to a dark eternity without His forgiveness, grace, and mercy.

Regardless of the knowledge gathered, no one can know Jesus without taking the certain leap of faith that salvation comes only from Him.

THE PERFECT LOVE OF GOD

The steadfast love of the LORD is from everlasting to everlasting.

PSALM 103:17 ESV

Behind every dealing God has with us is His perfect love. It was love that made Him create us, and it was love that caused Him to send His Son to redeem us. His love pursues us and draws us to Himself, and His love will someday take His children into His presence forever.

As with other aspects of His nature, we have a difficult time fully understanding God's love. For one thing, the word *love* has come to mean almost anything today. We say we "love" ice cream or the color of a car, or we say we "love" entertainers or celebrities. But God's love is far deeper than this. His love is not a passing fancy or superficial emotion; it is a profound and unshakable commitment that seeks what is best for us. Human love may change or fade; God's love never will. He says to us, "I have loved you with an everlasting love . . . with lovingkindness I have drawn you" (Jeremiah 31:3).

We must not sentimentalize God's love; it isn't a warm, fuzzy feeling that ignores sin or shuns judgment. God's holiness demands that sin be punished—but God's love has provided the way of redemption through Christ. If it weren't for God's love, we would have no hope, in either this life or the life to come. But there is hope, because He loves us!

A NEW PURPOSE

"Ask . . . where the good way is, and walk in it."
JEREMIAH 6:16

Some people are focused on using all their energies to reach their goals. Others drift through life with little purpose or direction, living for the moment and never thinking about where they are headed. Most people probably live somewhere in between. But they all have this in common: they are living only for themselves and their own happiness.

Down inside we all sense that this was not the way life was meant to be, and we want something better—and we search for it. We suspect there must be another way, a different path from the one we've been traveling. But why do so few people seem to find it? Can life be any different?

The answer is yes! No matter what our lives have been, the rest of the journey can be different.

When we come to Christ, God gives us a new purpose. He helps us begin again. He helps us confront our problems and deal with them, and this helps us avoid life's pitfalls and detours. More than that, God can help us make an impact on our world. When we begin to live according to His purpose, and not our own purposes, we see other people differently—not for what they can do for us but what we can do for them. Ask God for the good way—the better way—and walk in it.

No Rejection

The Lord is gracious and full of compassion.

PSALM 145:8

One reason many Christians aren't sure of their salvation is because they still sin, and they fear God may reject them because of it. But even when we sin, the Bible tells us that the Lord is gracious and compassionate. He's slow to anger and rich in love (Psalm 145:8).

Suppose someone is given the gift of a computer. The giver says, "This is my gift to you." The recipient would be delighted. Then they would become discouraged to hear the giver say, "If you make one mistake, I am going to take it back. You can only keep it if you operate it perfectly!"

Many people assume God's like that, giving us the gift of salvation—then taking it back if we aren't perfect. But this isn't true. When we're saved, Christ begins the work of transformation.

The story's told of a sculpture artist who was chipping away at a chunk of stone. A man asked, "What are you doing?" The artist replied, "I'm sculpting an elephant." The man responded, "How do you know what to chip away?" The sculptor smiled and replied, "I chip away anything that doesn't look like an elephant."

This is what God desires to do with our lives. When we place our lives in His care, He will chip away at whatever keeps us apart from Him.

God's View of Humanity

The carnal mind is enmity against God; for it is not subject to the law of God.
ROMANS 8:7

Humans view life from a personal point of time and space, but God views us from His heavenly throne in the light of eternity. We see ourselves as self-sufficient, self-important, and self-sustaining; God sees us as dependent, self-centered, and self-deceived. Our worldly wisdom has made us calloused and hard. Our natural wisdom, as the Scriptures teach, comes not from God but is earthly, sensual, and devilish (James 3:15).

There is the person you think you are. There is the person others think you are. And there is the person God knows you are and what you can become through Christ.

All truth is from God, and He wants us to believe His truth, which points us to the cross. It is there that we find forgiveness of the sins of "self," and we also find the solution to dilemmas and problems.

It is impossible for the "natural man" (the one who does not know Jesus Christ as personal Savior) to understand how God, in His grace and mercy, can forgive sinners and transform lives. It is also impossible for the natural man to comprehend how these changed lives can affect society. Those with their worldly wisdom do not understand the workings of God. But you can know the Lord Jesus today if you will receive Him by faith.

The Purpose of Pain

"I correct and discipline everyone I love."
REVELATION 3:19 NLT

God uses suffering and trials to discipline us. Jesus said in the Scriptures that He does discipline those He loves. It may be hard to understand but when we look at the parental role on Earth, discipline is part of raising a healthy and well-adjusted child. We don't want our children to keep making the same mistakes. Should we be surprised when the heavenly Father wants His children to mature?

God intends for the Christian life to make us what He wants us to be. God has a divine plan for shaping our lives. That plan often includes suffering in one way or another. It deepens our spirit; it strengthens our resolve to keep our eyes on Him and the path that He has put before us.

Have you ever considered that steel is iron plus fire; soil is rock plus crushing; linen is flax plus the comb that separates and the shuttle that weaves? Suffering includes many different elements of anguish known to man. We would all like to lead life free of pain and problems, but who really does? Such people would be impossible to find.

Read the Scriptures. You will not be able to find one person who lived without suffering. Then read the great chapter of Hebrews 11. You will see that victory awaits those who endured the fires of hardship and kept their eyes of Jesus.

OCTOBER

THE CONFLICT OF THE AGES

"Do I have any pleasure at all that the wicked should die?" says the Lord GOD.
EZEKIEL 18:23

Regardless of man's continual sin, the grace and patience of the Lord are overwhelming. You can't miss the countless warnings that come from Him. "I have no pleasure in the death of the wicked, but that the wicked turn from his way and live" (Ezekiel 33:11).

This is the conflict of the ages. Many people refuse to turn from sin because they're more afraid of man's ridicule than of God's judgment. Others think belief in Christ is foolishness. Well, let's see who is foolish. The whole world laughed at Noah when he boarded an ark on dry land. Lot's neighbors in Sodom and Gomorrah laughed when he ran from the cities, saying they would be destroyed because of rampant immorality. But these eternal judgments were fulfilled as scoffers drowned in the flood and burned in the brimstone of Lot's hometown.

But a greater judgment took place more than two thousand years ago on Calvary, when the sins of the world were placed on Jesus. He shed His blood on the cross to pay the penalty for sin.

Oh, friend, do not doubt the power of holy God, who calls out to the world to repent and find the mercy and love of the blessed Savior and Redeemer of the soul.

THE PURSUIT OF HAPPINESS

Godliness with contentment is great gain.

1 TIMOTHY 6:6

King Solomon was convinced he knew how to find happiness—and because he had vast resources at his command, he was able to pursue it. Wealth, fame, pleasure, power, lavish houses, a reputation for wisdom—you name it, King Solomon achieved it. And yet after gaining everything he had ever wanted, he reluctantly concluded that his life was still empty and without meaning. His search for lasting happiness had failed, and his soul was still empty.

This is a common story. Many people are in danger of making the same mistake King Solomon made—convinced that the things of this world will bring happiness and peace and pursuing them with vigor. Don't be deceived; they never will. And the reason is because we were made to know God. Later, King Solomon realized this. He should have known it sooner; after all, his father, David, was a man after God's own heart, and Solomon himself had vowed to live according to God's wisdom. Don't be misled (even as the wise king was), but make Christ the center and foundation of your life—beginning today.

The world makes a lot of empty promises concerning happiness—what it looks like and how to obtain it. But true happiness is really called joy, and it comes to those who delight in the things of the Lord and to those who meditate on God's Word—and obey it!

THE BARRIER OF SIN

We walk by faith, not by sight.
2 CORINTHIANS 5:7

Seldom do we doubt the stories of redemption that captivate us nearly every day. Whether it's someone being rescued from a fire or a flood, we praise the rescuers and sigh with relief for the victims wonderfully saved! The outcomes of rescue missions become part of history, even those that happened before we were born. We watch documentaries and movies of mighty battles down through the ages and believe them not because we were there as witnesses; we believe these stories by faith.

Down through the centuries, people haven't wanted to believe the accounts found in the Bible and have rejected truth. Human nature says, "We weren't there to witness these things for ourselves. How can we believe such a story that God created man and woman, they disobeyed God, they were tempted by Satan, they chose to believe Satan's lie over God's promise, and now all humanity must be saved from sin by Christ's sacrifice on the cross?"

Whether or not we believe doesn't change the truth. The problem is that human nature doesn't exercise faith in the truth of God's Word. God put within each soul a longing to know Him. But sin is a barrier that keeps us from knowing Jesus as personal Savior and Lord. We're bound by this barrier of sin unless we are freed from it. This is gloriously accomplished by the saving grace of Jesus Christ.

MORAL DETERIORATION

The time will come when . . . they will turn their ears away from the truth.

2 TIMOTHY 4:3–4

Naturalistic philosophers refer to the miracles of the Bible as "miraculous magic" and "oppressive absurdities." They're trying to hammer away at the very foundation of Christianity: faith in Christ as the Son of God.

Their philosophies have fed the moral deterioration throughout the Western world. If there's no such thing as a transcendent God who is interested in the affairs of men, then there's no moral law, and each person has a right to do as he pleases. We've sown the wind and are now reaping a whirlwind of cheating, lying, dishonesty, and immorality on a scale that hasn't been known in the history of this nation.

What are Christians to do? Stand fast in the Scriptures as Paul declared. "Take up the whole armor of God, that you may be able to withstand in the evil day, and having done all, to stand" (Ephesians 6:13). Greek scholars remind us that this phrase—the evil day—refers to a particular hour when evil will be manifested in an unusual way in the thoughts, activities, and pursuits of humanity.

We're also instructed to reexamine the foundations of our faith and know more of the abiding, unshakable rock of historic truth on which our faith and hope rest. We should learn, study, and digest the great absolutes of our faith.

THE MIGHTY WORKS OF GOD

The heavens declare the glory of God; the skies proclaim the work of his hands.
PSALM 19:1 NIV

I n the beginning God created the heavens and the earth" (Genesis 1:1). Everything in the universe—absolutely everything—owes its existence to God. Look up on a starry night and you will see the majesty and power of an infinite Creator. What astronomers and scientists have discovered about space shows the mighty works of almighty God.

Astronomers tell us that every star moves with precision along its celestial path. To ignore the detailed rules of the universe would spell ruin to a star. The laws of nature are fixed, and for a star to ignore those laws would be folly—if it were even possible. If the laws in His material realm are so fixed and exact, would God be haphazard in the spiritual realm, where the eternal destinies of billions of people are at stake? No! Just as God has equations and rules in the material realm, He also has equations and rules in the spiritual realm.

God's formula for the human race is to accept His Son, Jesus Christ, as "the way, the truth, and the life" (John 14:6). Without faith, the Bible says, "it is impossible to please Him, for he who comes to God must believe that He is, and that He is a rewarder of those who diligently seek Him" (Hebrews 11:6).

GIFTS AND TALENTS

Whatever you do, do it heartily, as to the Lord and not
to men . . . for you serve the Lord Christ.
COLOSSIANS 3:23–24

We may never know how God uses the talents that He gives to mankind. While many are acclaimed for the music they compose or canvas art or books penned, there are many testimonies unheard by the throngs but impact one soul at a time for eternity. We are responsible to be faithful in our witness for Jesus Christ, and it is He who blesses the work, though many will never know the outcome this side of Heaven.

In the twenty-first century, throngs of people acclaimed the newly discovered Leonardo da Vinci fifteenth-century painting entitled *Savior of the World*. The piece had been lost for five hundred years, disguised by layers of overpainting, and was painstakingly restored before going on exhibit in London in 2001.

Whatever we do in word or deed, the Bible says, do all to the glory of God. Our gratitude to Him can find expression in our service for others, but ultimately we use our gifts and talents to glorify His name, and He sees all that is done by human hands.

There is a powerful verse found in Genesis 50:20 that says, "You meant evil against me; but God meant it for good . . . to save many people." We never know how God blesses the works of our hands when we leave it in His capable hands.

The Power of the Christian Faith

No one has ever seen God, but [Jesus] . . . has made him known.
JOHN 1:18 NIV

Careful study of world religions reveals extreme contradictions and how impossible it is to take various ideas and draw them together into an intelligent system.

There is a problem to consider. Who would be the judge of which ideas to keep or throw out? Without a standard, the process would quickly fall apart.

Many religions in the world have developed because people have had various ideas about God. The Bible makes it clear that we don't have to guess what God is like. The Bible tells us. All we have to do is read it and by faith receive the salvation He offers. He transforms the sinner and brings new life. This is the tremendous distinctive of the Christian faith: Jesus died for the sins of man and stands ready to forgive.

The Christian life is not an idea—it's God's sacrificial gift of salvation to mankind. The power of the Christian faith is not in its ethics, ideas, or philosophies. It's found in the Lord Jesus Christ.

Many have tried searching the religions of the world to find peace but it ends in failure. But Jesus said, "I am the way" (John 14:6). God isn't an object to be studied and analyzed, like a butterfly or a chemical solution. He is almighty God who created us and loves us. And all people can know Him personally through His great salvation.

THE ANTICHRIST

You have heard that the Antichrist is coming.

1 JOHN 2:18

The term *Antichrist* is found several times in the Bible and refers to a person who will come in the days just before Christ returns to establish His kingdom. This person is not Satan, but he will use every evil device of Satan to oppose the work of God. The apostle Paul used the term "the man of lawlessness" to describe this individual (2 Thessalonians 2:3 NIV). He will be the embodiment of evil and will have great power to deceive those who choose to follow him.

When he is revealed, it will be in accordance with the work of Satan displayed in every sort of evil that deceives those who are perishing (2 Thessalonians 2:9–10). The time will come when someone who is totally opposed to Christ will rise to world dominance and achieve great influence. However, in the end, he will be defeated by the Lord Jesus.

At the same time, the Bible warns that there are many in the world who have the same spirit as the Antichrist and oppose the work of God. This means we need to be discerning and not be misled by those who oppose God's truth. How can we avoid being led astray into falsehood? The most important thing is to yield our lives to Jesus Christ and then to know the truth God has given us in His Word.

THE LORD'S MINISTERING SPIRITS

The angel of the LORD encamps all around those
who fear Him, and delivers them.
PSALM 34:7

The operation of angelic glory eclipses the world of demonic powers, as the sun does the candle's light. Throughout Scripture, God uses angels, and the Bible says, "Bless the LORD, you His angels, who excel in strength, who do His word, heeding the voice of His word" (Psalm 103:20).

It is God Himself who empowers angels to do His will. Angels speak. They appear and reappear. While angels may become visible, our eyes are not constructed to see them ordinarily any more than we can see the dimensions of a nuclear field, the structure of atoms, or the electricity that flows through copper wiring.

Demonic activity and Satan worship are on the increase in all parts of the world. The devil's demonic influence can turn many away from true faith; but we can still say that his evil activities are countered for the people of God by the Lord's ministering spirits, the holy ones of the angelic order.

Angels have been endowed with authority by virtue of their relationship to God through creation and continuing obedience. People are not yet perfect and therefore need what the Holy Spirit alone can give. We can be thankful for God's care over those who belong to Him, and we must always give the glory not to the angels but to Him who empowers them.

FREEDOM TO CHOOSE

When you offer a sacrifice of thanksgiving to the LORD, offer it of your own free will.

LEVITICUS 22:29

God set us apart for fellowship with Him. But He also gave us free will that was put to the test. One tree in the luscious Garden of Eden symbolized the knowledge of good and evil, and God said, "You shall not eat." Adam and Eve ate and violated what they knew to be God's will (see Romans 5:12–19; Genesis 3:1–8; 1 Timothy 2:13–14).

God could have created human robots who would respond mechanically to His direction. But instead, God created us in His image, and He desires that the creature worship the Creator as a response of love. This can be accomplished when "free will" is exercised. Love and obedience which are forced do not satisfy. God wants obedient followers, not machines.

A pastor friend once told of his son who was attending a state university and becoming "very wise." "Dad," he said to his father one day, "I'm not sure that when I get out of school I will be able to follow you in your Christian faith." The father looked at him with compassion and replied, "Son, that is your freedom—your terrible freedom."

Freedom to choose results in God's blessing or the consequences of disobedience to His will. We can exercise our freedom to love God with our obedience or we can rebel and build our lives without Him. Choose to follow Christ.

THE CONVERTED WILL

God is working in you, giving you the desire and the power to do what pleases him.
PHILIPPIANS 2:13 NLT

Thousands of people speak of having some form of emotional experience that they refer to as conversion, but they have never been truly converted to Christ. If a life does not conform to the Word of God, then there are reasons to doubt possessing true salvation in Jesus Christ.

Certainly, there will be a change in the elements that make up emotion when a person receives Christ as Savior. Someone who has been converted begins to hate sin and love righteousness. Personal affections will undergo a revolutionary change, and devotion to the Lord will know no bounds, and love and faithfulness will begin to grow.

Intellectual acceptance of Christ or an emotional experience is not enough. There must be the conversion of the will! There must be that determination to obey and follow Christ. Self must be nailed to the cross.

Our main desire must be to please Him. When a person is convicted of sin, the Holy Spirit sheds His truth in the heart and the face of sin is dealt with. When mankind opens its heart, a miracle of the new birth takes place and a new creation replaces the old creation, bringing to each redeemed soul a new beginning. Believers partake of God's own life, and Jesus Christ, when the Spirit of God takes up residence in the human heart.

REST IN THE LORD

*The LORD gave them rest all around, according to
all that He had sworn to their fathers.*

JOSHUA 21:44

For those who belong to Christ and have Him at the center of life, God is near. When we struggle, fight, and strive for our way, we are not "resting" in the Lord. "Rest in the LORD, and wait patiently for Him; do not fret" (Psalm 37:7).

We must let go of inner tensions that life sends our way, trusting in God moment by moment. A victorious Christian is confident that God is in control. Reliance on the Holy Spirit gives us physical and emotional rest as we set our minds on Christ.

The Bible tells us: "But the natural man does not receive the things of the Spirit of God, for they are foolishness to him . . . because they are spiritually discerned. . . . But we have the mind of Christ" (1 Corinthians 2:14–16).

We are the dwelling place of the Holy Spirit. Jesus promised that God the Father would send His Spirit to help us in all things. We must admit our weakness so that we can ask Him to take over. Standing with Christ means that we stand aside and let Him have His way in our hearts and minds.

What a comfort to know that our Savior is constantly praying for us. "[There is] no condemnation to those who are in Christ Jesus, who do not walk according to the flesh, but according to the Spirit" (Romans 8:1).

This should be a tremendous encouragement to every follower of Christ.

Doing Good

Encourage one another and build each other up.
1 THESSALONIANS 5:11 NIV

D r. Alan Redpath was pastor at the great Moody Church in Chicago. On the wall of his office, he had this inscription: "Beware of the barrenness of a busy life." There is always something to do. We can do good things, but we can also do better things. Often the answer to our dilemma is right in front of us—doing the better thing may solve a conflict. It could be that those who attend activities at church would be willing to move the activity to a person's house to minister in ways that reflect their desire to be used of the Lord.

Today, many people are looking for ways to comfort others, and this is commendable. There are shut-ins who need to see a smile. There are lonely people who long to hear a knock at the door. There are hospitals and nursing centers filled with long-term patients who could flourish if they only had someone who cared. And then there are many people looking for ways to reach out to others, providing the warmth of a handshake, a word of comfort, a message of hope. This can lead to one-on-one evangelism; it can also provide Christian fellowship. And as believers, we must reflect on wisdom from Scripture: "Let us consider how we may spur one another on toward love and good deeds . . . encouraging one another" (Hebrews 10:24–25 NIV).

OUR WORTH IN GOD'S EYES

"You are precious in my eyes, and honored, and I love you."

ISAIAH 43:4 ESV

People are often introduced this way: "This is Bob, and he works for . . ." as if where a person works determines his or her value. It seems that only the well-to-do or those who are thought of as "successful" are introduced this way. Yet God does not judge us by success. He loves each person the same because our value does not come from what we do or have, the clothes we wear, the house in which we live, or the type of car we drive. Our value comes from the fact that God made us and Christ died for us. And so, whether we have things or not, we are just as valuable to God.

God gave all that He had—His Son, the Lord Jesus Christ—because He valued us so highly, even when we did not value Him. Since God thought this much of us, shouldn't we show that we value Him by putting Him first in all that we do—our family life, our business life, and our spiritual life? There is a song that says, "Put Jesus first in your life, let Him handle all the problems that come your way." The actual value of an object is that which is placed on it by the owner or buyer. God has shown the value He has placed on you by sending His Son to redeem you.

REFLEXIVE ACTION

"You will call upon Me and go and pray to Me, and I will listen to you."
JEREMIAH 29:12

We've all had a doctor take a little rubber hammer and tap it on our knee to test our reflex. The lower leg gives a gentle kick, showing the reflex is good. It is a reflexive action that occurs automatically, and it is the same every time that nerve gets hit.

It's often the same when troubles come our way. Trials strike a nerve within us and our inner self comes forth. Our reflexive action tends to follow the pattern we've nourished. Many panic, react with anger, express confusion. Others react with an assurance that God is leading and giving a spirit of calmness.

The Bible writer James reminded us of what our reflexive action should be when trouble strikes. He wrote, "Is anyone among you in trouble? Let them pray. . . . The prayer of a righteous person is powerful and effective" (James 5:13, 16 NIV). Prayer is an acknowledgment of our helplessness.

Prayer is also an acknowledgment of God's power and love. We are not trying to manipulate God when we pray; but we are looking for Him to help us according to His perfect will. When troubles come, may prayer be our automatic response. For those who follow Christ daily, our attitudes and actions in seasons of difficulty show a watching world that we truly believe the promises given to us in Scripture.

NOT JUST ANOTHER GREAT BOOK

"Blessed are those who hear the word of God and keep it!"
LUKE 11:28

Simply put, the Bible is the source of all knowledge. It says, "People do not live by bread alone, but by every word that comes from the mouth of God" (Matthew 4:4 NLT). The Word of God is called the sword of the Spirit, and God Himself has provided His truth to mankind. He has given us His precious Word because He wants us to know Him, love Him, and serve Him. Most of all, He gave it to us to convict us of our sin against Him and repent and receive Him as Lord.

The Bible isn't just another great book. The Bible interprets the Bible. It tells how it came to be written—and it has stood the test of time. The Bible is actually a library of books—sixty-six in all. Behind each one, however, was the Author, the Spirit of God.

Someone has written, "Sin will keep you from God's Word—or God's Word will keep you from sin!" Which will we choose? While people today are searching for answers to life's problems, only the Bible has the answer to the deepest needs of men, women, and children.

The secret of the power of Christianity is not in its ethics. It is not in Christian ideas or philosophy; the secret is found in the Lord Jesus Christ and His truth.

LEAPING OVER WALLS

By You I can run against a troop, by my God I can leap over a wall.
PSALM 18:29

Extreme sports, like snowboarding and rock climbing, are difficult and risky. Athletes do tricks in midair or climb steep, smooth rock formations and count on their skills to help them survive. They wouldn't be able to take on the challenges of their sport if it weren't for all the time they've spent practicing and all the help they've received from coaches.

In one of his psalms, King David wrote, "By my God I can leap over a wall." We all can jump over some barriers in life by our own efforts. But some "walls" we face are higher and more challenging.

There are some people who have serious health problems or disabilities. Some deal with anger or anxiety. Others lose jobs, or worse, a loved one. We try to jump over these walls but repeatedly fail. Can we overcome our anger or losses, instead of constantly being overcome by them? Yes! With God's help, we can overcome.

Scripture reveals that even the apostles dealt with defeat, but they became "overcomers" when they began living life under the power of God (1 John 2:13).

Jesus can give us power to overcome every sin and habit that besets us. He can break the ropes that bind us, but we must repent, confess, commit, and surrender to Him. When we put Him first, He fills us with joy.

GOD'S SECRET SERVANTS

Bless the LORD, you His angels, who excel in strength, who do His word.
PSALM 103:20

In the late 1800s, a German composer and his sister wrote a musical version of the fairy tale Hansel and Gretel. Early in the opera, Hansel and Gretel become lost one night in a dangerous forest. Before they finally fall asleep, they sing their evening prayers, and fourteen angels come to surround them and keep them safe throughout the night.

Fairy tales come from fanciful imaginations, but angels themselves are God's secret servants and never fail at the tasks God gives them. Often when people talk or write about angels, they don't base their beliefs on what the Bible says about them. But angels are real and God has commanded them to watch over us. They are usually unseen and unrecognized, and only in Heaven will we know everything they did to keep us safe. Angels crisscross the Old and New Testaments, being mentioned directly or indirectly nearly three hundred times. We face dangers every day of which we are not even aware. Often God intervenes on our behalf through the ministry of His angels.

But we are not to worship angels; for it is God who empowers them, and they worship and glorify Him and stand ready to do His will. We can be glad about their presence and thank God for the ways He loves and protects through His angels.

THE RIGHT BUILDING MATERIALS

That you may be . . . filled with the fruits of
righteousness which are by Jesus Christ.
PHILIPPIANS 1:10–11

As an old man was dying, he told his grandson, "I don't know what type of work I'll be doing in Heaven, but if it's allowed, I'm going to ask the Lord to let me help build your mansion, so be sure to send up plenty of the right materials." This troubled the young man for some time until he realized what his grandfather was saying.

"Store your treasures in heaven. . . . Wherever your treasure is, there the desires of your heart will also be" (Matthew 6:20–21 NLT).

Obviously the grandfather was sending a message to his young grandson that if he lives according to God's Word, he will be sending up the right materials. God is busy at work preparing a place for each person who repents of sin and receives Christ as Savior. But what are these treasures? It is the fruit of our lives: obeying God, praying for others, witnessing to the truth of His Word, doing unto others in the name of Jesus.

Storing up the truths of God's Word in our hearts is also a key to walking in the right way. When we read and study His Word, it helps prepare us for whatever comes into our lives and helps us in the good and bad times.

Walk with God and be faithful every step of the way.

RESTLESS HEARTS

He who heeds the word wisely will find good . . . happy is he.
PROVERBS 16:20

This is the most entertained generation in history. Large-screen TVs pull in hundreds of channels. Sports teams take in (and spend) billions of dollars. Children are upset if they don't get the latest games on their devices, and adults are always on their smartphones even when in a restaurant for a meal.

There is a frantic search for entertainment, and it is a symptom of something deeper. Some have suggested that we are the most bored generation in history—and perhaps that is correct. Down inside is an empty place in our hearts—a restlessness, a search for inner peace. And the more we try to satisfy it with entertainment, the less content we become. People need something more to live for.

Only Jesus can fill that empty space in our hearts, and He will, whether it is a child's heart, a parent's heart, or the hearts of the elderly. As we open our lives to Him and live according to His ways, He brings us opportunities to serve Him—and others—and we find that boredom goes away and joy fills our hearts. God's Word points us to the future—to Heaven—where our hearts will be full and overflowing with thankfulness to God for what He has accomplished on the cross. And when we surrender to Him in this life, He fills us with peace and true contentment.

THE GREATEST NEED
IN THE WORLD

As far as it depends on you, live at peace with everyone.
ROMANS 12:18 NIV

Society is immersed in destruction brought about through slander, libel, and gossip. The strife in communities, families, business, politics, and even some churches is unbearable. What causes these behaviors? Sin. These are just samplings of what the Bible calls "works of the flesh" (Galatians 5:19–21).

Rebellion, waywardness, lack of discipline, confusion, and conflict prevent happy relationships, happy homes, and contented hearts. God is interested in all of these things, and that's why He has shown us the ideals for life on Earth.

How can we change? How can we become peacemakers? The formula is simple. We must first make our own peace with God by repenting of sin and turning to Him and living according to His ways laid out clearly in Scripture. When we receive His salvation, He begins to work in our lives to produce the fruit of the Spirit, which the Bible lists as love, joy, peace, patience, kindness, gentleness, goodness, faithfulness, and self-control (Galatians 5:22–23).

The trouble is that many want a society without God. When God is put aside, the result is indecency, bedlam, rebellion, and all that goes with it. Peace will be restored when individuals give God His proper place.

The greatest need in the world is the transformation of human nature. We need a new heart emptied of hatred and greed, and this is possible through Jesus Christ.

ALWAYS NEAR

"See, I have inscribed you on the palms of My hands."
ISAIAH 49:16

God could have created us and then abandoned us and forgotten all about us. There are many who believe this. They assume God isn't interested in them—so why should they be interested in Him? To them, God is distant, remote, and unconcerned about the problems they face every day.

But this isn't true! God not only put us on this journey called life, but He wants to join us on it, if we will only let Him. The psalmist asked, "Where can I go from Your Spirit? Or where can I flee from Your presence?" (Psalm 139:7).

When we take a stand for God's truth, some of our friends may drift away, not wanting to be reminded of the things of God. We cannot prevent them from walking away from us. But we can pray that they will not walk away from God. He will often use the life of a Christian to bring conviction to their hearts, which can result in them turning their hearts to Him.

If we understand this truth, it gives us assurance that God will use us to lift up His name to others in spite of the ridicule we might encounter. No matter what happens, God will never abandon those who faithfully live for Him.

Human friends may fail us, but God never will. Once we understand this, life is never the same.

A New Path

*No one can lay any foundation other than the one
already laid, which is Jesus Christ.*
1 CORINTHIANS 3:11 NIV

Whatever has happened in life so far—both good and bad—cannot be altered, and all the decisions and events that have made us what we are today are indelibly inscribed in the story of our lives.

But hope for better days is attainable. How? By looking to the Lord. The future doesn't need to be a copy of our past, nor does God want it to be. No matter what our lives have been like so far, God wants to put our feet on a new path—His path. And regardless of what we may think, His path promises joy, peace, and purpose—far beyond anything we could imagine.

We all go through life building. We build upon learning and experiences, and just as a careful builder lays a solid foundation before constructing a building, so God's Word gives us a solid foundation for building our spiritual lives.

The first pillar of turning life around is to recognize our sin and repent of it, asking God to forgive us and save our souls. Through His sacrifice on the cross, sin was conquered. Jesus' death and resurrection is the foundation of our hope, the promise of our triumph.

We must make it our goal to build strong foundations for life—foundations constructed from prayer and the truths of God's Word.

SOWING AND REAPING

You will always harvest what you plant.

GALATIANS 6:7 NLT

How many decisions do we make in a day? How many of those will be big, important decisions? Sometimes we think our small decisions don't matter, but all decisions have consequences. If we decided to eat nothing but junk food, eventually we would lose our health.

The Bible warns us that a farmer harvests only what he plants. He doesn't plant cabbage and get tomatoes. In the Old Testament, King Rehoboam stubbornly rejected wise advice and listened only to those who agreed with what he wanted to do. That caused conflict, and the nation of Israel split into two kingdoms.

Part of the human makeup that distinguishes us from other creatures is our ability to reason and make decisions. We are free moral agents. Becoming "new" in Christ is a beginning, but it isn't the end of our problems. It marks the beginning of our facing up to them. Being a Christian involves a lifetime of hard work and staying "in tune" with God.

Life is filled with decisions. How will we make them? Often He puts us in the path of others who will give godly counsel based on His Word. But the most important thing is to seek God's will in every decision. Pray. Turn to the Bible. The Lord waits to hear us call on Him, asking Him for the guidance of the Holy Spirit.

VICTORIOUS LIVING

God paid a high price for you, so don't be enslaved by the world.
1 CORINTHIANS 7:23 NLT

A comedian has said, "Enjoy as much as you can. Even if you live to be ninety, that's not as long as you're going to be dead!" We can laugh and throw it off, but there is a penalty to pay when God's Word is disregarded. Death brings an end to physical life, but the life of the human soul lives on for eternity, in either Heaven or Hell.

Godless influences are everywhere, persuading us toward idolatry and sexual immorality. Right moral living is not easy. We have at our fingertips every pleasure that mankind is capable of enjoying, and mankind has abused every gift God ever gave. Sinfulness and sensuality are inevitably destructive, dehumanizing, and demeaning to God's creation. At times, they may create tension between what we want to be for God and others, and what we crave for ourselves.

How do we overcome? By turning to God for His help by first repenting of sin and receiving His forgiveness. He enables us to live victoriously over sin that dominates the human heart. To His followers He says, "For you were bought at a price; therefore glorify God in your body and in your spirit, which are God's" (1 Corinthians 6:20).

He paid the penalty for our sin so that we can live righteously and bring glory to Him.

DISCERNING DOCTRINES

Test all things; hold fast what is good.
1 THESSALONIANS 5:21

Through Bible study and prayer, we are given discernment to tell the difference between what is of God and what is not. God's people are instructed to test the various doctrines that abound, and test them against the standard of the Word of God. This should drive us to daily Bible reading.

People sit in church week after week listening to sermons. Many slap the preacher on the back and say, "Your talk was wonderful this morning." But how many pause to think about what was really said, and did the teacher back it up from the Word of God? A trustworthy authority figure welcomes honest questions and will answer them frankly. A true person of faith is willing to be corrected by the Word of God. Those who speak against the authority of Scripture are not interested in questions; they only want loyalty and power over other people's lives.

Jesus warned, "Take heed that no one deceives you" (Matthew 24:4). Now who is behind this deception? It is none other than Satan himself. His method is to imitate God, often disguising himself as a minister of righteousness. Thousands of uninstructed Christians are being deceived today. False teachers that seem like the epitome of scholarship and culture are actually clever and crafty, adept at beguiling thoughtless people.

We must read the Bible for ourselves and seek God.

Tapping into God's Power

I have the desire to do what is good, but I cannot carry it out.
ROMANS 7:18 NIV

M any Christians know they should be better people, and they struggle with all their might to change their behavior. But most of their attempts at self-improvement fail, and they end up frustrated and discouraged. They can echo the words of the apostle Paul when he said that he desired to do good but often failed.

Why is this? The problem is that we rely on our own strength instead of the strength that comes from God's power. We not only need to know how God wants us to live; we also need the power to achieve it. God gives us this power through the work of His Holy Spirit within us. He is our constant, unchanging companion; He is our Guide. This is His promise: "He will guide you into all truth" (John 16:13).

Possessing God's Spirit within us isn't a once-for-all event but a continuous reality every day of our lives. But we must tap into His truth—the Word of God—asking Him to lead and guide our every step, our every thought, and our every action.

As we yield our lives to His lordship and give each day to Him through reading and believing His Word, and through prayer, we can look back each night and thank Him for fulfilling His promises to us.

STILL SMALL VOICE

Right behind you a voice will say, "This is the way you should go."
ISAIAH 30:21 NLT

T he Bible is God's textbook of revelation and speaks of having a pure conscience (1 Timothy 3:9). This is only possible when our minds are surrendered to the Lord and when we put into practice His commands and promises.

In God's great classroom there is an expansive library called Scripture. It speaks of nature and conscience and says God's law is "written in their hearts, their conscience also bearing witness, and between themselves their thoughts accusing or else excusing them" (Romans 2:15). It is so wonderful to think that God actually speaks to warn us when we are wrong and to bless us when we do right. This may be a "still small voice" that will not let us go until we settle in our hearts what is right according to Him. We must never silence that inner voice but always check what we believe according to God's Word.

Conscience is the detective that watches the direction of our steps and decries every conscious transgression. It is a vigilant eye before which each imagination, thought, and act is held up for either censure or approval. There is no greater proof of the existence of moral law and the Lawgiver in the universe than this little light of the soul.

We must remember that the human conscience is reliable only when it is guided by the Holy Spirit.

Meekness

"Blessed are the meek, for they shall inherit the earth."
MATTHEW 5:5

Eric Liddell, a missionary to China and an Olympic runner, was competitive and determined to use his abilities to the fullest. But his meekness, kindness, and gentle spirit won admiration even from people he defeated. He was described as "ridiculously humble in victory" and "utterly generous in defeat." That's a good definition of what it means to be meek.

The world has been successful in convincing society that meekness is a weakness. This is not true at all. Meekness involves being yielded. The word *yield* has two meanings. It can mean to let go (be passive) or surrender for something greater. Eric Liddell let go of pride whenever he won a race, and he also gave honor and respect to anyone who beat him in a race. He was gracious.

Jesus expressed this idea when He said, "He who loses [or surrenders] his life . . . will find it" (Matthew 10:39). When we surrender our will to the will of Jesus, it means that we let go of what we want and give ourselves to God to do whatever He wants for us. He blesses this obedience in ways that cannot be imagined, though it may not be what we anticipate. "He who believes in Him will not be disappointed" (1 Peter 2:6 NASB 1995).

Pride comes from looking only at ourselves; meekness comes through looking at God.

Jesus' Purpose

The message of the cross is foolishness to those who are perishing.
1 CORINTHIANS 1:18

A reading of the Gospels will reveal that Jesus did not impose Himself upon those who felt self-sufficient, righteous, and self-confident. People must come to the point of realizing their need for God's forgiveness and salvation. Those who feel capable of meeting life head-on and under their own power will never find Him.

While the Bible declares that people cannot earn salvation, there is a critical step that everyone must take in receiving Christ. "If we confess our sins, He is faithful and just to forgive us our sins and to cleanse us from all unrighteousness" (1 John 1:9). There must be a recognition and confession of sinfulness and spiritual need before there can be a response from Christ. He came to call not the righteous but sinners to repentance.

The natural man cannot comprehend the things of God, so how can people understand what happened at the cross when Jesus took our sins upon Him? It is only when we understand that Christ died in the place of sinners, for sin, that we find the elements of forgiveness. Jesus was born with the cross darkening His pathway. From the cradle to the cross, Jesus' purpose was to die so that mankind may live.

Jesus stepped out of glory and picked up His cross for us. Follow Him; He will never lead anyone astray.

THE HIGHEST PLANE

He is your example, and you must follow in his steps.
1 PETER 2:21 NLT

Did you know that the word *Christian* actually means "a partisan for Christ"? In our political culture the word *partisan* is a word that is understandable. It means to take sides. It means we are committed to something or someone. Partisans are not neutral. So this is a wonderful way to describe who and what a Christian is.

Many people have the wrong idea about this. They say, "A Christian is a person who prays" or "A Christian lives by the golden rule." But praying or living by the golden rule doesn't make someone a Christian. A person may be sincere, but that doesn't make him or her a Christian.

Being a Christian is serious business! It means to obey the gospel and accept Christ as personal Savior. It means to deny worldly pleasures and seek to please God in all things. It means to follow Jesus faithfully and joyfully. When Christians falter—and we do—we confess our sin to the Lord and ask Him to strengthen us.

We can never live the Christian life on the highest plane unless we are continually growing and moving forward. We should grow closer to God day by day as we strive to live as a shining light in a godless society and stand up for that which is right, just, and honorable.

NOVEMBER

GOD'S HOLY PERFECTION

His work is perfect; for all His ways are justice.
DEUTERONOMY 32:4

Jesus told the Samaritan woman at the well that "God is Spirit" (John 4:24). God isn't made of atoms or molecules. He exists in a wholly different realm. He isn't limited in any way. We should not try to confine Him to one place, or paint an imaginary picture of Him, or restrict Him to one way of doing things. We cannot put limits on His power.

God also is a Person. A person acts—and so does God. He feels, thinks, sympathizes, forgives, decides, acts, judges, and loves. God is not an impersonal force or power; He is a Person—the most perfect Person imaginable. There is, of course, a vast difference between God's personality and ours: He is perfect, but we are not. Emotions like anger, selfishness, hatred, jealousy, and pride overwhelm us. Our personalities may even become sick or self-destructive. But God isn't this way. He alone is perfect. Even His anger is righteous, because it is directed solely against evil.

God is also holy, righteous, and pure. We are weak and imperfect, and we can scarcely grasp the overwhelming perfection and holiness of God. We've become so used to sin that we can't imagine anyone being absolutely perfect. But God is! The Bible says, "God is light and in Him is no darkness at all" (1 John 1:5). Because God is holy, He never does wrong—ever.

THE ABUNDANT LOVE OF GOD

We love Him because He first loved us.

1 JOHN 4:19

God didn't make Adam and Eve because He was lonely or because He needed someone to love Him. His love far exceeds human love. We need to be loved and to have others to love, but this isn't true with God's love. God is complete in Himself, lacking nothing. His love is so abundant and so full of grace that He chose to express it to His creation by giving Himself.

Just as an artist has a compelling urge to create a beautiful painting, or a skilled woodworker has a compelling urge to create a fine piece of furniture, these are reflections of God's love, and He exemplified it by creating humanity in His image so that we would have the ability to love each other and especially Him. God is love, and now this wondrous characteristic of His personality has been bestowed on the human race.

God's love did not begin when He came to Earth as a Babe in the manger. His love began in eternity before the world was established, before the time clock of civilization began to move. No one can grasp the love of God without knowing His Son, Jesus Christ. "The Son of Man has come to seek and to save that which was lost" (Luke 19:10). If we truly love Jesus, we will want to please and honor Him by the way we live.

TRUE HAPPINESS

Delight yourself also in the LORD, And He shall give you the desires of your heart.
PSALM 37:4

Thomas Jefferson wrote about "the pursuit of happiness." But while Jefferson was correct that we should have a "right" to pursue happiness, a problem is created when people pursue it without knowing exactly what they are looking for or where to find it.

Happiness is a by-product, not an end in itself. Happiness cannot be pursued any more than one can pursue a cloudless day, grasp it, put it in a bottle, and then bring it out on a rainy day to enjoy again. True happiness is not superficial and fleeting, as a day at an amusement park might be.

True happiness begins when one is in a right relationship with God. In fact, God is the only source of true happiness, because He offers those intangibles that we mistakenly believe can be found on earth: contentment, security, peace, and hope for the future. None of these can be found in a job, a human relationship, money, power, or position. They are God's alone to give. That is why the Lord Jesus, in His Sermon on the Mount, told where ultimate happiness lies when He said, "Blessed are those who hunger and thirst for righteousness, for they shall be filled" (Matthew 5:6).

Happy is the person who has learned the secret of being content with whatever life brings and has learned to rejoice in the simple and beautiful things that come from the hand of God.

SALVATION STORIES

Salvation is found in no one else.

ACTS 4:12 NIV

People come to Christ in many different ways. Some conversions are sudden and dramatic. Some people are convicted of sin in church or at an evangelistic meeting in a basketball arena. Others find Christ through a television program where the gospel is clearly presented. Still others repent of sin at their bedside after reading the Scriptures. God speaks to the sinner's heart no matter where we are. But there is only one way to salvation, and that is through the Lord Jesus Christ (John 14:6).

Paul, before he became an apostle, approached the city of Damascus on a mission to arrest followers of Jesus, when a brilliant light suddenly blinded him. Later he recounted that he fell to the ground and heard Jesus say: "Why are you persecuting Me?'" (Acts 22:7). From that moment on, Paul began serving the One he had once rejected, and God used him to spread the gospel throughout the Roman Empire.

The important thing is not how we come to Christ but that we do come, and that we are sure we are now trusting Christ for our salvation. We must humble ourselves in repentance of sin and receive the forgiveness that Christ Himself offers. Don't let another moment go by without making that decision. Nowhere in the Bible are we promised a second chance after death, nor are we promised even one more day of life.

GROWING IN MATURITY

We are to grow up in every way into him who is the head, into Christ.
EPHESIANS 4:15 ESV

On a human level we know maturity isn't just a matter of age. We've all met people who were adults in terms of years yet acted like children. They are immature no matter their age.

A mature person isn't just physically mature but has grown up emotionally and socially. They've learned to be responsible and to realize that their actions have consequences. In a similar way, spiritual maturity isn't just a question of how long we have been a Christian. Sadly, far too many Christians never grow and develop in their faith. They are in spiritual limbo. They are like the Christians to whom Paul spoke: "I . . . could not address you as spiritual people, but as . . . infants in Christ" (1 Corinthians 3:1 ESV).

It is tragic when a child fails to develop into a capable, mature adult. Many times it's because the adults in their lives have set the bar low.

Even more tragic is a Christian who fails to develop spiritually. We weren't meant to remain spiritual babies. Instead, God's goal for us is spiritual maturity (Hebrews 6:1). The Bible also urges, "Like newborn babies, crave pure spiritual milk, so that by it you may grow up in your salvation" (1 Peter 2:2 NIV). The goal of a child's life is maturity—and the goal of a Christian's life is spiritual maturity.

A Beautiful Exchange

Put on your new nature.
COLOSSIANS 3:10 NLT

We shouldn't make the mistake of thinking that the Christian life is negative in a way that suggests we must give up everything we enjoy. While the Bible tells us what we shouldn't do, as in the Ten Commandments (Exodus 20), in order to live life to the fullest and in obedience to God, the Bible also tells us what to do, as in the beautiful message Jesus preached known as the Beatitudes (Matthew 5).

The same Jesus that said, "Go and sin no more" (John 8:11) is the same Jesus that said to His followers: I want you to be full of joy (John 15:11). God wants to give us that same quality of life.

When God takes away a sinful habit, He replaces it with a better way of living. When He takes away gossip or cursing, He replaces it with words of love and encouragement. God doesn't just want to remove the bad things in our lives; He wants to replace them with His goodness, to remake us from within.

Those who imagine that the Christian life is negative and cheerless and dull, they are gravely mistaken. God never removes something from our lives without replacing it with something far better.

Obey Him and heed what the Bible says: "Do not be conformed to this world, but be transformed by the renewing of your mind" (Romans 12:2). This is what gives us the strength to live a joyful life.

THREE CALLS

"Whoever is of God hears the words of God."
JOHN 8:47 ESV

God is a personal God. He is not lofty nor hard to find. His Word tells us that He calls out to sinners—that is anyone ever born.

God makes three calls. First, He calls us to the person of Jesus Christ: "'Come now, and let us reason together,' says the LORD, 'Though your sins are like scarlet, they shall be as white as snow'" (Isaiah 1:18). They can be made as white as snow because of the cross where He died to cleanse us and save us for eternity.

God also calls us to consecration. It means to "set apart." The Bible says, "Present your bodies a living sacrifice, holy, acceptable to God" (Romans 12:1).

God calls us to serve Him. Many people have the wrong concept of what this means. Put simply, it means to acknowledge Him and obey Him according to His Word.

If you are a dentist or a lawyer or a stay-at-home mother, get to know the Word of God and apply it daily to every phase of your life. Do not wait for a wind to come along and blow you in any direction. Make it your purpose in life to do the will of God, which is revealed in Scripture. It will change your life in remarkable ways that you cannot imagine. Surrender everything to Him because He has a plan for you.

Growing Our Faith

Faith comes from hearing, that is, hearing the Good News about Christ.
ROMANS 10:17 NLT

Faith grows when it is planted in the fertile soil of God's Word. Not only must we be saved by faith in God, but we must also live by faith, because we need God's grace and help at every turn. "We walk by faith, not by sight" (2 Corinthians 5:7).

God wants our faith to grow stronger, and He has given us the resources to achieve this. They are like tools in the hands of a skilled woodworker.

The first tool God has given us to strengthen our faith is the Bible. It is so essential that lasting spiritual maturity is impossible without it. If our faith isn't rooted in the Bible, it will wither like a plant pulled out of the soil. Only a strong faith—a faith based on God's Word—will protect us from temptation and doubt. Otherwise we will find ourselves "tossed back and forth by the waves, and blown here and there by every wind of teaching and by the cunning and craftiness of people in their deceitful scheming" (Ephesians 4:14 NIV).

For our faith to grow we need to let the Bible saturate our minds and souls. For centuries ordinary believers had no access to the Bible. Today it's readily available in hundreds of languages, yet most Bibles remain unopened. We must not let this be true if we are to grow our faith.

COMMUNING WITH GOD

In [Jesus] we have boldness and access with confidence through faith in Him.
EPHESIANS 3:12

For many people prayer isn't a joy but a burden. When they fail to pray, they feel guilty; when they do pray, they worry that they might not be doing it correctly. Or disruptions steal the time away. Or their prayers are wooden and lifeless. But prayer shouldn't be a burden but a privilege—a privilege God has graciously given us because He enjoys fellowship with His saints. Jesus Christ died to destroy the barrier of sin that separates us from God, and when we give our lives to Him, we have a personal relationship with almighty God.

But central to any relationship is communication. It's true on a human level; what kind of relationship do two people have who never talk with each other? In a far greater way, our relationship with God involves communication—not just an occasional brief chat but a deep sharing of ourselves and our concerns with God.

Prayer is simply talking to God, and God speaks with us through His Word. Both are essential—and both are gifts God has given us so we can know Him. Prayer is a gift from God's hand just as much as the Bible. Time for prayer should be paramount in our daily lives.

TEMPTATIONS AND GRAY AREAS

Search me, O God, and know my heart.

PSALM 139:23

People often react with the explanation: "I can't believe I said (or did) that. I didn't even realize what I was doing until it was too late." Satan had deceived them into thinking something wasn't really a sin.

Some claim there is no such thing as right and wrong. But God says otherwise. Giving in to temptation means to do wrong in the eyes of God.

Every day we are battered by messages from the media, advertising, entertainment, celebrities, even our friends, with one underlying theme: "Live for yourself." The world hammers away at us, trying to shape us into its mold. But God tells us not to conform to the pattern of this world (Romans 12:2).

When we belong to God, He alerts us when temptation comes knocking. We must be aware not only of obvious temptations but of the subtle ones—temptations of the tongue or emotions or thoughts or motives.

There are times we face "gray areas," things that aren't necessarily forbidden by the Bible but still may not belong in our lives. When conflicted, we can ask these questions: Does this glorify God? Does it draw me closer to Christ, or does it make me preoccupied with this world? Will it harm my health or hurt me in some other way? Will it cause hurt to someone else? Wise Christians are guided by this thought: when in doubt—don't.

HIDDEN MOTIVES

Stop trusting in mere humans.
ISAIAH 2:22 NIV

Once there was a woman who seemed to be a perfect example of Christian character: active in her church, respected in her community, above reproach in her personal life, always available to lend a helping hand to others. But when she received the news that she had only a few months to live, she became a totally different person. She quit her job, dropped her old friends, and turned her back on church, saying that she had been good long enough. She spent her last days catching up on all the fun she had missed. She found a new set of friends with no sense of morality and hung out with them at bars and nightclubs. Until the day she died, she scorned everything she had practiced most of her life. Her only appearance in church during those last months was on the day of her funeral, in her coffin.

How could someone who was apparently so upstanding and honorable suddenly throw it all overboard? Only God knows whether her professed faith in Him was genuine, or if it was only to impress others.

We must never set ourselves up as anyone's final judge. But one thing is clear: her faith had not changed her on the inside. The lesson is that we should not put trust in mere humans. They are as frail as breath. We must keep our eyes on the One who never disappoints.

THE KEY TO HAPPINESS

Having food and clothing, with these we shall be content.
1 TIMOTHY 6:8

A French philosopher once said, "The whole world is on a mad quest for security and happiness." A former president of Harvard University observed, "The world is searching for a creed to believe and a song to sing." A Texas millionaire confided, "I thought money could buy happiness—I have been miserably disillusioned." A famous film star broke down: "I have money, beauty, glamour, and popularity. I should be the happiest woman in the world, but I am miserable. Why?" One of Britain's top social leaders said, "I have lost all desire to live, yet I have everything to live for. What is the matter?"

The poet Amy Wilson Carmichael wrote:

The lonely, dreary road he trod. "Enter into My joy," said God.
The sad ascetic shook his head. "I've lost all taste for joy," he said.

It is the presence of sin that prevents people from being truly happy. People are told that to be happy all they have to do is think "happy thoughts." Such thoughts might cheer us momentarily, but they will never change us.

Jesus said, "[Happy] are the meek, for they shall inherit the earth" (Matthew 5:5). If we want the secret of happiness, meekness (humbleness) is a basic key. Happy is the person who has learned the secret of being content with whatever life brings and has learned to rejoice in the simple things.

SEEKING GOD'S WAY

To them [His saints] God willed to make known what are the riches of the glory
of this mystery among the Gentiles: which is Christ in you, the hope of glory.
COLOSSIANS 1:27

When your soul is saved, it is of utmost importance that you have a desire to be nourished from God's Word. Bring everything in your life to God in prayer and watch how He answers through the reading of Scripture. This is how God's children have fellowship with the Father and His Son Jesus Christ.

Be faithful in reading the Bible, praying for God's guidance and strength each day, seeking the fellowship of other believers as part of Christ's church, and share your faith with those who are still wandering in darkness. The church is the Body of Christ on earth, and it is important to join with other followers of Jesus Christ to learn from one another, to encourage one another, and to obey God's Word. You'll find yourself growing. Christ will work in you and through you and you will know His hand is upon you as He leads you along life's pathway.

Many struggle because they want Christ to walk with them; but believers are instructed to leave their own pathways and walk with Christ. He comes into a person's life with transformation, making forgiven sinners new creations in Christ. God will be busy conforming His children to the image of His Son. Salvation is the most important step anyone can take in life and is the only way to truth.

INNER PEACE

May the Lord of peace Himself give you peace always.
2 THESSALONIANS 3:16

Many people believe that if they follow Christ, their lives will be free of problems. After all, they say, didn't Jesus promise peace? Won't God take away our troubles and give us health and prosperity? The Bible, however, doesn't promise this. Yes, it promises peace, but it also promises tribulation. On the surface, this sounds like a paradox; after all, how can we be at peace and also be at war at the same time?

When warring nations sign a peace treaty, the fighting between them stops—and this is what has happened between God and us. At one time, we were at war with God, but now "we have peace with God through our Lord Jesus Christ" (Romans 5:1). The peace that Jesus spoke of tells of an inner peace. This is different from a problem-free life. Jesus said, "Peace I leave with you, My peace I give to you" (John 14:27), and He also said, "In the world you will have tribulation" (John 16:33). But in the midst of trouble, He is there with us. We do have peace when we follow Christ—an inner peace that comes from a deep and abiding trust in His promises.

The wars that once raged in our hearts have ended. This peace is real. It is an inner peace that keeps us calm even in the midst of life's worst storms.

GATHERING STORM

In the last days perilous times will come.
2 TIMOTHY 3:1

N o other book in the world utters such accurate prophecy as the Bible. The Word of God has predicted such a time as what the world is experiencing today. Neither Plato, nor Aristotle, nor Cicero, nor Plutarch, nor any of the ancients tells us of such a day as this, in which we see a tumult and upheaval of world conditions.

Jesus predicted in Matthew 24 and Luke 21 such days as these. He warned that there would be wars and rumors of wars. Then He spoke peace: "See that you are not troubled; for all these things must come to pass. . . . For nation will rise against nation, and kingdom against kingdom. And there will be famines, pestilences, and earthquakes in various places" (Matthew 24:6–7). For those who believe and follow Jesus, we are given a great hope, but also a warning, for Jesus also said that in these last days, iniquity will abound, and the love of many will grow cold.

A moving of the Spirit of God that would usher in true spiritual awakening must take place if we are to be spared the storm that is gathering on the horizon. For those who do not know Christ as personal Savior, God calls all people to repentance and obedience, for He stands ready to hear the prayers of those who will turn from sin and receive Him as Lord.

Two Become One

Those who obey God's word truly show how completely they love him.

1 JOHN 2:5 NLT

Two hearts give themselves to each other to be no longer two but one. A union takes place that makes the belonging of one the belonging of the other. Instead of being separated, the interests and paths of a man and woman are brought together. Love gives all and must have all in return. The wishes of the other party become binding obligations, and the deepest desire of each heart is to be fulfilled.

As a bridegroom rejoices over his bride, so God rejoices over His people. He has given us all and asks all in return. We should be so thankful for His salvation and abiding love that we are eager to throw ourselves unreservedly into His arms and hand over the reins to Him.

Because God knew that mankind was incapable of obeying His law, His love promised a Redeemer who would save His people from their sins. When we become His, our hands will not want to touch that which His hands cannot touch. Our eyes will not look where His eyes cannot look. Our love for Him makes necessary a separation from the world of which a less love could not conceive. This is the kind of love that we should desire toward Him, and He gives us the power of His Holy Spirit to help us be faithful to Him.

Our Inheritance

The earth is full of the goodness of the LORD.
PSALM 33:5

Imagine having a wealthy relative, and one day an attorney advises that he has died and left you $1 million that has been deposited in your name. You are told you can draw it out at any time. What would you do? Would you say, "Well, this cannot be true; I'll just forget about the call"? No, you would act on it, accepting by faith that what the attorney had told you was true; you were now a millionaire.

In a much greater way, God is rich in mercy and grace toward us and offers us the gift of salvation paid for with His blood, shed to cover our sins. He has done everything to provide for our eternal life, but we must receive it through repentance of sin and our faith in Him to save us.

He holds in His hand the gift of salvation, and He bids us to take it without money and without price, for He has paid it all.

God's generosity does not end there. He wants us to draw upon His riches every day—the riches of His wisdom, strength, truth, power, and presence. He offers us abundant life and He stands waiting for us to reach out our hands to Him.

Those who accept this gift do not owe God in payment for salvation, but we do owe God a life of undivided devotion and service.

O DEATH, WHERE IS YOUR STING?

Nothing can ever separate us from God's love.

ROMANS 8:38 NLT

With rapid changes in technology, communication, and lifestyles, the world created its breathless race into the future, and things such as funerals have changed. Over a period of time, people began to exclude children from deathbed scenes or even from viewing the dead. Death became a private affair. With this came the rejection of the grieving process, and communities felt less involved in the death of its members.

Geoffrey Gorer, an Englishman, began a study of this change in attitudes toward death and mourning as a result of a series of personal experiences. He lost his father on the *Lusitania* in 1915, so he was never able to see his body. It was 1931 before he first viewed a dead body and could experience and observe the conventions of mourning. However, in the late 1940s he experienced the deaths of two close friends, was struck by the rejection of traditional ways of mourning, and wrote about how death had become shameful to many in society.

For believers in Jesus Christ, death is the doorway to eternity with Him and therefore gives hope for what lies ahead after we finish our earthly journey. It's been said that death is not a period but a comma in the story of life. For the Christian, death can be faced with victory, because nothing can separate us from the love of God.

CLARITY IN THE WORD

There is no one on earth who is righteous.
ECCLESIASTES 7:20 NIV

The world is made up of sinners. The Bible isn't an idealistic fairy tale but rather a record of God's dealing with individuals from the beginning of time. There's nothing that indicates the truth of the Scriptures more than the factual record of mankind and its failures and sin against God.

One of the greatest men in the Bible is King David. Yet the Bible tells us he was guilty of adultery and murder. It also documents his repentance and turning back to God. All of these records are for our warning and instruction. They show us how sinful man needs God and His redemptive work in Christ. They tell us of many who accepted Him and were transformed. There's one thing about the stories in the Bible where sinful acts are mentioned: They do not glorify sin, nor do they make people want to go out and copy them. The Bible always shows sin for what it really is, an offense against God and something to be repented of and turned from. By the help of God's Spirit, He opens the minds and hearts of readers, giving clarity to mankind.

The Bible should be approached with the assurance that this is God-breathed literature and God has given us this enormous privilege of hearing His words that are filled with forgiveness and love.

THE RETURN OF CHRIST

"My kingdom is not of this world."

JOHN 18:36

We look for Jesus' return because He said many times that He would come again in glory. Jesus made it clear to His followers that He would send His Holy Spirit to remain with us and abide in us. Christ is with us today through His Holy Spirit, and He will be with His followers to the end of the age.

When He ascended into Heaven, two angels standing near told the disciples that Christ would return again as they were now seeing Him go (Acts 1:11). This climactic event of history is yet in the future. It will be sudden and final, the culmination of the ages. It will take the unbelieving world by surprise, and people will try to hide from His holy presence. At the return of Christ, the resurrection of believers will take place. They will be gathered together to be with the Lord forever. The Bible says all people must face Him at that time as either Savior or Judge. He is coming again and there is still time to trust in Him as Savior.

But in the meantime, for those who follow Him faithfully, He will be with us until the end of this world, and then eternity will begin. How wonderful to know that life on Earth is not all there is, but we must prepare to meet God! Be ready.

A Pattern to Follow

No good thing will He withhold from those who walk uprightly.
PSALM 84:11

Those who have traveled life's journey have come to understand that no husband or wife will be perfect. Every married couple will probably acknowledge this, but it is true that someone who is selfish will bring that into a marriage, and it can take a lifetime to rid oneself of this sinful way of life, apart from the salvation found in the Lord Jesus Christ.

One of the great truths of the Bible is that God loves us and has given us a pattern to follow. Because God loves us, He wants to give us what is best for us. God is pleased when we seek Him in everything.

Jesus posed this question: "What man is there among you who, if his son asks for bread, will give him a stone?" (Matthew 7:9). He goes on to teach that if a mere human father would give good things to his children, how much more will the Father in Heaven give good things to those who belong to Him and trust Him with their lives (v. 11)?

When people desire to honor the Lord in such important decisions, He provides wisdom to do what's right. Honor Christ first and above all, and life does fall into place. "In everything give thanks; for this is the will of God in Christ Jesus for you" (1 Thessalonians 5:18).

A DEBT WE CANNOT PAY

He was manifested to take away our sins, and in Him there is no sin.

1 JOHN 3:5

Suppose you owed someone a very large sum of money. What could you do? One possibility would be to pay them back. But what if you did not have the money and had no prospect of ever getting it? Then your only possibilities would be to undergo bankruptcy and suffer the loss of everything you had, or else go to the person and ask to have the debt forgiven. In human experience, that kind of forgiveness is very rare. But that is what God offers you—free and full forgiveness for your sins!

You see, you cannot "buy" God's favor, nor can you somehow do enough good deeds to balance your bad deeds. Why? Because God is holy, and even one sin is an offense to Him. The only hope is if God will forgive. But is that possible? Yes! It is possible because Jesus Christ took upon Himself the punishment you and I deserved for our sins.

We must not turn our backs on God's forgiveness any longer. Pray to the Lord and acknowledge and repent of sin and receive His forgiveness. Then turn from the old way of living. God helps us follow Him in obedience every day as we read His Word and depend on Him for guidance.

THE PRAYERS OF THE RIGHTEOUS

Devote yourselves to prayer, being watchful and thankful.
COLOSSIANS 4:2 NIV

The Bible says, "The prayer of a righteous person is powerful and effective" (James 5:16 NIV). It's important to notice the key word *righteous*. No human soul is perfect. Righteousness comes to those who repent of sin and let God turn their lives around. He points us in a new direction to help us walk according to His truth, and His Spirit helps us live according to His ways.

God doesn't always give us the answer we may want, but He always answers us for what is best because only He knows our future. Why would we not want to place our trust in the One who knows what is ahead? No matter what people may think they can do, they cannot predict the future or be certain of what is ahead in the next moment.

"Therefore, having been justified by faith, we have peace with God through our Lord Jesus Christ, through whom also we have access" (Romans 5:1–2). This doesn't mean that we can ask with selfish motives. We should seek God's will by reading His Word and depending on Him to lead and guide us to ask for the purpose of bringing glory to His great and mighty name.

One of the most effective ways to pray is to thank God for all His blessings and salvation and watch with expectation for how He begins to work.

SHINING THE LIGHT OF GOD'S LOVE

Our salvation is nearer than when we first believed. . . .
Let us . . . put on the armor of light.
ROMANS 13:11-12 NIV

J esus has not yet returned because God is not finished with this world! Someday Christ will come again to conquer evil and establish His perfect rule over all creation—but until then, "This gospel of the kingdom will be preached in all the world as a witness to all the nations, and then the end will come" (Matthew 24:14).

God wants to give everyone an opportunity to know Christ through repentance and faith in Him. The Bible says, "The Lord is not slow in keeping his promise, as some understand slowness. Instead he is patient with you, not wanting anyone to perish, but everyone to come to repentance" (2 Peter 3:9 NIV). At the same time, we are urged to anticipate Christ's return, because it is not the end of life for those who believe in Him. The last page of the last book of the Bible says, "Come, Lord Jesus!" (Revelation 22:20).

While only God knows when this will take place, we are told to be ready. Ready for what? For eternity.

We brush shoulders with darkened souls every day, so let us shine the light of God's love into the lives of those who may open their hearts to the one true God who is preparing eternity in Heaven for those who love Him.

ANSWERED PRAYERS

"Call upon Me . . . [and] I will deliver you, and you shall glorify Me."
PSALM 50:15

The Bible teaches that prayer is the privilege of those who have become the children of God (John 1:12). And of course He hears and answers the prayers of those who come to Him in repentance. God always answers prayer–not sometimes, but all the time. We may not always understand how God answers our prayers. At times He says "yes," while at other times He answers "no" or "wait."

But one of the greatest privileges of the child of God is the privilege of coming directly to God in prayer. "The prayer of a righteous person is powerful and effective" (James 5:16, NIV). This is possible because Jesus Christ has reconciled us to God through His death on the cross. We are separated from God, but Christ took away our sins, and when we come to Christ by faith, we are united with Him.

Our prayers must also be in accordance with the will of God for the simple reason that God knows better what is good for us than we know ourselves.

People often belittle prayer to God until they find themselves in trouble, but prayer opens the gates of eternity to sinners saved by grace.

TIMELESS TRUTH

The truth of the LORD endures forever.

PSALM 117:2

Truth matters. Just because truth is unpopular doesn't mean that it should not be proclaimed. The Bible is clear that Satan's purpose is to steal the seed of truth from people's hearts by sending distracting and deceptive thoughts. The difference between a Christian and a non-Christian is that though both may have good and evil thoughts, Christ gives His followers discernment and the power to choose the right rather than the wrong. The Holy Spirit takes God's word of truth and ministers to our deepest needs. And the person who discovers this truth has a serenity, peace, and certainty that others do not have (James 1:17–18).

Truth is timeless. The great all-prevailing truth stands for time and eternity. And we will see Him in all His glory when He comes again. His name is Faithful and True (Revelation 19:11), and He will reign from the City of Truth (Zechariah 8:3).

Here is an important lesson when we find ourselves among unbelievers: We must be a light for God's truth. We must pray that God will grant us favor with those who are watching our lives; that we will stand for the things of God without compromise, and perhaps the Lord will give us opportunities to demonstrate His power, love, and mercy to others.

ONE BODY, MANY PARTS

*Just as a body . . . has many parts, but all its many
parts form one body, so it is with Christ.*
1 CORINTHIANS 12:12 NIV

While much is said about Christian workers who are publicly visible, not much is said about the quiet works of the vast number of servants of God worldwide. We will have to get to Heaven before we will fully realize the army of prayer warriors that made others' work possible in Jesus' name. Just as the human body is made up of many parts, the church is the body of Christ; the work is never accomplished by the act of just one, unless it is Christ's alone.

Collectively the body of Christ operates in various ways—church volunteers help with parking, ushering, and teaching. Its members give financially, and, most important, everyone is instructed to pray for the lost souls that do not yet know the Lord as their Savior. All of these who have quietly and faithfully worked behind the scenes will be rewarded by the Lord Himself someday.

The people of God are to point others to the Savior by how they live, day in and day out. We are to be living examples who speak of Christ's virtues, instilling Christian character into the fabric of life so that when we are with others, no one can find fault in how we live. "For we are God's fellow workers; you are God's field, you are God's building" (1 Corinthians 3:9).

LIFE-GIVING WATER

O God . . . my soul thirsts for You.

PSALM 63:1

Everyone gets thirsty, and when that happens, what satisfies the most is a good cold glass of water. Our bodies are made up largely of water, and if we don't have enough water to drink, the cells and organs of our bodies can't do their jobs.

The first verse of Psalm 42 says, "As the deer pants for the water brooks, so pants my soul for You, O God." When deer are thirsty, they want water. Water is the only thing that will quench their thirst.

Just like our bodies need water, our souls need God. Even the best things in life can't be enough for us for very long. Only God can meet our deepest desires.

We must not let anything—or anyone—come between God and us. Just as our bodies need food and water, our spiritual lives need to feast on His Word—the water of life. Jesus Christ is the Source. He is the Bread of Life for our hungry souls. He is the Water of Life for our thirsty hearts.

Pray that the dew of Heaven may fall on Earth's dry, thirsty ground, and that God's righteousness may flood our souls as the waters cover the sea.

Jesus said that whoever will drink of the water that He gives will never thirst . . . that the water He gives will become in us "a fountain of water springing up into everlasting life" (John 4:14).

347

Spiritual Poverty

"Blessed are the poor in spirit, for theirs in the kingdom of heaven."
MATTHEW 5:3

When the apostle Paul went to Athens, Greece, he saw people who were like many in our world today: they were trying to put together the puzzle of life. The average Athenian of that day was a religious person who had numerous gods and followed numerous philosophies in their search for truth. One group of philosophers thought that happiness and pleasure were the goals of life. Another group, the Stoics, believed that the world was governed by reason or logic, and the goal of life was to accept whatever life sent to them. Some philosophers argued with Paul—others were searching for truth. We must not let anything—or anyone—keep us from Jesus, who alone is "the way, the truth, and the life" (John 14:6).

So what did Jesus mean by being "poor in spirit"—and how could it lead to blessing? Jesus was teaching that to be poor in spirit meant that we come to understand our spiritual poverty.

The soul requires as much attention as the body. It demands fellowship and communion with God. Unless the soul is fed and exercised daily, it becomes weak and shriveled. Spiritual emptiness comes before filling, and spiritual poverty before riches. Happiness comes from admitting our spiritual poverty and then asking Jesus to come into our lives, and we come to know what living the abundant life really means.

FLOURISHING LIFE

"They will be like a tree planted by the water that sends out its roots by the stream."

JEREMIAH 17:8 NIV

It is no accident that the Bible speaks of trees, even urging us to grow spiritual roots that are deep and strong. God placed the Tree of Life in the Garden of Eden in the beginning of time, but other trees grow from a small seed. Spiritual life also begins with a seed—the seed of God's Word planted in the soil of our souls that eventually sprouts and becomes a new seedling when we are born again.

We are not meant to remain spiritual seedlings, weak and vulnerable to every temptation, doubt, falsehood, or fear. God's will is for us to grow strong in our faith and become mature, grounded in the truth of His Word and firmly committed to doing His will (1 Peter 2:2).

When we give our life to Christ, we are taking the essential first step—but it is only the first step. God's will is for us to become spiritually mature, growing stronger in our relationship to Christ and our service for Him. Conversion is the work of an instant; spiritual maturity is the work of a lifetime.

Word studies from the Bible will teach us many things about ourselves, others, and most certainly the Lord Jesus. "He shall be like a tree planted by the rivers of water, that brings forth its fruit in its season" (Psalm 1:3).

DECEMBER

THE PRECIOUS HUMAN SOUL

"What will a man give in exchange for his soul?"
MARK 8:37

It was reported several years ago that it would take $100 billion to get one man safely to Mars. That is a staggering amount of money. It is interesting how people place great value on things and even experiences. But God in His outpouring of love for mankind placed the value of one human soul at an incalculable price— the blood of His only Son—in order to get just one soul to Heaven. Imagine: this priceless gift has not only saved one soul for eternity but a vast number that only God Himself knows. By tasting death for everyone, Jesus took over our penalty as He erased our guilt. This is God's amazing forgiveness and love toward mankind.

We humans cannot see or touch the soul, but God can and does because He created it.

Even as you read this you can submit your life to Christ Jesus by admitting your sin against Him and asking Him to forgive you and help you walk in a way that pleases Him. You can be filled with assurance that He is with you every step of the way and will grant you peace and eternal life. Don't delay. Exchange your sin for Christ's salvation. Receive Him today and He will begin to show you how to live a valuable life with purpose and thanksgiving.

THE INNER SPACE

Bless the LORD, O my soul.

PSALM 103:1

Inner space is defined in many ways, but when it comes to the inner life—something we all have—it deals with the dark side of the human spirit. From the vast number of questions on people's minds it is evident that a large proportion of the population is facing deep personal problems. They vary from person to person, but they do exist, and they are all problems of "inner space." Yes, we are the people who have been conquering outer space but are in danger of losing the battle of the spirit. Thankfully, there is a solution, and millions have already found it; that solution is in Jesus Christ. He said, in essence, "My peace, My liberty, My freedom, I give to you" (see John 14:27).

There are two natures within every person, both struggling for mastery. Which one will dominate us? It depends on which one we feed. There is a defect in human nature caused by sin, and it permeates our inner space until we give it up and let Christ come in.

Today, if we will turn on the searchlight of truth, it will reveal the dark side of our human spirits and help us recognize the need for Jesus Christ to become the Master of our lives. Submit the "inner space" of your life to Him, and you will come to know the inner peace of a loving God that will transform your life.

Our Friend, Jesus

*"Man shall not live by bread alone, but by every word
that proceeds from the mouth of God."*
MATTHEW 4:4

Jesus once told of a man who had been lonely and sick. For thirty-eight years the man had sat in the same spot, weary and tired, without a friend. This bundle of loneliness and human pain had been buffeted by the surging tides of thousands of people, but Jesus singled him out. He became the man's friend (John 5:1–9).

Jesus will become our friend if we will let Him.

The great hymns of the church bring great comfort because their lyrics are founded on the Word of God.

> *In times like these, you need a Savior / In times like these you need an anchor;*
> *Be very sure, be very sure / Your anchor holds and grips the solid rock!*
> *This Rock is Jesus, Yes He's the One; This Rock is Jesus, The only One!*
> *Be very sure, be very sure / Your anchor holds and grips the solid rock!*

Nothing else we cling to in this world will save our souls, only Jesus Christ. We must make Him Lord and Master of our lives and His Word will quicken our spirits and strengthen our faith in Him. Now is the day of salvation (2 Corinthians 6:2).

SPARKLING DIAMONDS

Live clean, innocent lives as children of God, shining like bright lights in a world full of crooked and perverse people.

PHILIPPIANS 2:15 NLT

When a jeweler places diamonds on dark velvet cloths, the dark background shows off the cut and sparkle of the stone.

Christians should stand out like sparking diamonds against a rough background. We should be wholesome, courteous, full of life and joy, but firm in the things we do or do not do. Jesus meant for His followers to be different from the world—refusing to allow the world to pull us down to its level.

The Christian has a great obligation to be ethical and gracious in all things, whether in victory or loss. The attributes of a Christian are noticed by how they respond.

But just being different is not enough. There's a purpose for who we are and how we live. We are to be the kindest, the most unselfish, the friendliest, and hardest working, the most thoughtful, the truest, and the most loving people on Earth.

Well, it might be said that all of that is impossible, but the Bible says that all things are possible with God (Mark 10:27). It takes God's power to develop these attributes in our lives, and we are to work toward this daily, keeping our eyes on Him and studying (through Scripture) His attributes that shine like the noonday sun in this dark world, and even in Heaven.

PERSONAL RESPONSIBILITY

He who covers his sins will not prosper, but whoever
confesses and forsakes them will have mercy.
PROVERBS 28:13 NKJV

Viktor Frankl, in his book *Man's Search for Meaning*, described the reactions of two brothers with the same heredity, the same environment, in the same concentration camp under the Nazis. One became a saint and the other a swine. Frankl tells us the reason why. He said, "Each man has within him the power to choose how he will react to any given situation." God has given us the power of choice. Some people today do not wish to accept the responsibility for their actions. They blame society. They blame circumstances. But Adam sinned in a perfect environment under perfect circumstances. We must accept the blame ourselves for our part.

The culture has developed a victim mentality that allows people to easily fall prey to casting blame on someone else or something else. We must get this fact firmly fixed in our minds: We live in an upside-down world. People hate when they should love, quarrel when they should be friendly, fight when they should be peaceful, wound when they should heal, steal when they should share, do wrong when they should do right.

While a good environment can be a positive influence, each person is responsible for what they ultimately believe. Each person has the freedom to look into God's Word and read it, and believe it, for themselves.

The Holy Spirit in Your Life

"For there are three that bear witness in heaven; the Father, the Word [Jesus], and the Holy Spirit; and these three are one."

1 JOHN 5:7

God the Father, Jesus Christ the Son, and the Holy Spirit make up what's known as the Trinity. This is at the heart of the Christian faith. The Holy Spirit isn't a thing, but God's Spirit.

The story's told of a young boy who asked his father, "How can I believe in the Holy Spirit when I've never seen Him?" His father, an electrician, took the boy to a power plant and showed him the generators. "This is where the power comes from to heat our stove and to give us light. We can't see the power, but it's in that machine and in the power lines." Then he asked his son, "Do you believe in electricity?"

When the boy answered yes, his father asked why. The boy answered right: Everyone believes in electricity because they see what it can do. Likewise, though we cannot see the Holy Spirit, believers in Christ know the results of His power in their lives. Surrendering our lives to the Lord Jesus opens up the power source.

When you yearn for God and desire His truth, that is the work of the Holy Spirit in your life. It is never a question of how much we have the Spirit, but how much He has of us.

New Life and Brotherhood

You are all one in Christ Jesus.
GALATIANS 3:28

There is a great deal of misunderstanding when it comes to the universal fatherhood of God and brotherhood. The majority of appeals made on behalf of peace are based on the idea of brotherhood. There is a wrong sense in which God is the Father of us all by creation. The truth is that He is our Creator. But the world seems to be blinded to the fact that for us to know God spiritually as Father, we must receive Christ as personal Lord and Savior and accept His forgiveness and His salvation. Only then are we brought into the family of God. His spiritual fatherhood belongs only to those who trust in Him.

Class warfare is another misunderstanding in society. The Bible says that there are only two classes of people: the saved and the lost; those who are going to Heaven and those who are going to Hell (Matthew 7:13–14).

Outside of Christ's work on the cross—His death and His resurrection from the grave—there is bitterness, intolerance, ill will, prejudice, lust, greed, and hatred. Within the efficacy of the cross of Christ Jesus, there is love and fellowship, new life and new brotherhood, no matter the race, nationality, or social standing.

There is no Jew, no Gentile. Those who belong to Christ are one great brotherhood in Him.

THE RESURRECTION AND THE LIFE

Arise from the dead, and Christ will give you light.

EPHESIANS 5:14

The great question of the ages has always been: "If a man dies, shall he live again?" The first part of that sentence is fulfilled every day. There is no "if" about it. "It is appointed for men to die once" (Hebrews 9:27). So the question remains: Shall man live again?

There are those who say that all there is to us is just bone, flesh, and blood. They say that when you are dead, when you die, nothing happens; you don't go anywhere.

Because many do not believe in life after death, their writings are filled with tragedy and pessimism. How different from Jesus Christ, who said, "I am the resurrection and the life. He who believes in Me, though he may die, he shall live" (John 11:25).

The Bible deals with the resurrection of Jesus as an event that could be examined by the physical senses. It involved the eyes, for the disciples saw the numerous appearances of Jesus under every conceivable condition. The resurrection involved the ears, for the disciples heard Jesus in conversation. It involved the touch, for the disciples were told to handle Jesus and to verify His physical reality. This is the basis of historical fact for our belief. Dust to dust, ashes to ashes for the physical body in death, yes, but when Christ says, "Arise," all of mankind will obey.

FICKLE FEELINGS

This is the promise that He has promised us—eternal life.
1 JOHN 2:25

It's amazing how quickly our feelings can change. One day we might be smiling because we were commended for a good deed. The next day we might be hurt because a friend said something unkind about us. Then before we know it, we're back to feeling on top of the world after we experienced something successful.

It's a good thing that when it comes to being saved, we don't rely on our up-and-down feelings. Only the facts matter—the fact that Jesus died for our sins and rose again, and the fact that if we have given our lives to Him, He has promised to forgive us and save us. The Bible says, "God has given us eternal life, and this life is in His Son. He who has the Son has life" (1 John 5:11–12).

God cannot lie. Our feelings will lie to us, and Satan might even use them to trick us into thinking God has left us all alone. But we must always remember what Jesus said about Satan: "There is no truth in him. . . . He is a liar and the father of [lies]" (John 8:44).

How wonderful it is to know that our faith is based on God's truth and not on our feelings. We need to stay close to Him, read His Word, and pray, asking Him to strengthen our faith.

God's Measure of Success

"This Book of the Law shall not depart from your mouth, but you shall meditate in it day and night. . . . Then you will have good success."

JOSHUA 1:8

Our world is obsessed with success. The world has its measures on what it means: financial success, athletic success, business success, professional success, social success, success in gaining popularity. The list is almost as endless as our search. Many people spend their lives pursuing at least one of these.

But how does God define success? His measure is very different from the world's measure, and it can be summed up in one sentence: success in God's eyes is faithfulness to His calling.

The apostle Paul was a failure in the world's eyes—but not to God. Even Jesus was a failure as far as most people were concerned, but He was faithful to the One who appointed Him—God the Father—and that is all that mattered.

May we refrain from comparing ourselves to others who experience success by worldly standards and rather pursue things that are successful according to God's Word. Even when the world mocks us or misunderstands us, may we seek to be faithful in all the small things and to walk humbly with God.

Time and the ravages of sin take their toll on noble achievements. Regardless of our cleverness, our intelligence, our ingenuity, and our achievements, we are spiritual paupers without God.

THE REAL YOU

Then the dust will return to the earth as it was, and
the spirit will return to God who gave it.
ECCLESIASTES 12:7

The human body is the house in which the soul resides temporarily. The soul is never completely satisfied and happy here, because it is not home yet. The true home of the soul is with Christ.

The Bible teaches that everyone has a soul (spirit) with certain attributes such as conscience, memory, intelligence, and consciousness. Your soul is the real you. One day our bodies will go to the grave, but our souls live on.

Jesus said our souls are more valuable than all the rest of the world put together. Why then do people spend so much time and energy pampering their bodies but ignore their souls? It only leads to spiritual starvation and malnourishment. God is calling out to all people to take care of their souls–the inner self–by receiving Him into their lives and feeding on the Word of God; letting His Spirit transform us from within.

Someday life will be over, no matter how much attention we give to our health. Will we look back with regret, because we nourished our bodies but starved our souls?

"Humbly accept the word God has planted in your hearts, for it has the power to save your souls" (James 1:21 NLT). This is true hope that only comes from the love of God.

GOD CARES ABOUT OUR FEELINGS

Our hearts ache, but we always have joy.
2 CORINTHIANS 6:10 NLT

The Bible tells us to be thankful to God in all things (1 Thessalonians 5:18). It is not that we thank God that loved ones have been taken from us, but that our loved ones who belong to Him are in Heaven where pain and death will never touch them again. Be thankful that God is with us in our own grief. God is still in control—even when we do not understand all that happens in this sin-scarred world.

It is important that we confess to God how we really feel. He already knows it, of course, but we need to be honest with Him and ourselves and face our own need of healing. We must always remember the pain that Jesus endured for us on the cross. He suffered unlike anyone in all of history. Christ was a man of sorrows and acquainted with grief (Isaiah 53:3). He knows about suffering, and He wants to help us in our own times of despair.

When we seize God's strength, we grow with a deeper sense of God's love, and we begin to feel His comfort. He came to "console those who mourn . . . to give them beauty for ashes, the oil of joy for mourning, the garment of praise" (Isaiah 61:2–3). When we know the Lord in a personal way, He will restore our joy and bring peace into our lives.

Persistent Prayer

[Continue] steadfastly in prayer.
ROMANS 12:12

The Bible says to persist in prayer and to pray about everything. God does not always answer the way we think He should, or when we think He should. (We should be grateful for this—He knows far better than we do what is best!) But the Bible tells us to always keep on praying. Jesus, in fact, told a parable about a persistent widow who constantly begged a judge to act on her case, which he eventually did (Luke 18:1–8). One reason Jesus told this parable was to encourage us to pray frequently.

Keep in mind two things. First, we cannot change God's mind about something that He has already answered. In other words, God will answer a prayer sometimes with a "no" rather than a "yes," and sometimes with a "wait." Are we willing to accept His will?

Second, there are times when we ourselves should take action as well as pray. Often we become the answer to our own prayers. Jesus told His disciples to ask Him to send workers into His harvest field, and in the very next verse we find that the disciples themselves went to the field to do God's work (Matthew 9:38, 10:1).

Prayer is one of the privileges of the child of God. God loves us and does not want us to be anxious about anything, but faithfully pray about everything with thanksgiving (Philippians 4:6).

TIME WITH GOD

"Abide in Me, and I in you."
JOHN 15:4

The first step to coming near to God is at the point of salvation. Those who enter into this relationship with Jesus Christ have been connected to the Source: "I am the vine, you are the branches. He who abides in Me, and I in him, bears much fruit; for without Me you can do nothing" (John 15:5). This is called "being in Christ."

When this happens, we also develop relationships with others who belong to the Lord. This helps us draw near to Him. The key to all of this, though, is spending time with God through the reading and studying of His Word and through prayer. This takes discipline, and God stands ready to empower us to do what we know we cannot do in our own strength or will. And when we do, we find strength for the journey, gaining wisdom each step of the way.

Every day has exactly 1,440 minutes. If we cannot find even ten minutes each day to spend with the One who has saved us from our past sin, we will never lead the kind of life God desires.

God deserves the best minutes of our day. Just as we set time aside to eat, or to work, or to enjoy a form of entertainment, we should first carve out time to commune with God and to meditate on His truth. This is the key to life.

THE RIGHTEOUS JUDGMENT OF GOD

"In that place there will be weeping and gnashing of teeth."
MATTHEW 13:50 ESV

Most people accept that Heaven is real, according to a Fox News poll. Many religious and nonreligious believe they will go there because God is a God of love.

Many of these same people, however, reject that Hell is real. Yet they reserve Hell as a very real place for people who have perpetrated some of the most hideous crimes in history. They are obviously judging that person's actions against their own merit. They believe they're good enough to pass judgment on another person, but they accuse God, who is holy, of condemning people to this foreboding place because they reject His Word.

"Please . . . write on anything but Hell!" This comes from bloggers who claim to be Christians. Responding to those who are sounding the warning about Hell, they write, "This makes Christians look like they serve a God filled with anger and wrath."

No matter how hard we try, we cannot escape the righteous judgment of God. But God, in His mercy and grace, wants to impart His righteousness through salvation to all people. Yet there are those who refuse such a gift and want to make light of Hell.

Herein lies the problem—we see ourselves as good and refuse to see that we, too, harbor wickedness within. Don't let Satan deceive you with his lies. Turn to God and live for Him.

THE NAMES OF GOD

I will . . . call upon the name of the LORD.

PSALM 116:13

Remember the story of the great exodus, when the Israelites fled Egypt? "Moses said to the people, 'Do not be afraid. Stand still, and see the salvation of the LORD, which He will accomplish for you today'" (Exodus 14:13). The Lord held back the water, and the people crossed the sea safely on dry ground. This miracle pointed to what would take place thousands of years later, when salvation's plan was fulfilled in the Land of Promise. When Jesus stretched out His arms on the cross, He secured salvation for all who receive Him.

Jesus is not only the Deliverer; He is the Provider. Just as God provided daily manna from Heaven to the children of Israel on their wilderness journey, so Jesus provides for the soul-hunger of people today. "I am the living bread which came down from heaven. If anyone eats of this bread, he will live forever" (John 6:51).

It is wonderful to learn the names of God, who calls Himself "I Am." "I am the light of the world. He who follows Me shall not walk in darkness, but have the light of life" (John 8:12). "I am the door. If anyone enters by Me, he will be saved" (John 10:9). "I am the good shepherd" (John 10:11).

Why would anyone resist the opportunity to be fed by God the Deliverer, the Sustainer, the Provider, and the Protector?

Heaven in View

The hope of the righteous will be gladness.
PROVERBS 10:28

Those who keep Heaven in view experience joy, even in the midst of trouble. Happiness can be fleeting, but joy runs deep; it is one of the fruits of the Spirit. The ability to rejoice in any situation is a sign of spiritual maturity.

But there is a sadness left behind for those still earthbound. How can we ever begin to know the rejoicing that takes place when a loved one is called into God's eternal presence? Someday, all who believe in Christ and follow Him will rejoice together when the Lord brings all of us home in immortal bodies. The morning stars will sing together, and the angels will shout for glory.

The Bible says, "In Your presence is fullness of joy; at Your right hand are pleasures forevermore" (Psalm 16:11).

Think of having complete fulfillment, knowing that our homecoming brings unspeakable joy to our wonderful Lord! Only when we stand in the joyful presence of Jesus Christ will this be realized. So why do we prefer lingering here? Because we are not only earthbound in body; we are earthbound in our thinking. Our imagination is limited to the things of this Earth. But when we leave this place, we will never dwell on it again. Our eyes and hearts will be fixed on Christ.

THE GOD WHO ANSWERS BY FIRE

"Put away the foreign gods . . . from among you, and prepare
your hearts for the LORD, and serve Him only."

1 SAMUEL 7:3

Uniting in prayer to the gods of this world will avail nothing. A clear demonstration of this is the story in 1 Kings 18 of Elijah and the prophets of Baal.

Elijah said to the people, "How long will you falter between two opinions? If the LORD is God, follow Him; but if Baal, follow him" (v. 21).

Elijah challenged both groups to prepare sacrifices and pray. "The God who answers by fire, He is God" (v. 24).

The people prayed from morning until evening, "O Baal, hear us!" (v. 26). But there was no answer. Then Elijah prayed, "'Let it be known this day that You are God. . . .' Then the fire of the LORD fell and consumed the burnt sacrifice" (vv. 36, 38).

The gods of this world will not answer prayer offered in their names because the gods are made by human hands. They cannot see, touch, hear, speak, comfort, deliver, or save. Pray in the mighty name of God. He hears. He answers. He saves.

There are many religions in the world, and they have developed because various people have had various ideas about God. Christianity makes a unique claim: we can know God because He came to us in human form in the person of His Son, Jesus Christ. That is why we proclaim His name unashamedly when we call on Him.

Before the World Began

He loved us and sent his Son as a sacrifice to take away our sins.
1 JOHN 4:10 NLT

God's love did not begin at creation, at the manger, or at the cross; God's love began in eternity past. Before the world was established, before the time clock of civilization began to move, God's love prevailed.

But not until the good news of Jesus Christ burst onto the human scene was the word *love* understood on Earth with such depth, as God coming down to us in human form, an expression of unmerited love.

Years ago, a pop duo sang a song that insisted they wouldn't live in "a world without love." Yet love came down from Heaven to the whole world, and the world rejected Him. It was God's love that knew mankind was incapable of obeying His law and loving Him. So in love He promised a Redeemer who would give true love away.

There is one thing that God's love cannot do: it cannot forgive the unrepentant sinner. For this reason, God sends things into our lives to block the route to destruction, with holy desire to drive us back to His love. The love of God that reaches us can be entirely rejected. We can also choose to accept God's love and receive His forgiveness. No one can do this for us. It is a decision for every individual soul. We can love Him because He first loved us (1 John 4:19).

TIME ALONE WITH THE FATHER

He Himself often withdrew into the wilderness and prayed.

LUKE 5:16

Imagine being part of a family and never spending time with them. Or having a close friend but never seeing or talking with them. Without fuel, a fire grows cold; and without the "fuel" of Bible reading and prayer, a Christian can grow cold. How can we walk with God if we cannot find time to listen to His words or pour our hearts out to Him?

Many people who say they love God don't want to spend time with Him. The question must be asked, "Why do we wait until the end of the day when we're tired and weary?" Do we consider the things throughout the day that just keep us "too busy" for God?

There's no set time to meet with God. The key is to begin the day with Him and end the day with Him, asking Him to be with us even in our minds as we sleep. Others find that setting special times aside helps discipline their time. Jesus rose early in the morning, long before daylight, departing to a solitary place to pray. If the Son of God needed time alone with His Father, how much more do we?

We must praise the Lord for the blessings of life. The wonders of life should drive us into His Word and into prayer that brings peace to our hearts.

WHY JESUS CAME

God . . . has highly exalted Him.
PHILIPPIANS 2:9

On that first Christmas night in Bethlehem, "God was manifested in the flesh" (1 Timothy 3:16). This manifestation was in the person of Jesus Christ coming in the form of a newborn Babe. The Scripture says concerning Christ, "In Him dwells all the fullness of the Godhead bodily" (Colossians 2:9).

This manifestation of God is by far the most complete revelation God ever gave to the world. If you want to know what God is like, take a long look at Jesus Christ. In Him were displayed not only the perfections that had been exhibited in the creation—such as wisdom, power, and majesty—but also such divine perfections as justice, mercy, grace, and love.

"The Word became flesh and dwelt among us, and we beheld His glory, the glory as of the only begotten of the Father, full of grace and truth" (John 1:14). To His disciples Jesus said, "You believe in God, believe also in Me" (John 14:1). This sequence of faith is inevitable. If we believe in what God made and what God said, we will believe in the One whom God sent.

We should not let the novelty of this holiday blind us from the truth of the Christmas story that will transform hearts and lives. The truth of the nativity that centers on why Jesus came to Earth—to save mankind—can be real in each heart.

PORTRAIT OF THE SON OF GOD

"I [God] will seek what was lost and bring back what was driven away."

EZEKIEL 34:16

Christmas is a time filled with anticipation and preparation. The thrill of wrapping and unwrapping gifts makes for a joyful time with loved ones. Even today, people who don't necessarily believe personally in Jesus as the Savior of the world send cards with pictures of what artists think Jesus may have looked like. There are images of the babe in the manger, shepherds, and animals. The world is fascinated with the grandeur of the greatest story ever told.

But it isn't just a story. It is truth. No matter how Jesus is imagined, He has no stronger portrait than the one in the Bible. It is a picture of the Man who is God. He is the foundation of Christianity. Since the quickest way to destroy any edifice is to tear out or weaken its base, people have always tried to disprove, ignore, or scoff at the claims of Christ. The hope of the world, however, is found only in the redemption from sin. This is dependent upon the deity of Christ.

While there are attacks on the celebration of Christmas in the twenty-first century, Christmas has been commercialized. The reality is that Jesus is truth and proclaims all people are sinners. This is why He came to seek and save those who are lost. This is the story of Christmas, and this is the portrait of the Son of God.

A Season to Give and Receive

"They shall call His name Immanuel," which is translated, "God with us."
MATTHEW 1:23

Christmas cards, the smell of pine drifting through the house, the fireplace crackling—all these things turn our thoughts to those we love. But often it is a sad time for those who are alone, without close friends or family. We all should look for others to reach out to, especially at this time of year, and extend a hand of fellowship, a heart of love. This is what Jesus did for all of us. He reached down from Heaven by giving Himself to us—a people in great need of a relationship with their God and Maker.

Christmas is the most thrilling season of the year because its message is that Jesus brings joy and love through His sacrificial gift of forgiveness and redemption. This, indeed, should be our focus. When we have people around us who need Christmas cheer, and we can't set aside time to invite them into our homes or around a table for a meal—we are too busy.

Christmas is about receiving and giving. Give the gift of the true Christmas story—that God gave His Son so that mankind would receive Him. Let's focus not on our own joys but making others joyful. The greatest gift we can give others is to tell them about the most wonderful Gift God has bestowed on the whole world.

VERY GOOD NEWS

[The wise men] saw the child with Mary his mother,
and they fell down and worshiped him.
MATTHEW 2:11 ESV

Christmas means something far deeper than human goodwill. There would be no goodwill at all if the birth of the Savior had not happened. Over two thousand years ago, on a night the world has come to call Christmas, a young Jewish maiden went through the experience countless mothers had before her and would since: she brought forth a Child. But this was no ordinary Child. This was the unique Son of God, sent from Heaven to save us from our sins.

Christmas should be a day when our minds go back to Bethlehem, beyond the noise of our materialistic world. We see the tenderness of a mother with her firstborn Son; and the angel said that His name is Jesus. The prophet Isaiah had announced this very good news centuries beforehand: "For unto us a Child is born. . . . His name will be called Wonderful, Counselor, Mighty God, Everlasting Father, Prince of Peace" (Isaiah 9:6). The angel announced, "Glory to God in the highest, and on earth peace, goodwill toward men!" (Luke 2:14).

This is the true definition of "goodwill." That Christ Jesus extended His goodwill toward us. We are not responsible for why others do "goodwill," but let's be faithful to announce this wonderful good news to all when we reach out to do the will of the One who exemplified it first.

THE REAL CHRISTMAS MESSAGE

I bring you good news that will cause great joy for all the people.
LUKE 2:10 NIV

In the midst of all upheaval, crisis, difficulty, problems, and fear comes the true message of Christmas with all its hope, goodwill, and cheer. The message of Christmas has been terribly misapplied and misunderstood for many years. Some think of business profits, shopping, gifts, tinsel, toys, and celebration. Others think only of Bethlehem, of the star in the sky, shepherds in the field, and angels singing.

The real Christmas message goes far deeper. It heralds the entrance of God into human history. It is Heaven descending to Earth. It is as though a trumpeter had taken his stand upon the turrets of time and announced to a despairing, hopeless, and frustrated world the coming of the Prince of Peace. It answers all the great questions that plague the human race. The Christmas message is relevant, revolutionary, and reassuring to us today. I believe it can be summed up in three words: a *cradle*, a *cross*, and a *crown*.

On that first Christmas night, the Bible tells us about the angel coming to those fearful shepherds and saying, "Fear not . . . I bring you good news" (Luke 2:10 ESV). This is the true meaning of Christmas—the good news—that God sent His only Son to Earth to save people from their sins. Christmas is not a myth, not a tradition, not a dream—it is a glorious reality.

God Over the Storms

He made the storm be still.
PSALM 107:29 ESV

Thunderstorms, tornadoes, blizzards—bad weather comes in many different forms. Florida winters are sunny and warm, while people in Pennsylvania may experience frigid temperatures and icy roads. People also experience different kinds of storms in life, but everyone experiences some form.

We don't have the same problems. Some experience marriage troubles, others deal with family dissension, difficulties at work, or health issues. We hear about conflicts around the world. And then there are storms of jealousy, rage, hatred, loneliness, selfishness; and storms that cause us to feel unsettled and insecure.

The Bible records the story of a violent storm that came upon Jesus and His disciples one night on the Sea of Galilee. The disciples were terrified—but Jesus was fast asleep. He was at peace because He knew God was in control. He was at peace also because He was the Ruler over the storm, and He knew it would stop at His command: "Peace, be still!" (Mark 4:39).

When we are faced with storms in life, we must ask ourselves if we are surrendered to Jesus. Do we place our trust in Him alone and not in our circumstances? When we put anything before Jesus, the storms will rage and overtake us.

We must look to Jesus, the One who calms our fears and settles our hearts. He is the One who goes before His children and brings His peace.

THIS MARATHON CALLED LIFE

"I am your God. I will strengthen you, yes, I will help you."
ISAIAH 41:10

Like the marathon runner, we are in the journey of life for the long haul, and it lasts as long as God gives us breath. We aren't meant to wander off the track, or quit and join the spectators, or decide we'll just slow down and take it easy while others pass us by. The Christian life is a process of learning and growing, and this is accomplished through the study of God's Word, obedience to it, and a life of prayer that brings us into fellowship with Him.

Our example is Jesus. "Looking unto Jesus, the author and finisher of our faith, who for the joy set before Him endured the cross, despising the shame, and has sat down at the right hand of the throne of God" (Hebrews 12:2–3). There, He works on our behalf and prays for us.

Jesus completed the journey God had prepared for Him, even at the cost of His own blood. This truth is our power to endure, when we feel like collapsing from exhaustion or drained by busyness. This happens when we run unwisely or depend only on our own resources. We may get by with it for a time, but eventually it will catch up with us.

God didn't intend for us to travel our journey in our own strength anyway, but only with the strength He supplies.

Our Guide and Advocate

The Spirit Himself makes intercession for us with groanings which cannot be uttered.

ROMANS 8:26

The Bible is clear that the Holy Spirit is God Himself! Many Christians do not realize that the Holy Spirit of God prays for us. The Spirit helps us when we are weak. God's Spirit helps us know how to pray correctly. And the Spirit of the living God speaks to God on our behalf, many times in ways that we cannot explain.

Believers have the wonderful gift of relying on the Holy Spirit because Jesus promised when He returned to Heaven that He would send His Spirit to help us through life (John 14:26).

Many times, we don't even know how weak we really are and how easy it is for us to make wrong choices. We forget how strong our enemy is. We may even doubt if God is going to really help us. Or we think we can fix everything ourselves. But we should ask the Holy Spirit to guide us in all our choices and decisions, because He will direct us to the will of our Father in Heaven.

When we turn our lives over to Him, we will know victory. Consecrated, Spirit-filled Christians can have victory over the world, the flesh, and the devil. It is the Holy Spirit who will be with us in the battle, and this is what transforms our lives from ordinary to victorious!

THE FULFILLMENT OF EVERY PROPHECY

"All things must be fulfilled which were written in . . . the Prophets . . . concerning Me."
LUKE 24:44

What do Socrates, Bach, and Shakespeare have in common? They are remembered as bigger than life, but they are dead and in the grave and can do nothing for you. Walk into the great cathedrals with spires that pierce the sky, and you will see paintings and sculptures memorializing robust men who are still revered and kind women who reach down to the lowly in compassion. But they, too, lie silent in death; they can do nothing for you.

Sadly, artists too often have depicted Jesus as feeble, weak, and dead—still hanging on the cross. This is not the truth; for the One who is depicted hanging lifeless and broken on the cross is instead full of the breath of life, full of glory. He emptied His life on the cross so that He could fill us with the gift of eternal life by His resurrection.

Christ's birth was no ordinary birth—it was marked by celestial wonders; His life was no ordinary life, for it was marked by many signs and miracles. His death was no ordinary death, for it was distinguished by great compassion, geological disturbances, and solar irregularities.

Such a life couldn't long be contained in a grave. Every important event in Jesus' life was described many centuries before He came in the flesh, and when Jesus came, He fulfilled every prophecy.

A Herald for the King

*Behold, upon the mountains, the feet of him who
brings good news, who publishes peace!*

NAHUM 1:15 ESV

Proclaim the acceptable year of the LORD" (Luke 4:19). This is the only hope for tomorrow. People always want to "turn a new page" when a calendar year advances. There is no better way to begin a new year than for a person to turn to Christ as Savior. The Bible says, "Behold, now is the accepted time; behold, now is the day of salvation" (2 Corinthians 6:2).

Jesus came as an infant King to bring new life—to draw people to Himself. But many walked away from Him. Why? Because they could not fathom that the One who proclaimed Himself King must lay down His life to bring about His kingdom. They wanted victory on their terms—not faith to believe that His way was the only way.

What constitutes "the only way"? Hearing and heeding the warning. Every true king has a herald. John the Baptist was the forerunner of Jesus Christ. He proclaimed, "Repent, for the kingdom of heaven is at hand!" (Matthew 3:2).

On the eve of the year, ask others to look back long enough to ask, "Do I belong to Jesus?" "Have I lived in obedience to the Savior?" "Am I serving Him for the sake of His eternal kingdom to come?" Become a herald for the things of God and be faithful to Him.

A YEARNING DEEP INSIDE

"I know the plans I have for you," says the LORD. "They are plans for good and not for disaster, to give you a future and a hope."
JEREMIAH 29:11 NLT

A new year is only a mark of time, a turning of the page. Mankind was not established on Earth just to be preoccupied with self, our own problems and pleasures. Mankind was not put here to make this a better world. Man was not made for himself but for God. The Great Designer planned that we would know Him forever.

Why are people so restless? Why are people constantly searching for lasting peace and contentment yet never fully satisfied? Many people express this particularly when a new year approaches. The Bible says this happens for a very good reason: we are incomplete without God. If we leave Him out of our lives, we have an empty place in our souls, a yearning deep inside us that only God can satisfy.

Man is not just a physical being; he is a spiritual being, created with a soul or spirit that gives the ability to know God. The Bible says that God implanted something of Himself inside us: "God created man in His own image; in the image of God He created him; male and female He created them" (Genesis 1:27). God has given us a unique spiritual nature, and we can know its blessings when we surrender completely to Him.

ABOUT THE AUTHOR

Billy Graham, world-renowned preacher, evangelist, and author, delivered the gospel message to more people face-to-face than anyone in history and ministered on six continents in more than 185 countries. Millions have read his inspirational classics, including *Angels*, *Peace with God*, *The Holy Spirit*, *Hope for the Troubled Heart*, *How to Be Born Again*, *The Journey*, *Nearing Home*, and *The Reason for My Hope*.

FIND AUTHENTIC PEACE
for YOUR SOUL

Beloved evangelist Billy Graham understood the flurry of modern life and the constant temptation of busyness. In a world in which everyone seems to be rushing to finish their to-do lists, answer their emails, and respond to their cell phones, peace is still possible. In *Peace for Each Day,* a 365-day devotional, Graham shares God's gentle, reassuring promise of spiritual calm.

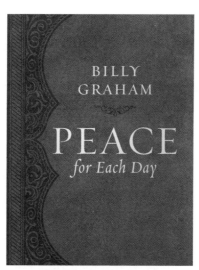

ISBN 978-1-4002-2411-1

GAIN *the* WISDOM YOU NEED *to*
LIVE BOLDLY *for* CHRIST

Billy Graham believed that Christianity is more than a system of beliefs or a series of moral guidelines. Christianity is a relationship—a personal relationship you can have with God through faith in Jesus Christ. In *Wisdom for Each Day*, Graham crafted 365 devotions to help you nurture and strengthen your faith.

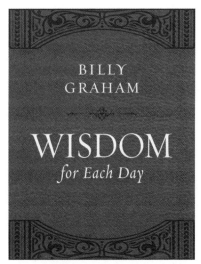

ISBN 978-1-4002-1123-4

May the God of hope fill you with all joy and peace . . .

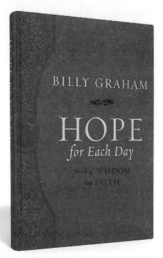

ISBN: 978-0-7180-7512-5

B illy Graham has touched the lives of countless people with the good news of Jesus Christ. Share that gift of hope with one of his best-loved messages, *Hope for Each Day*, available in a beautiful, deluxe leathersoft cover. This book of 365 daily devotions will encourage your soul as you revel in the hope of Jesus.

THOMAS NELSON
Since 1798

MY DEVOTIONAL THOUGHTS